Seeing the Elephant

SEEING THE ELEPHANT

The Many Voices of the Oregon Trail

Joyce Badgley Hunsaker

Texas Tech University Press

This book is typeset in Janson. The paper used in this book meets the minimum requirements of ANSI/NISO Z39.48-1992 (R1997).

Frontispiece: *Dancing elephant from Gold Rush lettersheet. "Seeing the elephant" became a popular phrase for describing the exotic, surprising, and adventure-filled experiences of the overland trails. To have "seen the elephant" and survived became a mark of great accomplishment for several generations of trail travelers.*

Digital chapter opening art by Laine Markham from photographs courtesy United States Department of the Interior, Bureau of Land Management, National Historic Oregon Trail Interpretive Center

Library of Congress Cataloging-in-Publication Data
Hunsaker, Joyce Badgley.
   Seeing the elephant : the many faces of the Oregon Trail / Joyce Badgley Hunsaker.
     p.   cm.
   Summary: Provides paintings, photographs, newspaper articles, and fictionalized diaries of real people who traveled the Oregon Trail throughout the nineteenth century.
   Includes bibliographical references and index.
   ISBN 0-89672-504-9 (alk. paper)
   1. Oregon National Historic Trail—Description and travel—Juvenile literature. 2. Pioneers—Oregon National Historic trail—Diaries—Juvenile literature. 3. Frontier and pioneer life—Oregon National Historic Trail—Juvenile literature. 4. Overland journeys to the Pacific—Juvenile literature. [1. Oregon National Historic Trail. 2. Pioneers. 3. Frontier and pioneer life—West (U.S.) 4. Overland journeys to the Pacific.]
   I. Title.
   F597.H86 2003
   978'.02—dc21

                                              2003004076

03 04 05 06 07 08 09 10 11 / 9 8 7 6 5 4 3 2 1

Texas Tech University Press
Box 41037
Lubbock, Texas 79409-1037 USA
800.832.4042
ttup@ttu.edu
www.ttup.ttu.edu

Printed in the United States of America

For all those who have journeyed far,
who have toiled beyond their strength,
who have stayed the distance.

For those who have seen the elephant in their everyday lives
yet have continued to put one foot in front of the other,
refusing to be vanquished, or to fail.

For people of all cultures.

You are heroes, every one.

In memory of
DONALD O. BADGLEY 1925–1993

CONTENTS

Contents

PREFACE

IT has been said that history has 20/20 hindsight. And indeed, the long view—generations removed from the actual events—oftentimes enables us to recognize flaws, weaknesses, or trends that were completely hidden to those who were, at the time, living that history.

Most Overland Trail primary source material existing today—letters, diaries, journals, and the like—was written by America's dominant culture in the mid-1800s. By and large, these were white, Anglo-Saxon, Christian people, certain of their superiority over other cultures and over the land. To them, Manifest Destiny was not only their prerogative, but it was their right, their God-given responsibility. When we judge them from a distance of more than a century and a half, we need to take into account the times in which they lived. This is not to excuse, but better to understand.

The faces of the Oregon Trail most shadowed, the voices most hushed (by virtue of their lack of written documents from the era) are nonetheless important to the overall historical integrity of *Seeing the Elephant*. Blacks. Hispanics. Orientals. Native Americans. We glimpse them in the sometimes distorted mirrors of other people's words, other people's prejudices. We see their reflections in laws that were passed to control them and regulate their power. Only with the 20/20 view of history can we hope to view them at all clearly and to understand their stakes in the westering experience.

Likewise, the land was a silent witness. Gone now are the hundreds of thousands of wagons; gone the millions of feet and hooves. Gone also are the countless campfires, the mass latrines, the disease-spawning common watering holes. But the land remembers. We have made our mark upon it, and in some places, the traces will never heal.

Today, scholarly research into these and other thorny issues strives to give us a more precise picture of how the Trail epoch has impacted the present. It is tempting to use the long view to differentiate ourselves from those historical travelers who saw the elephant and lived to tell the tale. But if 20/20 hindsight can teach us anything, it may be that we—as humankind—are more like one another than we are different, regardless of time frame or cultural orientation. Given the right set of circumstances, we all are capable of the very worst—and very best—of our species.

So why does the mythologized view of the Trail persist? Why do we, as a people, insist on elevating the mundane (flaws and all) to the sublime? Perhaps it is because in so doing, we can better justify, better integrate the Trail's common truths: that ordinary people make history; that *every* life—win or lose—toils in heroic struggles; that working together, differences or no, is better than working at odds.

In reading *Seeing the Elephant*, I would ask that you take these faces and voices for what they thought themselves to be; then judge them accurately and fairly, given what we know now. We can only hope history will do the same with us.

ACKNOWLEDGMENTS

H ISTORY is made by real people. Sometimes these people exhibit prejudice, poor judgment, and foolish, dangerous, or inflammatory behavior. They also exhibit kindness, curiosity, generosity, and selflessness. It is my intent that each person who speaks to you from these pages is portrayed fairly and accurately, within the context of a specific historical era, and according to the firsthand accounts still remaining of his or her experiences.

Permission has been granted to quote extensively from these primary sources and to paraphrase and interpret them in a way that accurately reflects the times in which these people lived. *Seeing the Elephant* does not attempt to whitewash or revise recorded history. Instead, this book allows these individuals to speak for themselves, thereby giving us—a century and a half later—insights into the human spirit of the history they created. Quoted material has been cited as to specific source.

Every attempt has been made to credit the original sources of the direct quotations found within the text and at the end of each chapter accurately. For ease in reading these quotations, modern spellings and punctuation have been used in most cases. Silent corrections have been limited to errors the diarist would have known to correct and to those instances absolutely necessary to eliminating confusion. Bracketed items within quotations are inserted by the author for clarity.

No written tribal diaries are known to exist from the Overland Migration era. Quotations within the Discussion Points that are attributed to tribal people were transcribed by U.S. Government and U.S. Army agents as the words were spoken to them or interpreted for them. Therefore, these words have been preserved in treaties, in logs of formal proceedings, and in trial transcripts. Tribal and oral tradition may offer variations on these same quotations.

In a few cases, direct quotations contain pejorative terms that are today unacceptable. In each case, their inclusion is addressed in explanatory notes.

I would especially like to acknowledge and thank:

Nellie Perkins Edwards, whose great grandfather, Edmund Perkins, rode on horseback five times from Kentucky to the Oregon Territory, bringing wagon trains to the West; Walter Love, who allowed extensive quoting from the 1853 unpublished diary of his great-grandmother, Helen Stewart; Ann Harman, who allowed extensive quoting from the unpublished papers of her great-great-grandfather, F. G. Burnett; Lois Comstock Franklin, who allowed quoting from the unpublished journal of her family ancestor, Margaret Dalton; Kenneth and Janice Sisson, Lucile Olson, and the Eastern Washington State Historical Society, who allowed extensive quoting from the original journal of Mrs. Lucy Alice Ide; the University of Oregon Library's Special Collections and Melissa Duniway for granting unlimited access to the original papers of the Scott/Duniway collection, and permission to quote extensively from them; the Arthur H. Clark Company, which allowed extensive quoting from the editorial content of its outstanding published series, *Covered Wagon Women, Diaries & Letters from the Western Trails, 1840–1890*; specifically, volumes 5 and 10; Ye Galleon Press, which allowed extensive quoting from the text of their published works: *Narcissa Whitman, My Journal; Letters of Narcissa Whitman; Journal Notes of Catherine Sager Pringle*; and *A Day in the Cow Column* by Jesse Applegate.

Also the Northwest Interpretive Association of Seattle, Washington, which allowed extensive quoting from the text of its published work, *An 1839 Wagon Train Journal, Travels . . . in the Oregon Territory*; the Ezra Meeker Historical Society of Puyallup, Washington (www.meekermansion.org), which allowed me to quote extensively from its archives of Meeker material and from its published work, *The Ox-Team or The Old Oregon Trail by Ezra Meeker*; the U.S.D.I., Bureau of Land Management's National Historic Oregon Trail Interpretive Center in Baker City, Oregon, for permission to reproduce images from its historical archives; graphic artist and photographer Jerry Gildemeister of La Grande, Oregon; research assistant Phyllis Badgley for her wealth of knowledge and her willingness to drop everything to go in search of just the right pieces of information time and time again, and also research sources Dr. Deane L. Root, Lt. Richard Hargreaves, and Nancy Harms Worthington.

Deep appreciation goes to my editor and friend Judith Keeling for her patience, her enthusiasm, and her vision; and most importantly to my husband David—my partner on the trail who has seen the elephant (and more) during the course of this manuscript—for his sense of adventure, his historical integrity, and his unfailing encouragement and support.

May the trails we make together be trails of honor.

INTRODUCTION

"What they dreamed, we live. What they lived, we dream."

T. K. WHIPPLE, 1931
Commemoration of the Oregon Trail

THEIRS has been called America's single largest voluntary, historical migration. Emigrants. Pioneers. Nearly half a million of them left farms and families, friends, and all that was familiar in the States to point their faces west: west to Oregon, west to California, west to the valley of the Great Salt Lake. All traveled the Oregon Trail. These were ordinary folk, just like you and me. By following their dreams and aspirations—by doing the best they knew how to do—they made history.

Whether viewed through the official policy of Manifest Destiny or through vision-dreams of tribal elders, their overland migration to the Land of Milk and Honey forever changed this nation. For all their imperfections, strengths, weaknesses, peculiarities, and prejudices, pioneers created a heroic image of American identity that exists to this day. In the forty short years covered by this book, the Oregon Trail left its indelible mark upon the American spirit as surely as it rutted the land over which it crossed.

Wagon trains—microsocieties traveling by wheel, heel, and hoof—brought out the best and worst in its members over their four- to five-month journeys. As the States were left behind, men, women, and children began to experience the adventure, and ordeal, of their lifetimes. The Oregon Trail was unlike anything they had ever seen or dealt with before. It would tax their discipline, their ingenuity, their perseverance and patience with every footfall, every lurch of the wagon. It would taunt their fears, magnify their sorrows, and inflame their prejudices. Day after mind-numbing and bone-jarring day, the Trail would wear them out with exasperating sameness. *Been There, Done That!* could have been the pioneers' motto. In short, the Trail was a rite of passage that would, in the language of the time, make them *see the elephant.*

There were many "faces" of the Oregon Trail. Each spoke with a unique voice. Today, each holds the potential to give us individual perspectives into the personality of history. As these personalities "speak" to us, the past ceases to be merely isolated bits of information. Instead, history becomes a cohesive dynamic that immediately transports the reader into the story. The text becomes, in effect, *living* history.

The voices of each chapter are real. These were historical persons who left written documents describing their adventures and misadventures while traveling the Oregon Trail. As much and as often as possible, their exact words or accounts have been used in the text. These are footnoted as to their sources.

In addition, factual historical information has been crafted into the chapters to give the reader a more immediate sense of the overall history presented. By using this interpretive format, we are better able to examine the individual truths of the Trail without losing sight of the bigger picture. In the words of Dan Prinzing, "The Trail represents a passage of attitudes as well as people."[1] The interpretive format allows us to examine these changing attitudes within the larger context without whitewashing recorded, historical fact.

Seeing the Elephant attempts to give you the genuine article, with all of its lumps and bumps and myriad truths, by letting the people of the Trail speak for themselves and their time.

The unflinching mirror of history shows us clearly now that grave mistakes were made in the push for Manifest Destiny. Tribal life along the Trail—and ultimately throughout the nation—was changed forever by this mass migration west; traditional lifeways were eventually completely eradicated. Buffalo were hunted to near-extinction. Streams and watering holes along the wagon routes became so polluted they bred fatal disease. The land itself was used up or worn out as if there were no tomorrow. Death was the Trail's constant companion. But, for the travelers, so was hope.

The U.S. government dreamt of an Empire of Liberty. Pioneers dreamt of Manifest Destiny. Conquest of the land and its peoples was their just due, their responsibility, their right. Tribal peoples dreamt of the Old Ways, disappearing as fast as smoke before the wind . . . or already gone. Then they dreamt nightmares: white men, as numerous as the stars, spilling over the land.

Seeing the Elephant is the true story of ordinary people who lived the history they dreamt.

"A most awful road: stones and rocks and the dust so bad, we could not see our train. . . . Water scarce, grass scant. Drove 28 miles and camped on the river bottom. Had to ford the river for grass. This is a trying time to the men and horses. I have just been to get grass, and got up to my 'tother end' in mud; I did not know whether I should [ever be able to] get out. First glimpse of the Elephant."

—GEORGE BONNIWELL, 1850
Along the Humboldt River²

NOTES

1. Dan Prinzing, personal communication with the author.

2. As cited in the *Northwest OCTA Update*, Oregon-California Trails Association, July 1996.

Seeing the Elephant

WHAT HAPPENED WHEN
A Brief Chronology of the Oregon Trail

Note: Chapters relating to chronology events are referenced within the chronology.

1792   American sailing ship captain Robert Gray claims discovery, on the western coast, of what he names the Columbia River.

1803   The Louisiana Purchase expands official United States territory to the Rocky Mountains.

1804–1806
        U.S. Army expedition, under leadership of Lewis and Clark, seeks river route from the "U. States" to the Pacific for the purpose of commerce.

1811   Fort Astoria is established on the Columbia River by the Pacific Fur Company.

1812   Robert Stuart and his party of Astorians discover what they call South Pass through the Rocky Mountains.

1812–1815
        U.S. and Great Britain fight War of 1813.

1818   U.S. and Great Britain sign treaty for joint occupancy of the Oregon Country.

1819   U.S. and Spain sign treaty establishing southern boundary of the Oregon Country.

1825   Hudson's Bay Company (British) establishes Fort Vancouver in Oregon Country.

1829   American Hall J. Kelley establishes a society for the encouragement of settlement of Oregon.

1830   First wagon caravan (Smith/Jackson/Sublette party) travels as far as Green River Rendezvous, the route that will become the Oregon Trail.

1832   First loaded wagons brought through South Pass by Captain Bonneville.

Nathaniel Wyeth's first expedition brings him to the Columbia River.

1834   Nathaniel Wyeth establishes Fort Hall in the Oregon Country on the Snake River (Idaho).

Jason Lee establishes the Willamette Methodist Mission in the Oregon Country (Oregon).

1836   Whitman/Spalding party brings what remains of their wagon—a two-wheeled cart—as far as Fort Boise before pushing on to establish Protestant missions among the tribes at Waiilatpu and Lapwai, deep in the heart of the Oregon County (later, Washington and Idaho). The wives are heralded as the first white women to traverse the Rocky Mountains and, subsequently, the entire route of the Oregon Trail successfully (see Chapter 1).

1839   Thomas Farnham, sponsored by *The New York Tribune*, travels the Oregon Trail from Independence, Missouri, to Fort Vancouver, Oregon Country, with the Peoria Party. His journals of the trek are published in 1843 under the title *A Wagon Train Journal: Travels in the Great Western Prairies, the Anahuac and Rocky Mountains, and in the Oregon Territory* (see Chapter 2).

1841   Jim Bridger establishes Fort Bridger trading post in what will later become Wyoming. Thomas Fitzpatrick guides a group of 80 emigrants across the route of the Oregon Trail (Bidwell-Bartleson party).

1842   Wagon train of 112 emigrants (Dr. Elijah White's party) travels as far as Fort Hall with their wagons.

1843   First mass migration of settlers across the Oregon Trail: more than 1000 emigrants, 120 wagons, and several thousand head of livestock. Among them was 7-year-old Jesse Applegate, traveling with his extended family from Missouri to Oregon. First provisional government is established in the Oregon Country at Champoeg (see Chapter 3).

1844   Henry and Naomi Sager begin their overland journey with their six children: John, Francis (Frank), Catherine, Elizabeth, Matilda Jane, and Louisa. En route, baby Henrietta would be born. By September, the children were orphans. With the help of other wagon train members, they completed their trek to the Whitman Mission (see Chapter 4).

1845   Over 3000 emigrants and 500 wagons head across the Oregon Trail. President James Polk, in his First Annual Message to Congress, pleads his case: "That it will ultimately be wise and proper to make liberal grants of land to the patriotic pioneers, who amidst privations and dangers lead the way through savage tribes inhabiting the vast wilderness intervening between our frontier settlements and Oregon, and who cultivate and are ever ready to defend the soil, I am fully satisfied. This is the best manner of securing national rights in Oregon. We have reached a period when Oregon must either be abandoned, or firmly maintained."

1846   Northern boundary for Oregon Country is finally settled at the 49th parallel by treaty with Great Britain. Over 2000 emigrants travel the Oregon Trail.

1847   The Mormon Trail is established as an offshoot from the Oregon Trail near Fort Bridger. Over 3500 emigrants head west across the trail.

1848   Oregon Territory established. Gold is discovered in California at Sutter's Ranch, and by the next year, the California Gold Rush is on. Gold seekers use the Oregon Trail as far as Fort Hall, then "jump off" for the gold fields on the California Trail.

1850   Donation Land Act goes into effect, offering what had formerly been government land to male U.S. citizens: 320 acres of land in Oregon Country to single males in return for residing upon and cultivating that land for four years. Married males could claim 640 acres.

1852   Over 50,000 emigrants travel the Oregon Trail. Among them are 17-year-old Abigail Jane (Jenny) Scott's family (see Chapter 5) and the 21-year-old new husband and father, Ezra Meeker (see Chapter 6).

1853   Helen Stewart and her family begin their trek across the Oregon Trail. Soldiers at Fort Kearny count 13,000 people, 3,000 wagons, and 90,000 head of livestock in the Stewart train, the largest wagon train to pass the fort yet (see Chapter 7).

1859   Oregon is proclaimed the 33rd state in America.

1861   Gold is discovered in northeastern Oregon, giving rise to *eastward* migration back along the route of the Oregon Trail and permanent settlement of the region's interior. America's Civil War begins.

1865   Civil War ends. Indian hostilities increase as settlers and gold seekers take up more and more land. Finn Burnett joins the U.S. Army's Powder River Expedition to guard wagon trains against attack. He travels the Mormon Trail, the Oregon Trail, and the Bozeman Trail in his duties (see Chapter 8).

1869   First transcontinental railroad is completed. United States now linked by rail in addition to the wagon road.

1878   Mass wagon travel over the Oregon Trail has come largely to a close. Those wagons that do use the route generally follow the railroads and stage roads since there are more settlements to offer supplies and safety. Mrs. Lucy Ide's family travels from Wisconsin to Washington Territory "under the flapping canvas of an emigrant wagon" (see Chapter 9).

1906   Ezra Meeker retraces his 1852 journey to bring attention to the importance of the Oregon Trail in American history. He continues on to Washington, D.C., to plead his cause with President Theodore Roosevelt.

1922   Ezra Meeker founds the Oregon Trail Memorial Association and is elected its first president. In 1924, Meeker retraces the Oregon Trail for the final time—this time by airplane. He makes his second trip to Washington, D.C., to meet with President Calvin Coolidge and to plead his case concerning national recognition for the Oregon Trail.

1978   Congress passes the National Trails System Act, which calls for the preservation, examination, and interpretation of important national trails. The Oregon Trail is one of those named.

Going to Oregon

FROM
Wagon Train By-Laws, 1849

RESOLUTION

Resolved: that inasmuch as immoral conduct and the use of profane language are useless, have an evil tendency and are hurtful to the feelings of many of the members of this Company, this committee respectfully suggests that all shall refrain from either, that we may move along in harmony and contribute to the happiness of each other.

COMMENTARY

From Journal entry of Joseph Warren Wood
May 27, 1849

"The whole was adopted unanimously, with the exception of the last resolution [above], which was adopted by a majority of 10. When it was adopted, the men from four wagons shouted that the Company was dissolved, and retired to their tents. They were a rough set and we were glad to be rid of them.

"It was customary among the emigrants to get up a constitution and code of laws after the style of the U.S., containing a Preamble, Declaration of Rights, etc. They elect their officers one day, and depose them [the next]; burst up, raise hob, go alone a day or two, and form another company."

ARTICLES OF AGREEMENT
Perkins Wagon Train, 1864

Made and entered into this 25 day of May, A.D. 1864, between the members of this emigrant train, known as the Perkins Train.

Article 1st: That all members shall obey the orders of the commanders chosen by the members;

2nd: That the Captain shall take command of the train and direct for them ordering the gearing and ungearing, yoking and unyoking, herding and corralling, and all road and camp duties;

3rd: That if any member become dissatisfied or complains, he has the right to withdraw at any time; and a majority of the members can dismiss a member by vote;

4th: That all members shall act at all times for facilitating the progress of the train;

5th: The second in command shall take command in the absence of the captain; and the clerk shall keep the roll and make out a just list of details that may be ordered by the commander;

6th: That we subscribe to the above rules and regulations and attach our names binding ourselves to observe and obey them as good men should do for the common benefit of all the train.

Signed

W. T. Ficklin,	Z. C. McCray,	H. Z. Perkins,	J. T. Starrett,
M. H. Wood,	R. P. Yantes,	Eli McCray,	J. E. Houston,
John Field,	J. H. St. Clair,	W. J. Nordyke,	F. M. Sidon,
W. H. McCray,	I. N. Warmath,	Nathan R. Tracy,	Fi Jett,

Wm. Purkins,	G.W. Warmath,	Y. J. Warmath,	C. P. DeVaul,
J. W. Wilson,	Scott Clark,	A. S. Baisley,	G. B. Falkner,
I. W. Field,	J. N. B. Wyatt,	Wm. Bosley,	W. L. McCray,
A.L. Wynne			

Clerk: Geo. W. Warmath.
Captain: J. P. Perkins.
Lieut.: James Houston.
Hardin Z. Perkins,
Wagon Master.[1]

NOTE

1. Transcription of original, by permission of Perkins family. Only the male heads of households were allowed to sign, which was typical for legal documents of this era. By signing the document, however, the men bound every member of their families to its conditions, as well as whatever hired help they may have brought with them or would acquire along the way.

OUTFITTING FOR OREGON

Letter to the Editor, *Gazette*, St. Joseph, Missouri,
March 19, 1847

Mr. Editor: Below you will find a list of the principle articles necessary for an outfit to Oregon or California, which may be useful to some of your readers. It has been carefully prepared from correct information derived from intelligent persons who have made the trip.

The wagons should be new, made of thoroughly seasoned timber, and well ironed and not too heavy; with good tight [wagon] beds, strong bows, and large double sheets [canvases]. There should be at least four yoke of good oxen to each wagon—one yoke to be considered as extra, and to be used only in cases of emergency. Every family should have at least two good milk cows, as milk is a great luxury on the road. . . .

No furniture should be taken, and as few cooking utensils as are indispensably needed. Every family ought to have a sufficient supply of clothing for at least one year after their arrival, as everything of that kind is high [in price] in those countries. Some few cattle should be driven for beef, but much loose stock will be a great annoyance. Some medicines should also be found in every family, the kind and quantity may be determined by consulting the family physician.

I would suggest to each family the propriety of taking a small sheet-iron cooking stove with fixtures, as the wind and rain often times renders it almost impossible to cook without them. They are light, and cost but little.[1]

All the foregoing articles may be purchased on good terms in this place.

[Signed] K. Conn, Proprietor

From *The Prairie Traveler: Handbook for Overland Expeditions, 1859,* as cited in the exhibit at National Historic Oregon Trail Interpretive Center.

"I once traveled with a party of New Yorkers en route for California [by way of the Oregon Trail]. They were perfectly ignorant of every thing relating to this kind of campaigning, and had overloaded their wagons with almost everything except the very articles most important and necessary. The consequence was, that they exhausted their teams, and were obliged to throw away the greater part of their loading. They soon learned that champagne, East India sweetmeats, olives, &tc., &tc., were not the most useful articles for a prairie tour."

NOTE

1. Of all articles noted in Trail diaries as being left by the side of the trail because they were too heavy and were taxing the oxen's strength, these sheet-iron cooking stoves were mentioned most. Obviously, this merchant didn't let the facts get in the way of a good sales pitch.

FROM
Emigrant's Guide to California, 1849

THE *Emigrant's Guide to California, 1849*, suggests the following for a group of up to three people heading west across the Oregon Trail toward California. Keep in mind these were 1849 prices, when $1.00 a day was considered a good wage.

Supplies

Three rifles at $20	$60.00	Dried fruit, 50 pounds[5]	3.00
Three pairs pistols at $15	45.00	Salt and pepper, 50 pounds	3.00
Five barrels of flour (1,080 pounds)[1]	20.00	Lead, 30 pounds[6]	1.20
Bacon, 600 pounds[2]	30.00	Tent, 30 pounds[7]	5.00
Coffee, 100 pounds	8.00	Bedding, 45 pounds[8]	22.50
		Cooking utensils, 30 pounds	4.00
Saleratus, 10 pounds[3]	1.00	Matches[9]	1.00
Lard, 50 pounds	2.50	Candles, soap, 50 pounds	5.30
Tea, 5 pounds	2.75	Personal baggage, 150 pounds	—
Sugar, 150 pounds[4]	7.00		
Rice, 75 pounds	3.75	TOTAL: 2,505 pounds	$ 225.00

Add to this a six-mule team to pull the wagon ($600) or an eight-oxen team ($200), harness for the animals (around $24), and the cost of the wagon itself (beginning at about $85 for a new one). Mule teams were considered the best, but many emigrants couldn't afford the price. Instead, they relied upon their oxen—cheaper, less prone to stampede, less likely to be stolen by Indians, and better able to cover long distances without complaint. In dire circumstances, the oxen could even be used as food. Mules, on the other hand—as everyone knew—were much more temperamental. *Stubborn as a Missouri mule* was an insult that became very popular in the mid-1800s. And no one, short of the Army, ever considered eating mule meat.

Settlers who traveled the Oregon Trail generally spent between $800 and $1,200 for their outfit and supplies. Many sold their farms to raise the money. Preparations for departure often took up to a year.

NOTES

1. Flour was most generally placed in double canvas sacks, each sack weighing a hundred pounds. These were then placed inside barrels for transport. The barrels not only kept the flour tidier, but also helped discourage animals and bugs from eating/burrowing their way through.

2. Bacon was stored in sacks and generally came in "sides of beef," not the separate strips we see today in the supermarket. Each sack weighed about 100 pounds. Emigrants were encouraged to store the sacks in boxes, surrounded by bran, to insulate the fat against melting in high temperatures.

3. Baking soda (sodium bicarbonate). This supply was often complemented by naturally occurring soda deposits at certain springs along the trail.

4. In addition to sugar's importance for cooking along the trail, it was known to be a good commodity for trading with the Indians. It was also sometimes used medicinally.

5. Consumed not only as food but also in preventing scurvy. Few other foods eaten by the emigrants contained enough vitamin C to keep them healthy. Vinegar was considered an excellent source of fruit nutrient in those days; hence, emigrant trail recipes include vinegar pie and lemonade made with vinegar.

6. For melting, to cast balls for use in their guns.

7. Most emigrants slept in their tents rather than in the wagons. The wagons were used primarily to haul goods and usually were so tightly packed there was little room for people inside.

8. Oregon and California Trail emigrants did not have the luxury of our high-tech thermal materials that keep us warm and dry yet do not take up much room. These travelers had to rely on woolen blankets, feather bed ticking (sewn mattress casings), and quilts. Fifteen pounds per person may seem like a lot to us, but to them it was getting by with the bare minimum. Temperatures on the journey easily varied from over 100 degrees by day to below freezing at night.

9. These would have been stick matches, often called *Lucifers* or *Lucifer sticks*. They were not as reliable as the matches we have today and were not as widely used by emigrants as the older techniques of starting fires. Flint and steel kits were available at this time, which came with char, or pre-burned fabric bits (easier to catch fire), and bits of punk, or dry tinder. The kits were generally brass with a magnifying glass in the lid. This glass could be used to focus the sun's rays onto a pile of tinder, thereby increasing the temperature until spontaneous combustion occurred.

SEEING THE ELEPHANT

FROM

The Prairie Traveler: Handbook for Overland Travelers, 1859

The *Prairie Traveler* calculates three months of clothing and personal items for one man (which could be stretched to the more likely four months of travel) as follows:

2 red or blue front-button flannel over-shirts
2 wool undershirts
2 pairs of thick cotton drawers[1]
4 pairs of wool socks
2 pairs of cotton socks
4 colored silk handkerchiefs[2]
2 pairs of stout shoes for walking
1 pair of boots and shoes for horsemen
3 towels
1 gutta percha poncho[3]

1 broad brimmed hat of soft felt[4]
1 comb & brush, 2 toothbrushes
1 pound of castile soap[5]
3 pounds of bar soap for laundry
1 belt knife and small whetstone[6]
1 coat and overcoat
Stout linen thread, large needles, beeswax[7], a few buttons, a paper of pins[8] and a thimble, with all the sewing products in a small cloth bag.

NOTES

1. Underclothes.

2. It isn't clear why silk was designated rather than other cloth, other than the fact that silk was very lightweight and didn't take up a lot of room. These handkerchiefs could be used for runny noses, as facemasks in the blowing alkali dust, as sweatbands, or as trading goods with the Indians.

3. This was a type of hard, rubberized cloth, the closest to waterproof as was then available.

4. Hats are still made from soft wool felt today. They are comfortable and flexible, and they can be crushed in a pocket or saddlebag without being ruined.

5. Castile soap is a fine-grained, hard soap that lasts a long time. It was milder on the skin than the often caustic homemade lye soap of those days.

6. The whetstone is an abrasive stone against which the knife's blade is sharpened.

7. Beeswax was commonly used to strengthen thread by coating it before the thread was used to sew. Lumps of beeswax were easy to come by and easy to carry in sewing boxes or kits. The thread was simply drawn over or through the wax. The end product was similar to today's waxed dental floss.

8. Straight pins were sold in quantities on small papers. Needles can still be purchased on papers today.

FROM
Ox Team Days on the Oregon Trail

T HIS IS Ezra Meeker's 1852 memorandum of outfit and eatables. Compare this with the 1849 and 1859 lists of supplies on pages 13 and 18.

2 light covered wagons—one for baggage, one for household goods
4 team of oxen (Tiger and Lion, Twist and Dave, Bright and Berry, Pollup and Popcorn)
3 sacks of flour (200 pounds)
150 pounds of bacon
55 pounds of sugar
7 pounds of tea
10 pounds of salt
10 pounds of coffee
75 pounds of beans and rice
20 pounds of dried apples
1 barrel of crackers
Bottle pickles
5 pounds saleratus [baking soda]
2 tin pans
2 tea kettles
1 coffee pot
1 coffee mill[1]
1 dish kettle

1 bake kettle [Dutch oven][2]
6 knives and forks and spoons
8 tin and iron cups, and tin plates
Frying pan
Tin and wooden pail
8 pounds of candles
2 candle sticks[3]
9 bars of soap
6 toothbrushes
6 woolen blankets
Bedding
Clothing and two pair of shoes for each person
Jeans
Bible
Arithmetic and grammar books[4]
1 large tent
Keg for water
3 rifles and ammunition
3 pistols and ammunition
Matches

Sewing needles, pins, and thread
Mirrors in gilt frames[5]
Calico cloth of dark color[6]
Maps and guidebook[7]

Medicine: box of physic pills, quart of castor oil, quart of rum, large vial of peppermint essence, citric acid, laudanum[8]

NOTES

1. For grinding coffee beans, which were purchased raw (green) then roasted in the frying pan as needed daily.

2. A Dutch oven is a cast-iron, flat-bottomed, lidded pot with feet and is designed to sit among the coals of a fire and cook or bake whatever is inside the pot. Stews, breads, cobblers, cakes—all could be made in this type of utensil that was called a bake kettle.

3. These are what hold the candles upright.

4. The arithmetic book was an especially valuable camp reference. Mathematic formulas were used in determining how many miles had been traveled that day, in determining doses of medicine or feed, and in keeping track of expenses, etc. Meeker most likely used the grammar book in writing the articles and journal notations that would later become published books. Both books would be useful for life at the end of the Trail.

5. Gilt frames were made of wood or plaster covered with gold leaf or gold paint. Certainly luxurious and risky to move, perhaps these were family pieces with great sentimental value. They would have been especially fragile for jolting Trail travel and would have required extra care to arrive in the Oregon Country unbroken.

6. The dark color would show the dirt less. It could also be used in patching clothes without showing up quite as glaringly as light-colored fabric.

7. It is not clear what kind of guidebooks Meeker took with him. By 1852, the year of his first trip across the Oregon Trail, there were many guidebooks for the route. Some had fold-out maps, some had milepost information, and most included descriptions of camping areas, rivers to be forded or ferried, and at what price. Many of these guidebooks had chapters on trail medicine, basic first aid, recipes using the limited wagon train supply of foodstuffs, and moral instruction for the children. It was clearly a case of *Buyer Beware* when it came to purchasing just the right guidebook. Some were written by men who had never set foot on the Oregon Trail, whose sole aim was to make money off the all-too-gullible pioneers.

8. The physic pills were evacuants used for purging, and castor oil was used as a cathartic and lubricant. The rum could be taken internally or could be poured on wounds and punctures as an antiseptic. Peppermint was commonly used to soothe the stomach, and citric acid prevented scurvy. Laudanum was an opiate drug—legal in 1852—that was used as a relaxant and sleeping aid. There are more than a few Oregon Trail diaries that tell of children getting into medicine kits, drinking the laudanum, and never waking up again.

The Voices

HISTORY AND INTERPRETATION

AS STATED EARLIER, the voices that speak to you from each chapter are real. Exact words, known to have been spoken or written by the subject of each chapter, are used wherever possible. Additional firsthand accounts of the time—recorded by others, but still documented as being true, and era-correct—have also been used. For purposes of this book, these are known as primary source material. Words written after the fact about these same people and their life events—by historians, scholars, researchers, etc.—are known as secondary source material.

Many times, however, these primary sources and secondary sources still leave gaps in the overall historical record. Interpretive material, founded in the historical record and garnered from well-documented sources, is sometimes necessary to fill these gaps, to help the story make sense as it is being told. Its main purpose is to weave raw data into narrative that (1) stimulates interest in the story, (2) creates opportunities for insight into both the story and the voice that tells it, and (3) establishes relevance to the reader.

Chapter endnotes lead to these primary and secondary sources that will enable the interested reader to determine which is which and to learn more about Trail life from both those who experienced it firsthand and those who have devoted their careers to studying it.

For example, Narcissa Whitman in Chapter One explains that the English she heard spoken on the Trail seemed far different from the English she had been taught in the States. The various expressions and meanings come directly from a letter Narcissa wrote to her sister on April 7, 1836, as cited in footnote number twelve. Hence, the passage is from a *primary* source: Narcissa's words, recorded by Narcissa herself.

Now examine the last sentence in that same paragraph: "I found their speech vexing to understand, but fascinating—just one more indication that we were, indeed, leaving behind all that was familiar." This *interpretive passage* contains paraphrasing of Narcissa's frustration (based on the tone of her April 7 letter), using the era-correct term "vexing." It also draws the conclusion that the difference in speech was one more sign that everything familiar was being left behind. That conclusion is historically correct, but it is something Narcissa, herself, did not record.

The verse about marrying in gowns of various colors is cited in footnote number four. This is *primary source* material, gathered from texts of Narcissa's time. The information is documented as being era-correct. We also know from family records—written long after the event, as a reminiscence—that the material of her wedding dress was black bombazine. Though less reliable, that is also considered *secondary source* material.

However, the framing of the color verse, Narcissa's remembrance of it on her wedding night, and wondering whether the words were true, is *interpretive*. We have no documented record as to what her thoughts were about her dress on that night, but it is certainly plausible that she might have thought about the verse. Reliable sources, both primary and secondary, document that many brides of the day chose the color of their dresses according to such associations. Hence, Narcissa's explanation of why she chose black is also *interpretive*, based on scholarly research (in itself an interpretation of the historical record) about her family's standing in the community.

You will find primary source material, secondary source material, and interpretive material blended within each chapter to give you a fuller understanding of the overall historical context. At no time was this done to change history or to try to fool you. Everything you will read in each chapter is accurate and true, as closely as we can recreate history from the distance of over a century and a half. Sometimes that re-creation requires filling certain gaps, so the story makes historical sense as you are reading it.

History, you will discover, really is full of holes. It is full of mystery. It's up to all of us—researcher, interpreter, writer, and reader together—to determine what *really* happened by trying to understand why.

NARCISSA PRENTISS WHITMAN
Into the Unknown

1836

I KNEW Mr. Whitman only two days before he proposed we marry. I immediately said, *Yes!* Then he disappeared for months, without a word. True, I had stipulated that he have a permanent mission post in the Oregon Country before I would submit to a ceremony. I would be a Missionary's Wife, and nothing less.[1] But I thought it impetuous, rudely abrupt, and singularly unromantic of him to leave without saying a proper goodbye.

It wasn't as though I was a lonely old maid with nothing better to do than sit and spin. I had had a string of suitors in my twenty-six years, before finding one whose looks I liked. Why, I had even turned down the proposal of Mr. Henry Spalding—and *he* was already attending seminary! Yet, Mr. Whitman took it upon himself to journey all the way to the Rocky Mountains and back, with no further word to me, his Betrothed, until the day he showed up again on my parents' porch, with two heathen Indians in tow.[2]

But then, that was typical of Husband.

Next, he demanded that the marriage ceremony take place right away. No time to sew a proper wedding dress. No time to observe the proper etiquette of festivity. Just *now, now, now! Before the fur caravans can leave St. Louis without us!* So I was married in black. Black bombazine, as is worn at funerals. Widow's weeds, they are called by some.

Are you shocked? Why? It was what I had on hand. Black was formal, with the proper decorum. After all, Father was a judge . . . and was ordained a church elder on the day of my marriage. We Prentiss women had always had a certain station to uphold, both in appearance and moral responsibility. Black bombazine served this bride fine. And my family followed suit.[3]

Yet, as we sang our final hymn together that February evening of my wedding and as I looked into the face of this stranger who was now my husband and weighed the prospect of what might truly lay ahead, I couldn't but remember the common ditty we girls used to sing:

> *Married in gray, you will go far away.*
> *Married in black, you will wish yourself back.*
> *Married in brown, you will live out of town.*
> *Married in red, you wish yourself dead.*
> *Married in pearl, you will live in a whirl.*
> *Married in green, be ashamed to be seen.*
> *Married in yellow, be ashamed of your fellow.*
> *Married in blue, he will always be true.*
> *Married in pink, your spirits will sink.*
> *Married in white, you have chosen all right.*[4]

Would I "wish myself back"? I pushed that thought out of my mind. In truth, I might have preferred to become a Missionary myself—if such a thing had been allowed. Reverend Parker knew of my zeal in this. It was from his lips I first heard about Indians coming from west of the Rocky Mountains, all the way to St. Louis in search of our Book of Heaven.[5] In search of the Word of the White Man's God. Imagine! I felt compelled to heed that call. The thought consumed me. I stepped forward then and there to become one of God's Anointed, a soldier in the mission army of the Almighty.

Reverend Parker, himself, wrote to the American Board of Commissioners for Foreign Missions, asking if I, as an unmarried woman of impeccable morals, could apply for their consideration. But of course, the answer was no. They wanted no unmarried females. I knew then I would have to find a husband—a Missionary husband—if I wanted to go among the heathen and bring those poor dark souls the Light of God. There was no time to lose.[6]

When Husband appeared, seeking marriage, I felt he was led by the hand of Providence.

After the ceremony, a collection of twenty-six dollars was gathered to be used toward our outfit of supplies for the journey. We embarked soon after, stopping to visit Husband's family in Rushville. There, Husband had his brother cobble a proper pair of boots for me.[7] The ladies of the church sewed shirts for him, and an additional two hundred dollars was donated for our cause. I think having the Nez Perce lads with us—the ones Husband brought back with him from the Rocky Mountains—helped loosen the congregation's purse strings immeasurably. Plus the fact that we were newlyweds. Everyone wanted to give us a proper send-off.

I was at once eager yet reluctant to set out for St. Louis and thence to our Rocky Mountain Mission. I knew we would be joined by others along the way; Husband had told me. But leaving Rushville seemed to me to be the beginning of the unknown.

I must confess some ill ease when pondering the months ahead in the company of my spurned suitor, Henry Spalding. Of course, as Christians, it shouldn't have made any difference at all now. But I wondered if we could all truly rise above our past petty differences. I wondered—ah, feminine vanity—how I might compare to the woman who *did* say yes, who became his wife: Elizabeth. I had heard some speak of her as "Eliza." I resolved to address her as "Sister" or "Sister Spalding" when speaking, in the manner of our larger mission family. Likewise, "Brother Spalding."

When we rendezvoused with them in Cincinnati, all seemed cordial enough. This, despite word coming to my ear previously of Brother Spalding stating in public that he did not want to go into the same mission with me, as he did not trust my judgment.[8] Perhaps he was still smarting from being refused in marriage. I certainly bore him no ill will of my own. Never did I mention the conditions of his scandalous birth, nor anything of his life before hearing the call of the Lord. Let the past be behind us and not start this arduous journey in rancor—that was my feeling. Of course, he never repeated his misgivings to me.

Once I met Sister Spalding, I realized at once she was the perfect partner for him in temperament. Perhaps now that he had a wife of his own, he would be more generous in his censure of others.[9]

Our party consisted of the Spaldings; the carpenter Mr. William Gray; Dr. and Mrs. Satterlee, missionaries to the Pawnee; Miss Emaline Parker, who was engaged to be married to a Missionary already amongst the heathen; and our Nez Perce boys.

Sister Spalding and I sewed a fine tent for ourselves out of bed ticking, and added this to our outfit of India-rubber cloth sheets, Mackinaw blankets, riding saddles, plates, knives, cooking forks, and tin cups. The India-rubber cloth we also had made into aprons and into life preservers that filled with air and kept us from sinking when held under our arms. All this we loaded into the Spaldings' wagon then acquired a second, plus some live stock. The prospect of what was to come still had the feel of adventure to me.

I was amazed at how suited to the task I felt. My health fairly blossomed! Sister Spalding, on the other hand, did not look to be quite up to our enterprise, even in the beginning.[10] Young Mrs. Satterlee became gravely ill while we were still on the river. She finally passed over, God rest her soul, without ever reaching the Pawnee mission.

Most of the others in our party felt the effects of drinking the river water. I was the exception. I never felt better! Everyone who saw me complimented me as being, in their judgment, the best able to endure our journey over the mountains. I tried not to let pride and vanity gain the upper hand.

All had the air of differentness, even the landscape. On April 1, the morning after we had left St. Louis, Husband and I discovered on the river bank a patch of what is called prickly pear, a type of cactus. Husband knew from experience the effects of handling them and cautioned me against them. But I thought I could take just one and put it into my India-rubber apron pocket then carry it back. This I did, but after rambling a little, I thought I'd take it out. And my pocket was filled with its needles, just like a caterpillar's bristles! I became considerably annoyed when I tried to take the needles out of the pocket and they covered my hands.

Husband would have laughed at me were it not for his own misfortune. He thought he'd discover what kind of sticky juice the prickly pear had by tasting it. He cut one in two, bit it, and covered his lips completely with its needles! We then had to sympathize with each other, and were glad to render mutual assistance in plucking the spiny needles out of each other's flesh.[11] So ended our misadventure.

Even the manner in which we heard English spoken now was different than in the States. The western people spoke so oddly, no New Yorker would understand! They used expressions such as *a heap of water*, meaning a great quantity . . . or *she is heap sick*, and so on. If you asked, *How does your wife today?* in the proper manner, the reply was likely to be, *O, she is smartly better, I reckon, but she is powerful weak; she has been mighty bad.* And then, with some impertinence they would ask, *What's the matter with your eye?* meaning the condition was obvious to all.[12] I found their speech vexing to understand but fascinating—just one more indication that we were, indeed, leaving behind all that was familiar.

By the time we caught up with the American Fur Company, just above the Forks between the North and South Platte rivers, our party had winnowed down to only those going to the Rocky Mountain mission: the Spaldings, ourselves, Mr. Gray, our Indian boys, and two young men we employed to assist with packing animals. With us, we had fourteen horses, six mules, and fifteen head of cattle. We started with seventeen, but the Fur Company took one of our cows for slaughter as their men had no meat, and we ourselves had killed one calf for beef. Four of the cows, we milked.[13] It proved a guessing game of sorts, as to what provisions one would truly need while traveling and making those provisions last until they could next be resupplied. We had purchased a barrel of flour before leaving the States. Sister Spalding and I baked enough every day to last us, if we killed a calf or two, until we could reach the buffalo and the prospect of fresh meat.

Between the Fur Company and ourselves, we really were a moving village—seventy men and nearly 400 animals, of which most were mules. The Fur Company had seven wagons drawn by six mules each, and one cart drawn by two mules which carried a lame man who was one of the proprietors of the Company. First in line was our Captain, Mr. Tom Fitzpatrick, then one they called the pilot. Next, came the pack animals—all mules—loaded with great heavy packs. Then came the wagons. And bringing up the rear, our company. Brother and Sister Spalding rode in one wagon with Husband and myself; Mr. Gray and the baggage were in the other. Our Indian boys drove the cows; Dulin, one of our hired men, drove our horses. Young Miles led our forward horses, four in each team. We covered quite a space. The pack mules always strung one after the other, just like Indians.[14]

At night, we camped in a large ring: baggage and men, tents and wagons on the outside, and all the animals except the cows within the circle. The cows, we fastened to pickets. Then a guard would be set every night.

In the morning, as soon as day would break, the first words heard were *Arise! Arise!* Then, the mules would set up a noise such as you never heard, which put the whole camp in motion. Every man would jump to his feet to turn the mules loose so they could be put out to feed and cease their braying.

While the horses were feeding, Sister Spalding and I would get breakfast in a hurry, and our party would eat it in just as much hurry. By that time, *Catch up! Catch up!* would be ringing through camp. We had to be ready to move by six in the morning, travel until eleven or so, lay by to rest and feed the animals, then start again about two. We traveled until six in the evening . . . or before, if we came to a good tavern, then encamp for the night.[15] We worshipped immediately after supper and before breakfast, every day.

I found it awkward work at first to bake out of doors over an open fire, but we women became so accustomed to it, we presently did it very easily. Yet, it was considerable work to supply our ten persons with bread three times a day! Where there were no trees for fuel, we gathered dried buffalo dung. There was plenty of it, and I found it gave a flame similar to the coal used in Pennsylvania. To those who make a face at this, I say if you had been there in that scarce timber country, you would have found yourself glad to have your supper cooked at all![16]

Sister Spalding and I became, of necessity, quite adept housekeepers on the prairie. Our table was the ground. Our tablecloth was an India-rubber cloth that doubled as a rain cloak when the weather turned. Our dishes were made of tin, so they would not break. We had basins as tea cups, iron spoons and plates, and several pans for milk or meat when we wished to set it on the table. Each of us—men and women alike—carried one's own knife in a scabbard worn upon the belt, so it was always ready for use. The forks we made for ourselves or simply used sticks to aid in eating our food.

We did not pitch our tent at noon. Instead, we took blankets and lay or perched by the table in the fashion of Turks, whether on a piece of baggage from the wagon or box, for those whose joints would not allow them to follow fashion.[17] I always tried to fix myself as gracefully as I could, not abandoning all of the subtler arts as we pushed on, deeper into God's wilderness.

From the first time I tasted fresh buffalo, I ate little else. When at last

SEEING THE ELEPHANT

our flour supply grew thin, we abandoned baking bread. We used it only to thicken buffalo broth, which was quite good. We had meat and tea in the morning for breakfast, then tea and meat again at noon. For the evening meal, more meat. Our only variety consisted in the ways of cooking it, which fell to Husband, and he seemed to relish the task. He had a different way for cooking every piece of meat. I was well satisfied with our Spartan diet, but Sister Spalding was adversely affected by it to the point of becoming quite sick. And finally—I must admit—the monotony of meat at every meal grew cloying, even for me.[18]

Then, in the middle of July, when we were still six weeks' travel from our Rocky Mountain Mission, suddenly we saw no more buffalo *on the hoof*, as is said here.[19] Thereafter, we had no game of any kind, to speak of, except a few messes of antelope, given to us by an Indian. We purchased dried buffalo meat from them, but it appeared so filthy, I could scarcely eat it.[20] A few times we had fresh fish, but the berries played out. We all became weary. We all longed for rest. Still, we were alive, so we gave thanks to the Almighty at every turn for his Mercies.

I pitied the poor Indian women, though, who were continually traveling in this manner during their lives, and knew no other comfort.[21] I made a little progress with their language yet knew not enough to converse with them about the Savior. Sister Spalding seemed more facile with their strange words than I. She made pictures for them with her watercolor paints and tried to teach them in that way.

We ladies were quite a curiosity to the Indian women we saw. Among the Pawnee, we were visited by them both noon and night. They would come and stand around our tent, peep in, and grin in their astonishment to see such strange-looking objects as ourselves. As we traveled, often a company of matrons would greet me, native women one after the other shaking hands and saluting me with a most hearty kiss! In one camp, a chief brought his wife and very politely introduced her to us. He said they all liked us very much, thanked God that they had seen us, and then invited us to come live among them![22]

It was truly pleasing to see our Nez Perce boys, Richard and John, with their Indian friends. In one place, Richard found several of his tribe and his brethren and was affected to tears. When they met, each took off his hat and shook hands, just as you would expect in civilized life.[23]

But I am getting ahead of myself in the telling. *First things, first,* that's what Husband always says. Let us go back to our travels along the Platte.

I swung between love and loathing for our little wagon. Sister Spalding and I considered it our home for the journey. We rode there, took refuge there and, within its canvassed confines, we tended to matters too personal to mention. But the wagon was always breaking down. Taxing our patience. Exhausting our ingenuity. Slowing us down, then slowing us down yet again as the way became more difficult. Husband decided at last that we had brought too many personal belongings with us in the wagons; they were overloaded. *Time to pare down,* he told us. *Time to winnow out.*

Even before reaching Fort William,[24] he, himself, decided to put off all the fine shirts so lovingly made for him by the Church ladies in Rushville. Those, plus his Sabbath black suit and overcoat. He thought to sell them, thereby enriching our coffers and lightening our load. At first I could not believe he was in earnest. Certainly these few articles of clothing could not weigh enough to be of any consequence. And what would he wear in their absence—the skins of animals, as the fur trappers did? I did not marry a mountain man!

All the reasons I could bring were to no avail. Until I stood firm. I told him I would sell off all my own clothing as well, if he persisted.[25] Then both of us would be clad as heathens! In the end, Husband finally relented. But, indeed, as the days wore on, we continued to have troubles with our land canoes, as the Indians call the wagons.

At the fort, we parted with many of the Fur Company with whom we had been traveling. We broke our baggage out of the heavier wagon and packed most of it on the mules. Then the sidesaddles were set upon the horses for Sister Spalding and me—no more riding in the lighter wagon. We were hopeful this meant it would be left behind, also, at long last. But no. Husband and Brother Spalding insisted we bring it forward with us. *For crossing the Rocky Mountains,* they said. Thus, we set off for the Green River Rendezvous[26] and the mysteries which lay ahead.

On July 4, Independence Day, we crossed what they call the Divide. This is the place which separated the waters flowing into the Atlantic from those that flowed into the Pacific. Quite honestly I cannot say it was much to gaze upon, though the men made much of it.[27]

Nothing could have prepared my eyes or senses, though, for the extravagant event that spread out before us on the Green. There must have been a thousand Indians of every kind. Tents and horses of every description: some painted, some adorned with finery of vivid color. Rough-faced trappers carrying animal skins. Mexican traders hawking their exotic wares. There were some of the American Fur Company men—those we knew from traveling and many more whom we did not. Even a few men from the Hudson's Bay Company, with their distinctive striped blanket-coats. All was clamor and noise. Languages of French, English, Spanish, and a Babel of Indian tongues . . . all shouted at once, each trying to out-voice the other. Dogs barking. Mules braying. It was bedlam of the most amazing and intriguing sort!

Husband warned us it had likely been years since some of these trappers had seen a white woman. He cautioned us to use care. But I found them most restrained around us and very attentive, particularly to me. So I set right to work, passing out Bibles amongst them. I gave away so many so quickly, Brother Spalding told me to stop. *Save some for the heathens at our mission*, he said.[28]

Sister Spalding, herself, was sick in the tent for a good part of our stay there. The Indian women seemed to flock to her in concern. They found even the most trivial items of her personal toilet of extreme interest; likewise, her sewing kit, and they spent much time with her. As Sister regained her health, she began collecting words they would speak to her in their languages and writing them down on paper. A dictionary, of sorts. By the time our party left Rendezvous the middle of July, she could speak some of the words back to them in their own tongues, which seemed to highly entertain and delight.[29]

But now, we had a problem. Reverend Parker was nowhere to be found! He, who had promised to meet us here, at Rendezvous, to lead us to the Rocky Mountain Mission. He, who had agreed to be our guide and sage. He, who had traveled to the Pacific Ocean and back, who knew of things we could only imagine—he was not there. There was no word of him. No letter, no instructions, no advice of any kind. Husband had never gone westward beyond this place. He could not lead us. Now what would we do? We prayed for Divine guidance.

The Indians seemed very anxious that we would go north with them, after the buffalo. They even fought amongst themselves for which tribe would have us, the Cayuse or Nez Perce. But to follow them would take months. And we had to set up our mission before winter.

Providence stepped in. The Hudson's Bay Company came to our rescue. Mr. John McLeod, Chief Trader of the Company as he called it, said he and his party would accompany us. They would take us all the way to Fort Walla Walla near our mission site before proceeding further west themselves toward the mouth of the Columbia River and their own Fort Vancouver. Some Flatheads, and Nez Perces, and members of the Snake[30] tribe would travel with us.

We commenced, July 18, on what would prove to be the six most grueling weeks of our long journey. What had been perceived before as adventurous or exciting, now became at best tedious and demanding; at worst, nearly impossible to bear. By now, I knew I was expecting.[31]

We ceased stopping in the middle of the day to rest and even traveled on the Sabbath! The ride became very mountainous—narrow paths winding on the sides of steep mountains, so narrow as scarcely to afford room for any animal to place his foot. One after the other, in single file, we passed along with cautious step. Even then, some of the pack animals were crowded off the side and were nearly lost, one severely injured.[32]

Husband was resolute that our wagon should accompany us all the way to our mission though daily it gave us more trouble. It got stuck in the creeks while crossing, and he was obliged to wade considerably when getting it out. After that, while going between the mountains and on the side of one—so steep that it was difficult for horses to pass—the wagon was upset twice. I did not wonder at this at all; it was a greater wonder that it was not turning somersaults continually.[33] It vexed me beyond words to see my husband worry so, to exhaust himself excessively over this silly wagon. During all of the most difficult part of our journey, he walked, in laborious attempts to bring it along. His rheumatism was greatly aggravated by continually struggling with it. Yet I dared not say a word aloud for fear of exciting his temper. The best I could do was write of my feelings in my journal and pray.

When one of the axle-trees of the wagon finally broke, both Sister Spalding and I were a little rejoiced, for we were in hopes the men would leave it and have no more trouble with it. Our rejoicing was in vain. They made a cart of the back wheels and lashed the fore wheels to it, intending to take it through in some shape or other.[34] Sister and I resigned ourselves in the knowledge they were so resolute and untiring in their efforts, they would probably succeed.

Our attentions were gratefully diverted at a place called Soda Springs. We went a full ten miles off our route in order to see them, but Mr. McLeod assured us the detour would be worth our trouble. He was right.

The first object of curiosity we came to were several white mounds on top of which were small springs of soda. These mounds were covered with a crust made by evaporation of the water that continually ran in small quantities from these springs. By the side of one of these, we saw an opening like a crater, about three feet in diameter. Below the opening, on the rocks, were dead flies and birds in abundance; they appeared to have been choked with the gas which the crater opening constantly emitted. We put our faces closer to the opening, and our breath was stopped instantly. Listening intently, we could hear a low rumbling noise like the roaring of fire coming from under the ground.[35]

Having satisfied our curiosity at the crater, we passed through a grove of juniper and pitch pine trees to discover a large spring of soda water—clear as crystal—effervescing continually. It appeared to be quite deep. At some distance below the surface, we could see two white substances, like lumps of soda in a concrete state. We drank freely of the water and found it very pleasant.[36]

Unfortunately, the ground all around in every direction was covered with lava. We gathered some specimens, but our horses had very difficult footing through the miles of coarse, grasping rock that made our path.

At last we reached Fort Hall. Granted, this place was very rough compared to Fort William on the Laramie Fork of the Platte. But this was Blackfeet country, after all, and attacks by the hostiles were many; even the Indians traveling with us were afraid of the Blackfeet. Here, at Fort Hall, there were no windows to the rooms, only a square hole in the roof; and in the bastion, a few port holes large enough for guns. And all the buildings were enclosed in a strong log wall.[37]

Yet, what a luxury it seemed. Log rooms with roofs covered in mud brick. Chimneys and fireplaces. Gardens! We felt as sustained and blessed as Christian in *Pilgrim's Progress*.[38]

When we left Fort Hall, all the Indians traveling with us—except one or two—left us. The whole tribe was exceedingly anxious to have us go with them. They used every argument they could invent to prevail upon us, and every strategy. But to go with them would have taken us two months or more out of our way. We declined, and started our way toward the Snake Fort, our last glimpse of civilization before we would reach Walla Walla,[39] twenty-five days away.

The way grew harder still. We got lost. Our livestock ran far afield. We came through swamps so swarmed with mosquitoes we could barely see, and the cattle ran mad. Then, barren desert stretched before us for hour upon hour, broken only by scatterings of a pale green wormwood called sage—a brush offensive to both sight and smell. In some places it grew in bunches the height of a man's head! Whether that height or just above the ankles, it was so stiff and hard it was a constant bother. The heat was oppressive, until I thought surely "the Heavens over us were brass, & the earth iron under our feet."[40]

Thankfully, the company of Mr. McLeod and McKay were excellent hunters and traders; otherwise, we might well have suffered, as many had, a diet of only dried meat from Rendezvous all the way to Walla Walla. As it was, we dined on fresh fish (called salmon) and on elk and antelope along our way, which fortified our strength for the challenges at hand.

Indeed, the hills were so steep and rocky that we began scattering our possessions as we went along. Husband thought it best to lighten the wagon as much as possible, to take nothing forward but the wheels. He told me I would have to leave even my precious traveling trunk there with the wagon box. I severely regretted leaving anything that came from home, especially that trunk. I had been cheered by its presence so long—it had been given to me by my sister, Harriet. It was my touchstone, my reminder of all most dear. Yet, Husband said leave it. So leave it at last I did. But Heaven took pity on my sorrowing heart. Mr. McKay retrieved the trunk and asked the privilege of taking it along for me.

It would have been better for me to have brought no baggage whatever, to have brought only what was necessary to use on the way. It cost us much in labor besides the expense of animals. To pack and unpack so many times, to cross so many streams where the packs frequently got wet, required no small amount of work and resulted in injury to the articles. *Possess nothing.*

Then you will have nothing to lose! That should be the motto for this wild country![41]

Especially when considering what was left of our wagon. In crossing the Snake River, Husband once again had considerable difficulty with it. Both cart and mules were turned upside down in the river and became entangled in the harness. The mules would have been drowned, but for our desperate struggle to get them disentangled and led ashore. Finally, after putting two of the strongest horses before the cart and two men swimming behind to steady it, they succeeded in getting it across.[42]

Sister Spalding and I rode across on the backs of two of the tallest horses, thus reaching our goal safely. Yet, the water was so deep and swift, I could only think of crossings previous where the horses and mules had to be driven across by the Indians. Then, the best Indian swimmer would mount a horse that was good for leading, to go before the other animals as a guide. Many others would swim after the animals, to help drive them over. Once underway, such a snorting and hallowing would arise, such as you never heard! At the same time, nothing could be seen except so many heads floating upon the water, all the way to the distant shore. On one such crossing, Husband took an elk skin and stretched it across himself as much as possible. Then, the Indian women carefully put him on the water and, with a cord in their mouths, they swam and pulled him over to the far side.[43]

I much preferred horseback, or better yet, a rush and willow canoe.

When at last we reached the Snake Fort on the Bigwood River, I laundered everything for the third time since leaving home. The chore took all day. Husband packed and re-packed the animals while reviewing our plans for continuing forward.

Here, our wagon-turned-handcart was finally set to rest. Those at the fort succeeded in convincing Husband that the Blue Mountains would claim it should he insist on pulling it through. The way was too tortuous. Only a fool would try. He could leave it there, they said, and at some future day once again claim it. So common sense won the day. I said not a word but breathed a prayer of gratitude. We set out with only the possessions we could carry on horse or mule.

The land began to change yet again, and the flat, sandy, interminable plains gave way to great rolling dun-colored hills, then steeper bluffs skirted by timber, and beyond that, jagged blue-shadowed mountains. The Blues. We separated from Brother and Sister Spalding, choosing to go forward with Mr. McLeod at a faster pace. We came to the place known as The Lone Tree in a beautiful valley of the Powder River.[44] We took our rest beside the solitary giant for which the valley was named then pushed on.

When at last we allowed ourselves to rest, Husband and I lingered together on top of a hill. We gathered berries and had no distressing apprehensions, having passed entirely out of dangerous Indian country. I treasured these rare times together, away from the camp. We could ride and talk together. We reminisced about home and much-missed friends. It was then that the tedious hours were sweetly decoyed away. Then, that my heart would be sure there could be no husband finer than mine; he was one of the best the world ever knew.[45]

All too soon we were back on our path, and a fearful path it was! We began to descend one of the most terrible mountains for steepness and length I had yet seen. It was like winding stairs in its descent and in some places almost perpendicular. The horses appeared to dread the hill as much as we did. They would turn and wind in a zigzag manner all the way down. We no sooner gained the foot of this mountain, when another more steep and dreadful was before us! The way was stony and we had to step over logs. In many places, it was covered with jumbles of black, broken rocks. Our horses' feet were very tender—all unshod—so that we could not make good progress. And there was no water.[46]

Yet, when we gained our first view of the Columbia River valley that would be our new home, our difficulties were largely forgotten. It was beautiful. Just as we gained the highest elevation and began to descend, the sun was dipping behind the western horizon. Beyond the valley we could see two distant mountains, Mount Hood and Mount St. Helens. These lofty peaks were of a conical form and separated from each other by a considerable distance. Behind Mount Hood, the sun was hiding part of his rays, which gave us a more distinct view of this gigantic cone. The beauty of this extensive valley contrasted well with the mountains behind us and, at this hour of twilight, was enchanting. It certainly diverted my mind from the fatigue under which I labored.[47]

By that time, our horses were in as much haste to see camp as we were. Mine made such *lengthy* strides in descending the mountain, that it shook my sides surprisingly![48]

We had crossed the Blue Mountains in only a day and a half. Before us lay Fort Walla Walla, and the site of our Rocky Mountain Mission. We stopped a day to prepare ourselves. Some of the men shaved their faces; some cut their hair. Husband and Mr. Gray stretched out flat on the ground and slept. I tried to divert myself by doing mending for Husband and trying to write in my journal. Mother was so wise when she suggested I keep one. It had been my constant companion, my listening ear, my comfort, my friend all these months. And now that we were but one day away from our destination, I could barely get the words to flow across the paper. I was too excited!

September 1, 1836. Our arrival day. You can better imagine our feelings that morning than I could describe them. I could not realize that the end of our long journey was so near. We arose as soon as it was light, ate hurriedly, and dressed for Walla Walla. We started out early, for all were anxious to reach our desired haven. Both man and beast alike appeared propelled by the same force. The fatigues of the long journey seemed to be forgotten in the excitement of being so close, and the whole company galloped almost all the way to the fort.[49]

The end of our travels, at last! Two days later, Brother and Sister Spalding arrived with the rest of the company, having made better progress than we anticipated. The animals all came in as well, except one horse that had been injured in packing and had entirely given out.

Here we all were at Walla Walla through the mercy of a kind Providence, in health and all our lives preserved. What a cause for gratitude and praise to God! My heart was ready to leap for joy at the thought of being so near the long-desired work of teaching the benighted ones a knowledge of a Savior, and for having completed that hazardous journey under such favorable circumstances. The Lord had been with us, and provided for us all the way. We proposed a day of mutual thanksgiving, and praised His name.[50]

I was home. I had reached my Promised Land.

Narcissa Prentiss Whitman

Almost immediately, it was decided that the Whitmans and Spaldings would proceed by boat down the Columbia River to Fort Vancouver with the Hudson's Bay Company men, since (in Narcissa's words) "nothing can be done by either . . . party about location [of the missions] until the Indians return from their Summer hunt."[51] At Fort Vancouver, they could send and receive packets of letters, acquire the supplies they needed for setting up their mission schools, and gather equipment, seeds, and cuttings for their farms. There was such an abundance of supplies available at Fort Vancouver, in fact, Narcissa wrote her parents,

> If anyone wished to come by land . . . let them send all their outfit [around the Horn] to Oahu by ship [thence, to the West Coast], and take only the suit they wish to wear and a few changes of undergarments, packing their provisions only . . . and they will make an easy pleasant trip, and less expensive than the one we made. . . . We see now that it was not necessary to bring any thing because we find all here.[52]

Narcissa and Eliza were left by their husbands at Fort Vancouver for some weeks while the goods were ferried back to Fort Walla Walla in the boats. Dr. McLoughlin, Chief Factor for the HBC, tried to persuade the ladies to stay the winter as his guests at the fort while their husbands built suitable homes for them back at the mission sites. They, however, preferred to return to their husbands' sides, finally settling 110 miles from one another at the missions of *Waiilatpu* and *Lapwai*.[53] They were the first nontribal women to successfully traverse the entire length of what would become known as the Oregon Trail.

There seemed to be a fundamental difference between the two women and between the two missions. To Narcissa, at least, bringing "the Light of God to those dark souls" (see Note 6) was paramount. Judging from her writings, she viewed the *heathen* as quite apart from herself and her husband. Whether she was referring to the Cayuse or the other tribes of the region, one gets the feeling they were more of a curiosity and moral challenge to her than individual human beings. Her rhapsodic idealism over her "dear Indians" in the early days of her journey quickly faded to complaints, negative judgments, and sometimes harsh rebukes once the mission was established. She never successfully bridged the gap. And indeed, one gets the impression from her letters home that she never wanted to. Eliza Spalding, on the other hand, openly admired much of the Nez Perce culture and responded to the tribal people on an emotional and intellectual level that enriched both.

The resulting number of converts and recorded baptisms reflected the difference, which only fueled the growing competition between the two missions.

In spite of their basic differences, however, both women missed the company of other white women. Of the two missions, Spalding's was by far the more remote and isolated. But until the Oregon Trail began regularly bringing emigrants to the area, Narcissa, too, keenly felt the absence of "a woman's civilized communion and conversation."[54] She and Eliza, therefore, agreed they would maintain a spiritual bond with one another by spending a certain hour of every day thinking about and praying for one another.

When Narcissa and Marcus's daughter was born at the mission in March of 1837, the Cayuse called her *te-mi*, or Cayuse girl, because she was born on Cayuse land. The Whitmans recorded, "[T]he whole tribe are highly pleased because we allow her to be called a Cayuse girl. . . . [We were told by them] her arrival was expected by all the people of the country—the Nez Perces, Cayuses, and Walla Wallapoos Indians, and now [that] she has arrived, it would soon be heard of by them all."[55]

Evidently the political implications and tribal importance of having their daughter called a *te-mi* was lost on her proud parents. Was it a prime opportunity to forge deep familial bonds with the Cayuse? Yes. Was it a verbal reminder that this territory was—and always would be—Cayuse territory, regardless of the changes the Mission might bring? Maybe. Whatever its original intent, the issue of the Whitman's *te-mi* came to a sad and abrupt close when Alice Clarissa accidentally drowned. She was only two years old.

After that, according to tribal oral tradition and other missionaries along the Columbia River, the Whitmans hardened their hearts against much, including tribal ways. They continued to take in (adopt) mixed blood children and orphans of Trail travelers, but their approach to tribal matters was described as proud, inflexible, and haughty. Even Richard—the young Nez Perce man who had accompanied Marcus Whitman to New York State to fetch his bride then was spoken about in such glowing terms by Narcissa during the return journey—was finally driven out by them. He had lived in their home since the beginning of the mission station, but when he was forced out, he said they had become very harsh, very strict and stern, and quick to punish.[56]

Dr. Whitman himself was said to have

> looked down upon [the natives] as an inferior race & doomed at no distant day to give place to a settlement of enterprising Americans. With an eye to this, he laid plans and acted. . . . Indeed, it might almost be doubted whether he felt half the interest in the natives that he did in the prospective white population. He wanted to see the country settled. . . . Where there were scattered . . . Indian huts, he wanted to see thrifty farm houses . . . the cow, the ox, and the sheep of a happy Yankee community.[57]

Now, how much of this assessment was purely objective and how much might have been colored by personal or ecclesiastical opinion, we cannot say for certain. We do know that there was a progressive falling out between the Whitmans, many among the tribes, and other missionaries in the area. Still, to Oregon Trail travelers, they remained godsends.

Their mission established at *Waiilatpu* served for eleven years as a resting and resupplying station for the emigrant wagon trains. Then, in November 1847, Narcissa, her husband, and some of her extended mission family were killed by a group of disenchanted Cayuse in an event that became known in the newspapers of the time (and history books thereafter) as the Whitman Massacre. See Chapter 4 for a detailed discussion.

Discussion 1

"You have still fresh in mind the story of those Indians who came to St. Louis to try & obtain religious instruction & teachers to come & teach their people. There were . . . seven chiefs, some Nez Perce & some Flat Head. They went to the States with the traders of the American Fur Co. & spent the winter at St. Louis. . . . They were introduced to the Roman Catholics. . . . A Methodist minister however happened by some means to learn something of their intention & published it. And so at length their wishes became known to the public. This was the origin of all the missions in this western wilderness."[58]

—MARY RICHARDSON WALKER, Missionary, 1838

"The Presbyterian Church is a Missionary Society, the object of which is to aid in the conversion of the world, and every member of this Church is . . . bound to do all in his power for the Accomplishment of this object."[59]

—PRESBYTERIAN GENERAL ASSEMBLY, 1847

What reasons might have prompted the seven chiefs to visit St. Louis in search of religious instruction by white men? Tribal people already had systems of religious belief. Why might they seek the power of Roman Catholic or Protestant faiths? Could there be reasons other than—or in addition to—religious ones? Keep in mind that tribal alliances often included formalized acts of accepting and adopting one another's ceremonies or rituals. How might the rivalry between the Catholics and Protestants for the tribes' loyalty have made those tribes feel?

Discussion 2

"I wish you were all here with us going to the dear Indians. I have very much attached to [Nez Perce] Richard Sak-ah-too-ah. [He] is the one you saw at our wedding; he calls me mother. I love to teach him, to take care of him, and hear [the Nez Perce] talk. There are five Nez Perces in the company, and when they are together, they chatter finely."[60]

—NARCISSA WHITMAN, June 3, 1836

"In the morning, we met a large party of Pawnees going to the fort . . . to receive their annuities. They seemed to be very much surprised and pleased to see white females; many of them had never seen any before. They are a noble Indian—large, athletic forms, dignified countenances, bespeaking an immortal existence within. . . . The next day, we passed all their villages. We, especially, were visited by them both at noon and at night; we ladies were such a curiosity to them. They would come and stand around our tent, peep in, and grin in their astonishment to see such looking objects. . . . I was met by a company of matrons, native women one after another, shaking hands and saluting me with a most hearty kiss. This was unexpected and affected me very much. They gave Sister Spalding the same salutation."[61]

—NARCISSA WHITMAN, June 27, 1836

"It does not concern me so much what is to become of any particular set of Indians. . . . I have no doubt our greatest work is to be able to aid the white settlement of this country and help found its religious institutions. Providence has had its full share in all these events. . . . It cannot be hoped that time will . . . mature either the work of Christianization or civilization before the white settlers will demand the soil and seek the removal of both the Indians and the Mission. What Americans desire of this kind they always effect, and it is . . . useless to oppose. . . . The Indians have in no case obeyed the command to multiply and replenish the earth, and they cannot stand in the way of others doing so."[62]

—MARCUS WHITMAN, May 16, 1844

Narcissa seems to have begun her missionary work with a very idealized notion of her "dear Indians." Even the Pawnee, whose traditional lifestyle by this time was already modified to the point of regularly going to the fort to receive government annuities, were described by Narcissa as, essentially, the noble savage. How does that perception conflict with her husband's assessment, written eight years later? When Dr. Whitman says the Indians have not made the earth "multiply and replenish," he is, of course, speaking of farming. How many tribal peoples traditionally had a farming lifestyle? What conflicts might come from idealized expectations (from either culture) and realities that fell short of those expectations?

Discussion 3

"Brothers! I have listened to a great many talks from our Great Father [President of the United States]. But they always began and ended in this—'Get a little farther; you are too near me.' I have spoken."[63]
　　　　　—SPECKLED SNAKE, Creek, 1825

"When we were put here by the Creator, we were given our ground to live on, and from this time, these were our rights. We had the fish before the Missionaries came, before the white man came. . . . This was the food on which we lived. My mother gathered berries; my father fished and killed the game. My strength is from the fish; my blood is from the berries. . . . I was not brought from a foreign country, and did not come here [as did the white man]. I was put here by the Creator."[64]
　　　　　—WENINOCK, Yakima, 1855

"I remember when I was a small boy, I used to see so many wagon trains going west. I knew these were white people, but at that time I did not know where they were going. I saw these wagons going through [our lands] nearly the whole summer, and my folks told me these people were going west [to] live there, and that I must not injure them in any way, and that I must have respect for them, because they were always kind to my folks."[65]

　　　　　—UMAPINE, Cayuse, recalling the mid-1840s

Though some tribal people at first welcomed the white missionaries, traders, and emigrants, others did not. What are some dangers or misconceptions that might result from assuming all people of a certain cultural, ethnic, or religious group are the same? Take the viewpoint of a tribal person, talking about the Whites. Now take the viewpoint of a white missionary, talking about the Indians. Consider various tribes. Consider various religious groups. Consider the political rivalry between the *King George men* of Great Britain and the *Bostons* of the United States at this time. How do you deal with one another effectively on the basis of misinformation, stereotypes, and hearsay?

Discussion 4

"Mrs. Whitman was a large, stately, fair skinned woman, with blue eyes and light, auburn—almost golden—hair. Her manners were at once dignified and gracious. She was by nature and education, a lady, and had a lady's appreciation of all that was courageous and refined; yet, not without an element of romance and heroism in her disposition strong enough to have impelled her to undertake a missionary's life in the wilderness. Mrs. Spalding, the other lady, was more delicate than her companion, yet equally earnest and zealous in the cause they had undertaken. The Indians would turn their gaze from the dark haired, dark eyed Mrs. Spalding to . . . the golden hair and blue eyes of Mrs. Whitman, and they seemed to regard them as beings of a superior nature."[66]
—MOUNTAIN MAN ISAAC P. ROSE, recalling 1837

"The truth is, Miss Prentiss, your lamented sister was far from happy in the situation she had chosen to occupy. . . . If I may be allowed the liberty of expressing my own opinion, I should say unhesitatingly that both herself and her husband were out of their proper sphere. They were not adapted to their work. . . . That [Narcissa] felt a deep interest in the welfare of the natives, no one who was at all acquainted with her could doubt. But the affection was manifested under false views of the Indian character. Her carriage towards them was always considered haughty. It was the common remark among them that Mrs. Whitman was 'very proud.' . . . What contributed still more . . . to increase the distance between her and the natives was her ill health and increasing nervousness. Her constitution was a good deal impaired toward the close of her labors. . . . Her hopes of success also, were very much weakened and melancholy musings occupied her more than at her first setting out in missionary life."[67]
—REVEREND H.K.W. PERKINS, October 19, 1848

How do you tell the difference between factual observation and opinion? The two quotations above paint two differing pictures of the same woman. Is one true, and the other untrue? Could they both be true, given the ten years which separate them? Could either—or both—be colored by the observer's expectation of womanhood? Isaac Rose was a mountain man, whose observations may have been affected by the unexpected presence of white women (and all they symbolized) in the wilderness. What might have influenced the Methodist Reverend Perkins' observations? Now consider Narcissa herself. What influences or beliefs might have colored her own view of her life?

NOTES

1. Marcus Whitman was trained as a doctor, not a preacher. To meet the criteria of the American Board of Commissioners for Foreign Missions in establishing a recognized mission site—thereby officially carrying the coveted title of Missionary and receiving ABCFM support—Whitman had to be in reasonably good health, had to be married, and had to enlist a preacher to serve at the mission. In saying *yes* with these stipulations, Narcissa may have been trying to secure her future somewhat, both in prestige and in material support, upon marrying this total stranger.

2. *Heathen* was a term typically used at this time in missionary circles for any who did not profess to Christianity, particularly tribal peoples. Whitman had scouted the feasibility of what he called the Rocky Mountain Mission in the Oregon Country during his many months away from Narcissa. While in the far West, he had treated cholera among the mountain men he encountered at Rendezvous and successfully cut a three-inch arrow tip from Jim Bridger's back. When he returned to New York State, he brought with him Nez Perce youths from the Rocky Mountains, tribal members he had used as interpreters on his travels. Now, they served as effective visual aids in his appeals for financial donations and volunteers for his project.

3. February 18, 1836, in the Anglica Presbyterian Church, Allegheny County, New York. Narcissa's family is said to have worn black at the wedding as well. While it was not at all unusual in this era for brides to wear colors other than white, the choice of black was relatively rare. The color and the fabric (a silk/wool blend) would have proven practical in traveling to St. Louis, but as evidenced in the cited folk verse, it would have been considered a rather undesirable color for a wedding dress by Narcissa's contemporaries. For a more detailed discussion of this event, see Carlson's *On Sidesaddle to Heaven*, 51.

4. Traditional verse. It was common for young girls to learn such verses and songs by heart to help them understand society's rules for acceptable behavior. Obviously, red was the least acceptable color in which to be married. Green ran a close second, followed by black.

5. Samuel Parker preached about an incident published in the *Christian Advocate Journal* detailing an account of Indians from the Pacific Northwest who, in 1831, traveled two thousand miles to St. Louis in search of the Book, or Bible. Today, historians debate whether this incident actually took place in the manner described or whether the cause of their visit was simply (as cited in one news journal of the day) "to inquire for the truth of a representation which they said some white men had made among them, that [Christian]

religion was better than theirs, and that they would all be lost if they did not embrace it" (H. Jackson, 105). At any rate, the Indians' journey and inquiry (however packaged) was widely circulated to justify the Christian missionary movement's directive "to aid in the conversion of the world." And it proved highly effective. The story was told and retold in women's magazines, men's pamphlets and newspapers, and in meeting societies until it reached the epic proportions of a folk myth.

6. When Narcissa spoke of the Word of God, she was speaking about a Protestant God, specifically a Presbyterian. There was fierce competition at this time between the Christian denominations for ecclesiastic territory among the Native tribes and even more pointed competition between Protestant and Roman Catholic missionary efforts. Narcissa subscribed to the Presbyterian doctrine. She was most eager to spread that particular interpretation of Christianity to the heathens before other doctrines could be established.

7. Rushville, New York. These boots would have been made of tough, durable leather and most probably cut from a standard pattern for men's boots since Narcissa describes them as gentlemen's boots. There was no differentiation at this time between right and left footgear. Typically, to achieve proper fit, the booted foot was soaked in water then allowed to dry before the boot was removed. It wasn't until after the War Between the States (the Civil War) that specific right-foot and left-foot shoes/boots were commonly available in America.

8. As quoted in Jeffrey's *Converting the West*, 60, Spalding said, "I do not want to go into the same mission with Narcissa Prentiss, as I question her judgment." Whether this was based upon Narcissa's overall quality of judgment or whether this was in response to her refusal of Spalding's proposal of marriage is not clear. Spalding was widely known to have been born illegitimate. This scandal condemned Spalding to the lowest stations of polite society. The only way to become respectable by the definition of the day was through the Church. This he did, but he doubtless was deeply affected by the experiences of his early years.

9. In his application to the ABDFM for Missionary status, Spalding requested that one of his professors at Franklin Academy write a letter of recommendation. The professor reported to the Board that Spalding didn't possess any particular academic brilliance, that he didn't display much judgment or common sense, and that he seemed quick to criticize those whom he deemed to be "less zealous than himself" in spreading the word of God. He added, however, that Spalding was a decent man and that his wife, Eliza, was "much beloved" and "one of the best women for a missionary's wife with whom I am acquainted" (as cited in Drury's *Henry Harmon Spalding*, 64).

10. What Narcissa did not (and would not) know was that Eliza Spalding had suffered through a debilitating stillborn birth less than a year before, from which her health never fully recovered. Such topics were not discussed in those days among any but immediate family members and then only with the greatest circumspection. That Eliza successfully completed the grueling journey was a testament to her faith and to her fortitude.

11. Narcissa Prentiss Whitman, *The Letters of Narcissa Whitman, 1836–1847* (Fairfield, WA: Ye Galleon Press, 1986), March 31, 1836, 12, letter to her sister Jane.

12. Ibid., April 7, 1836, letter to her sister Jane.

13. Ibid., June 4, 1836, 15, letter to her sister Harriet and brother Edward. "Just above Forks" in Narcissa's notation refers to the point in present-day Nebraska where the Platte River divides into the North and South Platte.

14. Ibid, 15.

15. Ibid, 16. Tavern in this usage probably means an inn or overnight structure of some kind. There were yet occasional amenities of civilization at this point along the Platte River, as this was a well-known and well-traveled route by fur traders.

16. Ibid., June 4, 1836, 16, letter to her sister Harriet and brother Edward. The use of

dried buffalo dung as fuel became so commonplace on the treeless plains that the French coined a phrase for the chips, calling them *bois de vache*, or buffalo wood.

17. Ibid, 16.

18. Ibid., June 27, 1836, 21, letter to her Whitman in-laws. Today, this type of high protein diet sets up a super-acidity in the body which is very hard on the kidneys and often results in diarrhea. In the long-term absence of nutrients usually gained from vegetables, fruits, and grains, the body can actually begin feeding upon itself to maintain function. As Eliza Spalding was less robust than Narcissa to begin with, one assumes her body was quicker to feel the impact of this all-meat diet.

19. Narcissa Prentiss Whitman, *My Journal* (Fairfield, WA: Ye Galleon Press, 1994), July 27, 1836, 17. Her journal was intended to be transcribed at a later date with other journal entries and mailed to her family "back in the U.States."

20. Ibid.

21. Ibid.

22. Whitman, *The Letters of Narcissa Whitman*, June 27, 1836, 22.

23. Ibid. Richard and John are doubtless the names these tribal males were given upon their baptism into Christianity. We have only Narcissa's phonetic spellings of their tribal *last* names in her letters to indicate about whom she was talking. In addition to the two Nez Perce tribesmen traveling with the Whitmans and Spaldings, there were apparently at least three others traveling with the American Fur Company, as well as the tribal peoples who made their appearance along the route.

24. Now called Fort Laramie in Wyoming.

25. Ibid, 22.

26. Often called simply Rendezvous in what is now southwestern Wyoming. This was the annual American Fur Company congregation of fur trappers and traders, hundreds of tribal peoples, and revelers of every description. It was the biggest trading/swapping/buying opportunity of the year, as well as being an enormous social event. In addition to

business, there was horse racing, gambling, visiting, drinking, contests, and hijinks of every kind—both harmless and lethal. As cited in Carlson's *On Sidesaddles to Heaven*, one such Rendezvous even featured jousting in medieval armor!

27. This was considered a first in U.S. history: white women crossing the Rocky Mountains. Eliza Spalding wrote of it in her journal; Narcissa made no notation that survives.

28. As described in Carlson's *On Sidesaddle to Heaven*, 69. Apparently, these men flocked around Narcissa simply to be in the company of a civilized woman. They were hungry for such attention and protracted their stay as long as possible. It is dubious many were overly pious, but to receive anything in the wilderness from such a woman's hand would have been much sought after and highly prized.

29. William Gray, who was part of this mission party, spoke of Eliza's efforts among the Indians in glowing terms, as cited in Drury's *Marcus and Narcissa Whitman*, 198. Of Narcissa, however, he was highly critical, saying she was "too busy flirting with dazzled and savage mountain men to pay much attention to her charges."

30. Those commonly called the Snakes from Lewis and Clark times through pioneer emigration were the peoples today called the Shoshones. Their homelands were, like the Nez Perce and the Flatheads, west of the Rocky Mountains. The term Snake came from nontribal misunderstanding of the hand sign by which they designated themselves. They themselves made the motion of the salmon's tail (sometimes also referred to as the waving grass from which they wove their baskets). This hand sign was misinterpreted as the movement of a snake; hence, the name. Some ethnohistorians also include the Northern Paiute peoples in this classification of Snake.

31. There is no direct mention in any of Narcissa's journal entries or letters of this pregnancy, which is in keeping for proper etiquette of this era. However, when the months are counted back from the birth of her daugh-

ter, Alice Clarissa, on March 14, 1837, one realizes Narcissa most probably became pregnant sometime in early June. By the middle of July, she would have realized the fact.

32. Whitman, *My Journal*, July 25 and August 6, 1836, 16, 25.

33. Ibid., July 25, 1836, 16.

34. Ibid., July 28, 1836, 18.

35. Ibid., July 30, 1836, 18.

36. Ibid, 20.

37. Ibid., July 28 and August 4, 1836, 17, 22.

38. Ibid., August 4, 1836, 22. Christian was the principal character in the hugely popular religious allegory, *Pilgrim's Progress*. The book was first published in England in 1678 by John Bunyan as moral instruction in living a Christian life. In the book, Christian wandered a long and dangerous route, facing many moral dilemmas and temptations along the way. He was sustained by his faith, ultimately arriving at a Divine destination where he was amply rewarded for his steadfast commitment to his God.

39. Ibid., August 4, 1836, 22. What Narcissa calls the Snake Fort was also called Fort Boise and sometimes McKay's Fort for the HBC employee who was in charge there. Narcissa says, "The Snake Fort is built and owned by Mr. Thomas McKay, one of our company" (*Journal*, August 19, 1836). Walla Walla was the term used by Narcissa both for the fort at that location and the general vicinity (in present day Washington State). The modern city by the same name grew up around the old fort grounds.

40. Ibid., August 2, 1836, 20. Whitman's description of the landscape and citation of the Bible (Deuteronomy 28: 23).

41. Ibid., August 12, 1836, 29.

42. Ibid., August 13, 1836, 29.

43. Ibid.

44. Now called the Baker Valley, in far northeastern Oregon. This Lone Tree served as a guidepost for travelers long before the Oregon Trail migration. John C. Fremont, in his journal entry of October 15, 1843, lists it as "felled by some inconsiderate emigrant's axe." But the Lone Tree Valley remained a vivid memory for many, as it presented their first breathtaking view of what emigrants called the Promised Land: fertile land for farming, abundant water, great quantities of wild game, and, during the time when most emigrants came through it, moderate temperatures.

45. Whitman, *My Journal*, August 28, 1836, 34.

46. Ibid., August 29, 1836, 36.

47. Ibid.

48. Ibid.

49. Ibid., September 1, 1836, 39.

50. Ibid., September 3, 1836, 42.

51. Ibid., September 5, 1836, 44.

52. Ibid., November 1, 1836, 60.

53. *Waiilatpu*, place of the rye grass, near what is now Walla Walla, Washington; *Lapwai*, place of the butterflies, near what is now Lewiston, Idaho.

54. Whitman, *The Letters of Narcissa Whitman*, May 2, 1840, 93.

55. Ibid., March 30, 1837, 47.

56. Clifford Merrill Drury, *Marcus Whitman MD* (Caldwell, ID: Caxton Press, 1937), 174.

57. Thomas E. Jessett, *The Indian Side of the Whitman Massacre* (Fairfield, WA: Ye Galleon Press, 1985), 10, letter of October 19, 1849 from Reverend H. K. W. Perkins, who was the Methodist missionary at the Dalles Mission.

58. Mary Richardson Walker, 1838 letter to parents upon arrival in Oregon Country. *Christian Advocate Journal* as cited in Laurie Winn Carlson, *On Sidesaddles to Heaven: The Women of the Rocky Mountain Mission* (Caldwell, ID: The Caxton Press, 1998), 26.

59. Carlson, 47.

60. Whitman, *The Letters of Narcissa Whitman*, letter to her sister Harriet and brother Edward.

61. Ibid., June 27, 1836, letter to her Whitman in-laws, June 3, 1836.

62. Drury, Marcus Whitman letter to his father and mother, May 16, 1844

63. Speckled Snake, from his speech to the Council of Indian Chiefs on June 20, 1829,

SEEING THE ELEPHANT

Edwin L. Jackson, *The Georgia Studies Book* (Athens, GA: University of Georgia, Carl Vinson Institute of Government, 1991), 155.

64. Joyce Badgley Hunsaker, *Oregon Trail Center: The Story Behind the Scenery* (Las Vegas, NV: KC Publications, 1995), 12.

65. Jos. K. Dixon, *The Vanishing Race* (New York: Bonanza Books printing of original manuscript and photographs, 1913), 53.

66. Isaac P. Rose, *Four Years in the Rockies* as cited in Whitman, *The Letters of Narcissa Whitman*, 6.

67. Jessett, 8, October 19, 1848, Reverend H. K. W. Perkins' letter to Narcissa's sister, Jane, recounting Narcissa's death.

THOMAS JEFFERSON FARNHAM
Go West, Young Man!

1839

THE FAMOUS Horace Greeley, who coined the phrase *Go West, Young Man!* sent me on my adventure across the Oregon Trail.[1] He hired me to relate my experiences in journal form so that he could publish them in his newspaper. Why? To stake our claim to the Oregon Country, of course! To excite America's imagination! To incite the common man to catch the fever and journey west. Settle there. Spit in the eye of the English, who still say the land is theirs. This nation aims to carry our boundaries from sea to sea, one day.[2] Why not now?

Spain ceded her rights to the Oregon Country in the Treaty of Florida, twenty years ago. But the English . . . ah, the English. When Jefferson bought the Louisiana Purchase, doubling the size of America, England started getting nervous. Well, now, we've squeezed the Russians out of Oregon in the past, and we'll do the same to the Queen![3]

On the 21st of May, 1839, I arrived in the town of Independence, Missouri, with sixteen other men. Our destination was the Oregon Territory. Our aim was to settle. Some of our number sought health in the wilderness. Others sought the wilderness for its own sake. And still others sought a residence among the ancient forests and lofty heights of the valley of the river, Columbia. Each, driven by his own peculiar reasons, began his preparations for leaving the frontier.[4] They called us the Peoria Party, as we harkened from that region in Illinois.

Pack mules, pack horses, and saddles were purchased and prepared for service. Bacon and flour, salt and pepper (sufficient for 400 miles) were secured in sacks. Our powder casks were wrapped in painted canvas; large oil-cloths were purchased to protect the casks and our clothing from the rains. Our firearms were thoroughly repaired. Bullets were molded, powder horns and cap-boxes were filled,[5] and all else was done that was deemed needful before we struck our tent for Indian Territory.[6]

Nine days later, we found ourselves prepared to move from the States[7] toward Indian Lands. With pack saddles girded upon the animals and our provisions snugly lashed upon them, we commenced in highest spirits. We had traveled only three miles when such torrents of rain fell upon us, we had to take shelter in a neighboring school house for the night. The storm howled over, and under, and throughout, sounding as though it would never stop. It was a dismal beginning.

The next morning, however, dawned clear and pleasant, and we were early on our route. We crossed the stream called Big Blue[8] about noon, and approached the border of Indian domain. We lingered over every object that reminded us we were still on the edge of civilization. It was painful to approach the last frontier enclosure—the last habitation of the white man—the last semblance of home. Finally, we came to the last cabin. We drank from the well and traveled westward.[9] Everything familiar was now behind us.

Before us were the treeless plains of green—beautiful, unbroken by bush or rock, unsoiled by plough or spade. We traveled about twenty-five miles over this prairie before stopping on the banks of a small stream at a place called Elm Grove. Here, we pitched our tent, tied our horses to stakes, and after considerable difficulty in finding fuel for a fire, we cooked and ate for the first time in Indian Territory.

The Grove was a crossroads of sorts, filled with those coming and those going. We met traders coming from the mountains who told us the buffalo had not yet come so far north as to furnish us with their fine hump-ribs. After leaving this camp, it could be a week or even a fortnight[10] before the buffalo would be in their accustomed gathering grounds. So we decided to remain here until we could send some of our party back for 200 pounds of extra flour. Until their return, we took account of our common stock: provisions, arms, ammunition, packs and pack saddles, and goods for trade with the Indians. We chose officers for our party and defined their powers of authority.[11] We hunted unsuccessfully for deer, searched to retrieve strayed animals, and regaled ourselves with the strawberries and gooseberries which grew in abundance near camp. We wondered and wondered again what excitements the future would hold in store.

At last the provisions arrived, and we set our faces westward once again. As the days passed, we fell into a routine: travel fifteen to twenty miles a day, then camp. Each night, a certain portion of the company unpacked the mules of the common-stock property, provisions, and ammunition. Another portion pitched the tent; another gathered wood and kindled a fire. Meanwhile, others brought water, and still others put pots and frying pans to their appropriate duties.[12]

Our messes[13] were divided into two shifts: seven men in one, eight in the other. We ate upon the ground, each with a tin pint cup and a small, round, tin plate. The cup was most usually filled with coffee, tea, or water; the plate piled high with fried side of bacon and dough fried in fat. Each of the men had a butcher knife in hand and ate sitting—tailor-like—around the campfire. The first wild meat we killed was a turtle, which provided an excellent supper. It was the only game of any description we had seen since leaving the frontier.[14]

Occasionally our camp fell near other wagoners, most of which were on their return to Missouri. With these men, we passed very agreeable times around the campfire, listening to their yarns and legends of mountain life. At one camp, two Indians came within close distance of our tents. They watched us narrowly, characteristic of caution, as they waited for our invitation to approach. When we signaled that we were friends not foes, they took seats near the fire and commenced smoking their customary blend of willow bark and tobacco. The evening passed without incident. Then, when we left the ground, one of our men threw away a pair of old boots, the soles of which were fastened with iron nails. Our Indian visitors eagerly seized upon the boots and in their language of pantomime and grunts, congratulated themselves upon becoming the possessors of so much wealth.[15]

If only all could be so happy with so little! It was here that three of my valuable men became disillusioned with the difficulty of our trek and turned back to the States with the wagoners. As they filed off and bade us adieu, every face among those remaining was etched with discouragement.

The days wore on, and the expressions of doubt grew more grave. We scoured the country all day, every day, in search of game.[16] There was none to be found. We had only 100 pounds of flour and a side of bacon left, and the buffalo—by best estimates—were still three hundred miles away. The country between us and the buffalo was constantly scoured by Indian hunters as well. We had little prospect of making a kill. So we put ourselves on short allowances and looked at our horses as the means for preventing starvation, if it came to that.[17]

It rained almost daily. The men grumbled mightily for the lack of food, and the abundance of mud. Until the day we found elk.

We were ten miles into the day's march. Our animals were tugging lustily through the prairie mud, when the advance guard shouted: *Elk! Elk!* and *Steaks broiled!* and *Ribs boiled!* and *Marrow bones!*[18] *No more hunger!* and finally *Oregon Forever, starve or live!*

We filed off to the chase, splitting into two parties. The hunters circled down-wind, around the point of the sharp ridge upon which the elk were feeding, so their scent would not be detected. Then, lying close to their horses' necks, they rode slowly and silently up the ravine towards them. Meanwhile, the rest of us moved quietly along the trail, hoping to divert the attention of the elk. Thus, the hunters crept undetected within three hundred yards of the game before they were discovered.

But the instant—that *awful* instant to our gnawing appetites—the instant the elk perceived the crouching hunters nearing them, they tossed their heads in the air, sniffed loudly and disdainfully at our poor attempts to deceive their wakeful senses, and put hoof to turf in fine style.

Our hunters attempted pursuit, but as they had to ascend one side of the ridge while the elk were descending the other, they were at least four hundred yards behind their quarry. Ball after ball whistled after them, only to sleep in the earth instead of in the panting hearts which were their target. In the end, no elk were killed. Not even one.[19]

Then it began to rain again. We spent that sleepless and hungry night trying to dry our drenched bodies and clothes, accompanied by a symphony of stomach rumblings and the howling of wolves.

Have you ever seen a prairie storm? Ever felt its fury? On the 12th of June, we were assaulted by one the likes of which I could never have imagined. It was about three o'clock in the afternoon when a great, black cloud arose in the southeast, another in the southwest, and still another in the northeast. They looked like those that spawn tornadoes, rising and surging, and merging into dreadful masses over our heads. They struggled so terrifically against one another that they sounded like artillery. It was terrifying. Deafening. Then suddenly, all was hushed. Not a breath of wind stirred.

We looked up for the coming of the catastrophe surely foretold by that awful stillness.

And at that moment, the clouds were ripped apart. A terrific explosion of electricity split the sky. Peal upon peal of thunder rolled around, and up, and down the heavens. Burning lightning bolts leapt from cloud to cloud above our heads; then from heaven to earth with such ferocity that the glare of one would scarcely fall upon the eye before another of still greater intensity would follow. We were stunned. Absolutely stupefied.

Our animals madly huddled themselves together and became immovable. They heeded neither whip nor spur but turned their backs to the tempest and dropped their heads as if awaiting their doom. The hail and rain responded by slamming down upon them in torrents. The plains were converted into a sea and the sky into a continual blaze of electric fire. It was a scene no pen can adequately describe.[20]

The rain fell for hours in cold, shivering floods. When, at last, the storm grew thin, we tried to pitch our camp. But all of our packs were sodden. That night, we huddled together for warmth as we ate our scanty suppers. We drank the water from the puddles and sought rest. Once again, we had to be content with spreading our wet blankets upon the mud, putting our saddles under our heads, and musing and shivering until morning.

But in the morning—that and every morning on the over-watered plains—as the sun rose high in the heavens, so did the swarms of mosquitoes. The most gigantic and persevering mosquitoes that ever gathered tribute from humankind lighted upon us and demanded blood. They fixed themselves around our eyes, inside our noses, over every inch of skin—on both man and beast. They attacked in such numbers, we found ourselves in frenzies of flailing and whipping and jumping about.[21] Consequently, we often lost the trail.

At least we were not murdered. Yet. Not by Nature, nor by man. And we reminded ourselves: Oregon was drawing closer with every sunrise.

The nearer we drew to buffalo lands, the more evidence of Indian encampments we saw. Across Pawnee Fork, we visited the Caw[22] camp. There appeared to be about 1,500 of them. It was their custom to make a yearly hunt here in the spring, lay in a large supply of dried meat, and return to their own territory[23] in harvest time to gather their beans and corn, make their buffalo hides into tents, and prepare for a long winter.

On these hunting excursions, they would take with them all their horses and mules that could be spared from their labors in the fields and head south until they met the buffalo. There they would build their wigwams and commence their labor.

The work was divided between the males, females, and the children. The men killed the game. The women dressed and dried the meat and tanned the hides. The boy children of the tribe watered and guarded the horses and mules, changing their stakes from one spot of fresh grass to another. They crouched along the heights of camp to notice the approach of foes and sound the alarm. The girl children attended the women in their duties.[24]

The Indian male's sole duty as a citizen of the tribe, and lord of his woman's life, was to ride the horse which she saddled and brought to his tent; to kill the game which she then dressed and cured; to sit and slumber on the couch which she spread for him; and to fight the enemies of the tribe. The wife was expected to take care of the horses; to manufacture the saddles and bridles, leash ropes and whips, her husband's moccasins, leggings, and hunting shirts by her own hand; to beat the buffalo robes with a wooden adze until they were soft and pleasant for her husband's couch; to tan the hides for his tent coverings, and to drag from the distant hills the poles to support it; to cook his daily food and place it before him.[25] Ah, the glory of being born an Indian male!

We watched with keen interest as the Caws hunted buffalo. The weapons used in killing varied with the rank and wealth of each man. The high chief carried a lance with a handle six feet long, and upon that, a blade that measured another three feet. This in hand and mounted on a fast horse, he rode boldly to the side of the stampeding buffalo herd. He thrust it again and again toward the livers or hearts of as many beasts as he could, before his horse could no longer keep near them. In this way, five or six were killed at a single heat.

Some of the lesser chiefs also had these lances, but their lances were all shorter than that of the head chief. The common Indians used muskets and pistols. Rifles were an abomination to them. The twisting motion of the ball as it enters, the sharp "crack" when discharged, and the mournful singing of the lead when it cuts the air—these were considered symptoms of witchcraft, unsafe for the red man to meddle with. They call them Medicines.[26]

The poorer classes still used the bow and arrow. But I have seen these— in the well trained hand of the Indian—a highly effective weapon, equal to the others in hunting buffalo. Astride a good horse, beside a bellowing band of these wild beef, many a naked hunter used bow and arrow with astonishing dexterity and success. They would lean forward on their horses' necks, and draw their limbs close to their sides. Then they ran until every man had a buffalo at his side. Frequently, the arrows passed entirely through the running buffalo, hitting no bones on their course! They seldom failed.[27]

When the hunt was over and great numbers of the noble beasts lay upon the dusty plain, a cloud of women from the camp descended. They hurried to the site on pack animals, stripped the hides off the carcasses, cut off the best flesh. Then they loaded all upon their pack saddles, mounted themselves on top, and moved slowly back to camp.

The meat was cut into long, narrow strips and wound around sticks standing upright in the ground, or laid over a stack of twigs under which a slow fire was kept burning. This cured the meat and dried it. Then they stretched the hides upon the ground and staked them and with a blunt wooden adze, hewed them into leather.

We were told they would load up every animal with meat and hides about the first of August and travel back to their fields on the Konzas River. Thus it had been since before memory and would continue until Pawnees or other enemies might interfere.[28]

How I envied the predictability of their lives! Particularly when later, two of the most quarrelsome men in my company—released from the restraints of society and law—came to a sudden and unforeseen disagreement that resulted in the shooting of one. An accidental wounding, that's what we called it.

Everything was done for the wounded man that his condition required and that our circumstances permitted. Still, it was thought best to send for the doctor who was traveling with some wagoners, eight miles ahead. In the meantime, the Caw high chief visited our patient and administered some sort of colored water and salve. When Dr. Walworth finally examined the chest wound, he announced he could do little that had not been already done and said he thought our man would live. The good doctor furnished us a carriage and advised us to travel on at once, for Comanches and Pawnees were on the prowl.

We covered the bottom of the carry-all with grass and blankets, laid our invalid upon them, and bolstered him with yet more blankets so the jolting of the carriage would not roll him.

I left my lieutenant[29] in charge of the company, ordering him to follow after me as fast as camp could be broken. Then I took the reins of the carriage in my hands and drove out into the waning light toward the camp of the wagoners.

The trail was continually crossed by deep paths made by the buffalo. These, and the tracks from the forty-odd wagons ahead, jolted the carriage at every turn. My patient groaned aloud. He screamed with pain. Then the rains began. And when the water streamed through the carriage upon him, he cursed the stars; consigned to purgatory the thunder, lightening, and rain; cursed the wagon. Finally, gathering up strength, he shook his fists at the storm, quoting Shakespeare at full voice. Then he fell back, silent, and ground his teeth until daylight.[30]

When the rest of the company caught up to us, there was a mutiny in the making. Here was repeated, for the twentieth time, the quarrels of the company. Here was repeated the argument for—and against—who should be leader, who follower, and in what order. There were those who wanted to go on to Oregon and those who wanted to go back. Those who wanted to leave behind our invalid; those who swore they would carry him on their backs if need be. The traveling babel stopped only when Bent's trading post came into sight.[31]

Our hearts, weary of the tensions of our camp, leapt for joy. The gates were thrown open and *Welcome to Fort William* greeted us from the lips of our countrymen. Peace again—roofs again—safety and relief again—and bread . . . ah, bread again at Fort William.[32]

Two of the Bent brothers were at the post when we arrived. They seemed to be thoroughly initiated into Indian life. They wore moccasins decorated with beads and porcupine quills. Their trousers of deer skin were hung with long fringes from ankle to hip. Their splendid hunting shirts were made of the same material, with sleeves fringed from the wrist to the shoulder. They were ornamented with figures of porcupine quills in many colors and leather fringe around the lower edge. The Bent brothers dressed like chiefs, and chiefs they were in the authority they exercised over this wild and lonely fortress.[33]

A trading establishment must be seen to be truly known. It was the solitary abode of men seeking wealth in the teeth of danger and hardship, rearing its towers over the uncultivated wastes of Nature like an old baronial castle that had withstood the wars and desolations of centuries. Indian women in their glittering moccasins and long deer skin wrappers,[34] accompanied by their mixed-blood children, chattered now in Indian, now Spanish or English. The owners and their clerks and traders would sit in the shade, smoking the long native pipe, passing it from one to another, drawing the smoke into the lungs by short, hysterical sucks then blowing it out through their nostrils. Sometimes they sat around a crudely-fashioned table, spread with coffee or tea, jerked buffalo meat, and bread. Sometimes they lay comfortably upon their pallets of straw and Spanish blankets, dozing to the sweet notes of a flute.[35]

There would be a congregation of old trappers, withered from their life in the elements; half-tamed Indians and half-civilized Mexican servants, seated on the ground with their only rations—a large pan of dry meat and a tankard of water. Adventures about the shores of Hudson's Bay, on the rivers Columbia and Mackenzie, in the Great Prairie Wilderness, and among the snowy heights of the mountains would be told and retold. Sage opinions would be voiced about the destination of certain bands of buffalo, of the distance to the Blackfeet country, and whether my wounded man was hurt as badly as Bill the mule was when the meal party was fired upon by the Comanches.

Business within the walls of the post was done by the clerks and traders. The clerks were most commonly young gentlemen from various cities in the States, whose duty it was to keep the accounting books. The traders were generally selected from among those daring men who had traveled the

SEEING THE ELEPHANT

prairie and mountain wilderness with goods or traps, and understood how best to deal with the Indians. Their duty was to weigh the sugar, coffee, powder, etc., in a Connecticut pint-cup; to measure red cloth, beads, and trinkets; and to speak several Indian languages that had a name for beaver skins, buffalo robes, and money.

Fifteen or twenty of them were employed to take the buffalo robes and animal pelts collected at the fort to market then to return with new stocks of goods for future purchase. Another party was employed in hunting buffalo meat in the neighboring plains. And still another, under the command of an experienced trader, was charged with going to some distant Indian camp to trade. Each party knew danger well.[36]

The fort was situated in a country common to several tribes, all which were unfriendly to one another and to the whites. The Utahs[37] and Cheyennes of the mountains near Santa Fe and the Pawnees of the Great Platte River came here to meet the buffalo in their annual migrations north. And on the trail of these animals followed the Comanches. From June through September, there were in the neighborhood of the fort from fifteen to twenty thousand savages,[38] ready and panting for a fight. If they engaged in battling out old feuds and grudges among themselves, the Bent brothers felt comparatively safe in their fortress. But if they spared each other's property and lives, there were great anxieties at Fort William. Every hour was pregnant with danger for the white man.[39]

Yet we, ourselves, felt safe. The fine days spent there restored our energies and refreshed our weary animals. Even our wounded invalid recovered astonishingly. We were loathe to leave the place, but Oregon would not wait. It was time to push on. How many would leave with me?

The company disbanded. Property held in common was divided and each individual left to his own choices and resources. Only three good men and the one wounded man chose my course. The others—the mutineers—turned their backs upon us and headed away.

Five miles above Fort William, we came to Fort Puebla. It belonged to a company of American and Mexican trappers who, weary of the unpredictable life, had retired to this spot to raise grain, vegetables, horses, and mules for the trading posts. But these, like the results of so many honest intentions, were wholly crippled by a scarcity of money and a superabundance of whiskey.

Here, the independent trappers congregated. After the spring hunt, they came down from the mountains and took rooms free of rent. Here, they stored their furs and opened a trade for whiskey. One skin, valued at four dollars, bought one pint of liquor; no more, no less.[40]

Not all were in their cups, however. One trapper was from New Hampshire. He had been educated at Dartmouth College and was altogether one of the most remarkable men I ever knew. He was a splendid gentleman, a finished scholar, a critic on English and Roman literature, a politician, a trapper, and an *Indian!*

He stood more than six feet tall; his shoulders and chest were broad, and his arms and legs very muscular. His forehead was high; his hair as black as jet,[41] two and a half feet in length. He was clothed all in deer leather. But it was his eloquence that held me fast.[42]

The enthusiasm and power with which he spoke of his people impressed me with an awe I had never known. I began truly to appreciate the dignity and independence of the American Indian. Enfeebled and reduced to a state of dependence by disease and by the crowding hosts of civilized men, the Indians still possessed too much of their own character to adopt that of another race. They possessed too much bravery to feel like a conquered people. And they preferred annihilation to the abandonment of that way of life which had been consecrated by a thousand generations of their venerated ancestors.[43]

He said he never intended to visit the States again. "I will live and die in the wilderness," said he. And assuredly, he should thus live and die. The music of the rushing waters should be his requiem, and the Great Wilderness his tomb.[44]

After Puebla, day trudged into weary day. The grasses gave way to broken hills; these, to barren knolls, sparsely covered with shrub cedars and pines. Then rocks and gravels littered our way through limestone bluffs and crumbling sandstones. At last we were at the gateway to the mountains. Nothing could be more perfectly wild. Their summits were capped with ice; their wooded ravines were a profusion of eternal, sublime confusion. What a joyful occasion this was! The storms, the mud, the swollen streams, the bleakness and the barrenness of the Great Prairie Wilderness were behind us. And the deep, rich vales, the cool streams and breezes of the Rocky Mountains were just ahead.[45]

If only our expansiveness of spirit could have made the way seem easy! But the mountains had other plans. The steepest part of our trail was a loose, moving surface of sand and pebbles, constantly falling under its own weight. Other portions were precipitous, lying along overhanging cliffs and the brinks of deep ravines strewn with fallen rocks. Our progress up was pull after muscle-burning pull. Thirty yards of a zigzag clambering and slipping and gathering and tugging. Then, all halted as we gathered breath and strength for a new effort.

All too soon the shout, *Go on! Go on!* started the cavalcade again. Our pack animals, each with 150 pounds weight, struggled and floundered, as step after step gave way in the sliding sand. The track wound around a beetling cliff, crowding the animals upon the edge of a precipice, with a drop-off of 300 feet directly below. We skirted pines two feet in diameter and a hundred feet high. It was a bed of rocks: at one place small and rolling, at another large and fixed, with deep openings between.[46]

At last we reached the pass and pitched our camp by nightfall. We ate our simple supper of tole, or water porridge, and we tried to sleep. But the cold wind from the mountain snows soon drove us from our blankets to the fire, where we turned ourselves like Christmas turkeys until morning.

Tole had been our only food for nine days. It seemed strange that we should have traveled 180 miles since leaving Fort William without killing an animal. Our guide informed us, *It is a starving country; never any game found in it.* And certainly, that seemed to be so.

Until the next morning, when Providence shone upon us and a lone buffalo bull stumbled into our cooking pot. We ate and ate until we could hold no more; rested, then ate again. The blows of our guide's hatchet cracked the marrow bones into pieces, and laid bare the rolls of trapper's butter inside. A pound of marrow was extracted and put into a gallon of water heated nearly to the boiling point. Then the buffalo's blood was stirred into the water until the mass became the consistency of rice soup. A little salt and black pepper finished the preparation. It was a fine dish. Excellent . . . most excellent, indeed.[47]

It was decided around that stew fire we might, by packing what meat we could, be able to reach more game on the tributaries of the Grand, some days ahead. Our choice was unanimous. Pack, or perish from hunger.

We followed Indian trails through the mountains for nearly two weeks.

Thomas Jefferson Farnham

The meat played out, so we cut thistles, and ate the inner portion of their stalks, as we had seen Indians do. How quickly man's fortunes changed in the wilderness! From gluttony to want in a matter of only days. Was this the story of the trail to Oregon?

We had heard from trappers that the Arapahos were fattening on buffalo in the Bull Pen on the north fork of the Platte, but the Shoshones or Snakes were starving on roots on Great Bear River. They said there was no game in the mountains except on the headwaters of Snake River. They warned us that the Blackfeet and Sioux were in our neighborhood; we might reasonably expect starvation *and* the arrows of the Sioux. The grass on the Columbia, they said, was already dry and scarce; and if there should prove to be enough of it to sustain our horses between here and there, the snows on the Blue Mountains would prevent us from reaching Vancouver until spring.[48] Yet we pushed on.

We passed over Little Bear River. We caught three or four small trout and ate them. The next day brought only worm wood[49] and prickly pear to the expanse of rugged desolation before us. Then another day and yet another. A week. The face of the country was a desert. Neither tree, nor shrub, nor grass, nor game in sight for mile upon dreary mile. Then there was no water. Our faithful hound could be eaten as a last recourse, but we had to find water. At last, turning from our track and following a deep ravine, we came upon a filthy, oozing sulphurous puddle that our horses—though they had had no water the entire day—refused to drink. We men were not so particular. We drank.

There followed forty-eight hours without food of any kind—not even thistles. We were near the throes of death. We held council and decided our noble dog must die. He was accordingly shot, his hair burnt off, and his forequarters boiled and eaten. Some of the men declared that dogs made excellent mutton. To me, it tasted like the flesh of a dog. A singed dog. Whether cooked or barking, a dog is still a dog, everywhere.[50]

We pursued our journey over the gray, barren wastes of perpetual sterility. At long last, we reached Brown's Hole on the Green River,[51] and Fort David Crockett. Here, we rested both ourselves and our animals. Here we soaked up hospitality like a parched desert, the precious rain. Among those I met at Brown's Hole was an old Snake Indian who saw Messrs. Lewis and Clark on the headwaters of the Missouri in 1805. He said he was the first of his tribe to see the explorers. He and his nation had never seen men with faces pale as ashes. "The head rose high and round, the top flat; it jutted over the eyes in a thin rim. Their skin was loose and flowing, and of various colors," he said.[52] He recounted the entire story of the white men's coming, including the fact that ever since that time, he had been much honored and loved by his tribe and—he said—by every white man in the mountains. He was then eighty years old and poor. But he could always be found about Fort David Crockett, and he was never permitted to want.

On the 17th of August, the old Yankee woodsman, Paul Richardson, arrived from Fort Hall. He had been on one of his favorite summer trips from St. Louis to the borders of Oregon, acting as guide and hunter to a party of missionaries to the Oregon Indians. Several other persons from the States had accompanied them: one with the lofty intention of conquering California; others with the intention of trading and farming on the lower Columbia; and others to explore the Rocky Mountains and the wonders of Nature along the shores of the Pacific.

Richardson gave Oregon a terrible name. He said it was not nearly as productive as New England; rain fell incessantly five months of the year; the remainder was unblessed even with dew. He said the Indians and whites residing there had the ague, or bilious fever, the year round. And what little human life was left after these maladies was consumed by mosquitoes and fleas. He told us the Columbia River was unfit for navigation, fit only for an Indian fish pond.[53] He had lived in the Territory for two years and traveled it well. We were shocked at his description.

The next day, two of my companions turned back for the States in discouragement. Now there would be only three of us, alone in the heart of the Wilderness, alone in Blackfeet country. I was completely disheartened. Yes, I was kindly offered quarters for the winter at Brown's Hole, but I was determined to reach the Columbia River this season, no matter what the risk.

Immediately, we laid in supplies. I purchased a good horse, obtained a quantity of dried buffalo meat, and had a dog butchered. Then I hired a Snake guide, whom the whites called Jim, for the sum of fifty loads of ammunition and three bunches of beads. He would pilot me to Fort Hall, two hundred miles ahead . . . two hundred miles to the edge of the Oregon Country.[54]

August 19, we were ready. Blair, Smith, and my guide Jim, constituted my whole party. Numerous war parties of Blackfeet and Sioux were hovering over my trail. If discovered by them, death was certain; if not, and starvation did not assail us, we might reach the waters of Snake River. In all events, we were going. And by ten o'clock in the morning, we were winding our way most determinedly toward our goal.

Our trail now was frequently populated with mountain men, as they called themselves. Some had lost their relish for a life of chasing beaver and were preparing to descend to the Columbia and open farms in the valley of the Willamette. Some were former Company men;[55] some, remnants of the American Fur Company's trapping parties. Some told us of caches[56] they had left along the trail and offered them to us, should we pass that way and have need. One even offered a horse he had been obliged to leave down by Beer Springs. When he heard we were traveling to the Columbia, he suggested we might go down with the Nez Perce Indians who were now encamped on Salmon River, one day's journey from Fort Hall. These Indians would be leaving their hunting grounds for their homes near the Columbia in about ten days, he said, and we could go with them.

We pushed hard, averaging twenty to twenty-five miles' travel per day. On the 29th, we camped near the Soda Springs. These, called Beer Springs by the fur traders, were most remarkable. There were six groups of springs: six small hollows sunken about two feet below the ground, about seven or eight feet in diameter. In these hollows, fountains sent up large quantities of gas and water and emitted a noise like the boiling of immense cauldrons. The pools were usually clear and had a gravelly bottom. The water bubbled so invitingly, I was tempted to drink at one of them. But as I proceeded to do so, the suffocating gases instantly drove me away. I tried again at a more open fountain and found the waters extremely pleasant to the taste. They appeared to be more full of soda and acid than those of Saratoga[57]; these fumed from the stomach like the soda water found in shops.[58]

Three days more and we beheld Fort Hall. Oregon Territory! We halted within sight of it. Our wardrobes were overhauled, our razors put to duty, our sun-burned bodies bathed in the river. Then, equipped in our best, we rushed to the plains, our hearts joyfully beating back the rapid clattering of our horses' hooves. Jim told us that we should discharge our rifles in salute, as was the custom. This we did.[59] Welcome to Fort Hall!

Inside the gates, there were handshakes and salutations all around. A generous flagon of Old Jamaica rum, wheat bread, newly-churned butter, and buffalo tongues fresh from the neighboring mountains appeared as if by magic for these trail-weary travelers. The next two days passed most comfortably and agreeably. But there was no time to lose. We must press on. We acquired fresh horses, fresh supplies, and a guide to lead us to Walla Walla.

The guide, Carbo, was of the Walla Walla tribe. He stood five feet nine inches in height. The front of his head had been pressed flat in infancy; his eyes were forced out upon the corners of his head; his nose hugged his face closely like a bunch of affectionate leeches. His hair was as black as a raven, flowing over a pair of Herculean shoulders.[60] And his feet—the likes of which I had never seen. I was told he was considered most attractive among his native people.

The face of the country over which Carbo led us had scarcely grass enough to feed our animals, and that was dried to hay. There had been no timber since we left the immediate vicinity of Fort Hall. All the rocks more or less fused together; there were many large tracts of lava, broken only by cut rock and worm wood deserts. Then, the soil became even too poor to bear the worm wood. Baked, impenetrable. It was a graveyard of desolation. Here, we saw those they call the Digger Indians and along the river, some Snakes. Many were employed in laying by their winter store of salmon. For one large fish hook, we bought one fish; for one paper of vermillion,[61] six bunches of spawn; for one butcher knife, one leather braided rope.

When, on September 14, we entered into Boisais,[62] we determined to stay only long enough to rest our horses then push on. Mr. Payette, the person in charge, plied us with salmon and excellent bread spread with butter from an American cow that he had obtained from some of the missionaries. He insisted upon seating us at our table and serving us himself. After a long and satisfying meal, he urged us to tour his establishment.

Among the curiosities we saw there were the front wheels, axletree, and thills[63] of a one-horse wagon, said to have been run by the American Missionaries from the eastern States through the mountains thus far on their way toward the mouth of the Columbia. It was left there under the belief that it could not be taken through the Blue Mountains.[64]

Lest we grow too comfortable with Mr. Payette, we left on the second day of our visit. The hills grew higher and more rocky. Those in the distance to the west and northwest appeared partially covered with pines and cedars. These gave way to high mountains thick with aspen, pine, and spruce. We saw many beautiful valleys among the highlands. We heard the song of the meadow lark and the honking of wild geese.

Temperatures grew much colder at night. Often, frost greeted us in the morning. During the day, we were reminded of Indian summer time of New England. How much snow, we wondered, might be waiting for us on the Blues?

When at last we reached *L'Arbor Seul*,[65] the Lonely Pine, we could see from the plain there was not the snow we had been told to fear. We looked upon the beautiful heights of the Blue Mountains and later ate among its summer blossoms, its singing pines, and lofty crags, ten thousand feet above the seas. All afternoon, we continued to ascend. Vast rolls of mountains lifted themselves over one another higher and higher, until in the distance their tops mingled with the blue of the sky.[66]

Carbo pushed us forward, forward. We stopped to eat when darkness fell. But as soon as the moon peeped over the eastern heights, Carbo roused me to say in his broken French that the horses had nothing here to eat and that we, being rested, must climb the mountain to find food for them. My first impulse was to order him to sleep, but a hungry whinny from my roan pony changed my mind. I summoned my weary limbs and bruised, ulcerated feet to their best efforts, and at twelve o'clock midnight we were on the march. To label this forced scramble in the dark heart of the Wilderness as harrowing would be pale. Suffice it to say that a very long three hours later, we finally encamped in a grove of pines that crowned the mountain. The Man-In-The-Moon was the only one who smiled.

The next afternoon, we encountered a Skyuse Indian[67] en route to Dr. Whitman's mission, where a considerable number of his tribe had pitched their tents for the approaching winter. I decided to leave my companions and accompany him there. Carbo would take the others to Fort Walla Walla.

At the end of our first day together, my Skyuse host and his family set camp for the night. His wife presented a dish of meat to her husband and one to me. There was a pause. Then, the Indian bowed his head and prayed to God! He called upon Jehovah in the name of Jesus Christ!

After the meal came a hymn in the Nez Perce language. That finished, they all knelt and bowed their faces upon the buffalo robes and prayed long and fervently. Afterwards, they sang another hymn and retired. I was astonished! This was the first breathing of religious feelings that I had seen since leaving the States. Clearly, the Oregon Country was beginning to bear the rose of Sharon upon its thousand hills.[68]

Another half-day's ride brought us in sight of the groves around the mission. The plains far and near were dry and brown. Every form of vegetation appeared dead, save the ancient forest trees. We crossed the river, passed the Indian encampment, and were at the gate of the mission fields in the presence of Dr. Whitman. He was speaking Skyuse at the top of his voice to some Indians who were driving their cattle out of his garden then giving orders in English to others to yoke their oxen and get the axes so trees could be felled for the sleeping quarters of the new mission house. Mr. Hall, printer from the Sandwich Islands,[69] soon appeared with an axe on his shoulder. Next came Mr. Monger, pulling pine shavings from the front of his planing tool.

All welcomed me warmly, asking in jest how long a balloon line had been running between the States and the Pacific by which a single individual such as myself should successfully cross the continent. But, the oxen were yoked and axes were glistening in the sun; there was little time for idle banter. The doctor introduced me to his excellent lady, Mrs. Whitman, and departed with the men to their labor.[70]

That evening, we all ate together and took tea. The hours were passed away in conversation about home and friends left there, of the pleasure the missionaries derived from their occupation here, and of the trials that had befallen them while establishing the mission and afterward. Among the most sorrowful was the drowning of their only child in the Walla Walla River the year before, a little girl named Alice Clarissa, just two years old. Yet they held fast to their faith and, grieving still, had confidence in a merciful God.

The next morning, I strolled the mission grounds. In addition to the extensive garden and fine yoke of oxen I had seen the day before, now I observed two cows, an American bull, and the beginning of a stock of hogs. On the far side of the river stood a grist mill for grinding flour. Dr. Whitman said it would grind enough in a day to feed his family for a week and that it was better than beating it with a pestle and mortar.

It seemed quite remarkable to me that the doctor could have made so many improvements since the year 1834.[71] In five years, one man without funds or other aid (save the help of a fellow missionary from time to time) had fenced, ploughed, planted an orchard, and built a mission school on the face of that wilderness. Not only that, he learned the Indian language, doctored among them on occasion, and fulfilled his duties as physician to the associate missionary stations on the Clear Water and Spokane Rivers. The doctor's untiring energy of character—and the very efficient aid of his wife in administering the school—have made all possible.

In the afternoon, Dr. Whitman and Mrs. Whitman assembled the Indians for instruction in reading. Mrs. Whitman rang a hand-bell. Forty or fifty children between the ages of seven and eighteen—plus several older people—gathered on the shady side of the new mission house and seated themselves in an orderly manner on a variety of wooden benches. The doctor then wrote syllables, words, and sentences in the Nez Perce language on a large blackboard suspended from the wall. He proceeded to teach the sounds of the letters, the construction of the words, and their uses in forming sentences. The sentences written during these lessons were at last read aloud—syllable by syllable, word by word—and explained, until the meanings were comprehended by the students.

It was delightful to see the undisguised enthusiasm with which these people would devour a new idea. A hymn in the Nez Perce language, learned by memorization and repetition from their teachers, was then sung. The exercises closed with a prayer by Doctor Whitman in the same Indian tongue.[72]

The course pursued by the Whitmans and other Presbyterian missionaries was to teach them in their native language, opening to them the arts and religion of civilized nations. They also taught them practical agriculture. By these means, they hoped to make the Indians a better and happier people. Mrs. Whitman, particularly, appeared a tireless instructress as she taught from a Nez Perce primer which had been lately published at the Clear Water mission station.[73]

I did not stay long with the Whitmans, though their company was most elevating and pleasant. On the 29th of September, I hired my same Skyuse guide to take me to the Chutes of the Columbia River and from there, to the Dalles. Mrs. Whitman filled my sacks with bread, corn meal, and other edibles. These I lashed upon my pony and, the next day, headed once more westward.

A brief stop at Fort Walla Walla—some fifteen miles from the mission—gave me time to survey the landscape ahead, which had been described to me in the States as being fruitful and beautiful. Not so. It was an ugly desert. Desert accurately described it, as sterile and inhospitable as the wastes of Arabia. Everything was brown and desolate, a treeless expanse of vast sandy swells too poor even to bear worm wood. Was this Oregon? Should I have heeded Richardson's dire warnings after all?

We made our way to the river, which appeared to be a long line of liquid fire blazing with the light of the western sun. The rush wigwams of the Walla Wallas dotted the sands of the opposite shore, beyond which rose barren rocks and bluffs. In the distance, these gave way to buttresses of volcanic basalt with Indian trails so narrow that a misstep of four inches would have plunged horse and rider hundreds of feet into the boiling flood of the river below. High dykes of basalt and sand hills intruded upon the river's course in several places, and a series of rapids could be clearly seen.[74]

Shortly after, my guide decided he must leave me and turned back. I was convinced this sudden change was due to his fear of what was called in Indian-English, *tum-tum-orter,* or thundering water of the Chutes. These were the only perpendicular falls of the Columbia. And they did, indeed, thunder. A thick layer of black rock rose there above the river in an abrupt precipice, hanging sixty feet in height over the water below.

The river, when I passed, was at its lowest stage; still, the Chutes were terrible and grand. The main body of water swept near the river's southern bank. There, it compressed into a narrow rough channel that chafed its angry way to the brink. Then, bending in a massive curve, it plunged into a narrow cavern sixty feet deep, with a force and volume which made the earth tremble. The noise was enormous. Deafening. And it echoed in an awful tumult throughout the barren mountains.

Toward the other shore, smaller jets of the river rushed from rocks clustered near the brow of the cliff into other caverns. Close under the north bank, further down, another chute thundered, nearly equal in grandeur to the first.

Just below, were the huts of perhaps a hundred Walla Walla fishermen who were taking salmon from the whirling waters with scoop nets and bone-pointed spears. I made my way past them on a fast trot, followed by some of their tribe on foot who demanded a tribute of smoke, or tobacco, for the privilege of passing their domains. Having none at hand, I pushed on to the Dalles.[75]

The Dalles is a French term for flat stones and was applied to a place in the river where the water had cut channels through an immense layer of volcanics. At low stages, these gigantic black flat rocks were exposed. But the annual floods completely overflowed them, producing—I was told—a lashing and leaping and swirling of waters as grand as Niagara Falls.

I took a birds-eye view of the Dalles and region around it, when I spied Lee House, the mission of the American P. E. Methodist Church.[76] Messrs. Lee and Perkins, who were in charge, were formerly connected with the mission on the Willamette. Eighteen months before, they had come to this spot with axes upon their shoulders. They felled trees, ploughed, fenced, and planted twenty acres of land with their own hands. Their location could not have been more perfect for a mission house. Indians from many quarters and nations already flocked to the Dalles and the Chutes after salmon. The movement of commerce between the States and the Pacific would soon pass their very door. And surely, in the future, emigrants from the States would stop—as did the Pilgrims at Plymouth Rock—to give grateful praise to Him who brought them safely thus far on their way to the woody glens and flowering everglades of Lower Oregon.[77]

I spent a week at the Dalles mission, eating salmon and growing fat before putting onto the river for my descent by canoe down the Columbia to the Willamette. I thoroughly enjoyed the ease with which this portion of my journey passed. With Indians manning the oars and Mr. Lee at hand for civilized conversation, I had no duty but to drink in the breathtaking views of the wild gorge of Columbia.

Mr. Lee pointed out the Island of Tombs, where stood cedar board houses of the dead. On them and about the houses were stacked the cooking utensils and other personal property of the deceased. Within were the dead bodies, wrapped in many thicknesses of deer and elk skins, tightly lashed with leather thongs and laid in a pile with their heads to the east. Underneath the undecayed bodies were many bones from which the flesh and wrappings had fallen. Three or four of the tombs had gone to ruins, and the skulls and other bones lay strewn upon the ground. The skulls were all flattened. I picked up one, with the intention of bringing it to the States. But Mr. Lee assured me the high veneration of the living for the dead would make such an attempt very dangerous. I reluctantly returned the skull to its resting place,[78] and we continued downriver.

At the lower falls of the Columbia, we portaged. Baggage was put ashore, and the Indians conveyed our canoe upon their shoulders around the rocks of the great rapid. The whole descent of the rapid here was about 150 feet; the volume of water that passed, incalculable. The velocity was so great—even at this lowest stage of the river—that the eye had difficulty following objects floating on the surface. The water rose and bent like a sea of molten glass over channels of ragged rock. How must it have looked in June at its highest, when the melted snows from 700 miles of western mountains swelled its banks to overflowing?

Beyond the falls, we could see immense and gloomy forests, tangled with fallen timber and impenetrable underbrush, covering the mountains. Above rose the shining glaciers and massive grandeur of Mount Hood, a perfect cone. And to the north, Mount Adams.

It was here we met the legendary Doctor McLaughlin of Fort Vancouver. Thirty years he had resided in this virgin country, had taken an Indian wife, and had created a wilderness empire for the Hudson's Bay Company. He had just returned from London with dispatches from the Company's Board in England, he said, and with letters from friends at home to the hundreds of Britons still in H.B.C. employ within the Oregon Country. He was a stoutly-built man, about five feet eleven inches in height, weighing perhaps 200 pounds. He had a ruddy complexion, hair of snowy whiteness, and large green-bluish eyes.

This evening he was in high spirits. We had spent scarcely ten minutes with the doctor before he invited us to be his guests at the post when we should arrive. Soon, we assured him. Soon. Then we parted company.

It was nearly sunset when the three barges of Doctor McLaughlin swept swiftly by us under their sapling masts and Indian blanket sails. They would reach Fort Vancouver well before us.

Thomas Jefferson Farnham

Night was creeping into the valleys, and we had twenty miles yet to make. The tide of the Pacific was setting up and the wind had left us, but our Indian oarsmen suggested that the force of their paddles might be strengthened by a small present of shmoke, or tobacco. We gave our promises to pay the required bribe upon arrival at our destination. Then, we wrapped ourselves in blankets and dozed to the music of the paddles until a shower of hail aroused us. It was about ten o'clock. An angry cloud hung over us and the rain and hail fell fast. The wind cut through our blankets and chilled us to the bone.

The wooded hills on both sides of the river were wrapped in swirling brown clouds. The owl and wolf answered each other on the heights. Enough light lay on the river to show dimly the islands that divided its waters, and in the distance we could make out the fires of distant wigwams with naked groups of Indians around them. It was a scene that the imagination loves.[79]

A few hundred yards below, nearly obscured in fog, floated a ship and a sloop. On shore rose an earthen breastwork, beyond which we heard voices in English speaking of *home*. We landed, ascended the levee, and entered a dark lane between cultivated fields. A quarter mile further, we entered Fort Vancouver.

It was nearly midnight, October 16, 1839. My five-month trail to Oregon—my adventures in the Wilderness—came to a close. The goal of my wanderings, the destination of my weary footsteps, at long, long last, was at hand.

SUMMARY

Within a week of his arrival at Fort Vancouver, Farnham traveled farther down the Columbia and Willamette Rivers to inspect them for suitability toward commerce and settlement. As he was still under the employ of Horace Greeley, he wanted to gather all possible information about the area and its inhabitants to be serialized in *The New York Tribune* upon his return. He found much evidence of what he called civilization in the Willamette Valley: churches, schools and academies, courts, hospitals, mills (both sawmills and gristmills), and all manner of farms and cultivated fields. He stated that "a military corps was about to be formed for the protection of the settlers," and cited a local petition "signed by 67 citizens of the United States" that embodied their wishes that "Congress and the Federal Government should extend over them the protection and institutions of the Republic" (Journal summary, October, 1839). American Democracy—as defined by Farnham—was alive and well in the Oregon Country.

Farnham's original intent was to winter over in the Willamette and to return to the Green River Rendezvous the following summer, where he planned to meet the American Fur Company traders. He reasoned that he could travel back to the States at the end of the season with them. But when he discovered a ship was already at anchor at Vancouver, bound for the Sandwich Islands (Hawaiian Islands) with a cargo of lumber, he abandoned his overland plan. From the Sandwich Islands, he could book passage on a ship for either California or New York and see his journals published within the year.

On December 3, he bade the Oregon Country farewell. His journals, as expected, caused quite a furor in the States when they were published, firmly attaching the stamp of high adventure upon the overland journey west.

Farnham was an astute observer of the landscape and its people. He was also an entertaining storyteller. Yet, one should not forget that he was writing with a specific objective in mind: to encourage American emigration and settlement of the Far West in order to help bolster the United States' claim to the land itself.

His highly detailed—and sometimes, highly romanticized—descriptions of tribal camps and fort life tend to read like armchair traveler pieces. They are exotic, they are fascinating, and they have just enough danger to keep the pages turning. His battles with nature carry with them a sense of the heroic . . . and patriotic. Here is an *American* carrying civilization across the continent! Farnham was a masterful salesman who knew his audience well.

The tribal peoples he met en route were generally categorized in the journals as helpful or hostile; noble or simply savage. Those who were half-civilized (who had extensive contacts with whites, or adopted white ways), were good, in Farnham's estimation. Tribes that were yet wild (resistant or overtly hostile to white culture), he termed as bad. The Hispanics and mixed-bloods he observed at the forts, Farnham largely dismissed except as quaint and romantic stage dressing. This was completely in keeping with his time.

Most (Anglo) Americans of that day considered themselves to be the highest embodiment of God's image. They were the anointed, the chosen culture. So it was their *duty* to prevail, their *responsibility* to master . . . whether they were talking about the land itself, or the peoples who lived upon it. In this quest for mastery, they saw themselves as elevating everything around them to its greatest (Anglo) good. Hence, the push to emigrate carried with it not only a political mission but a moral mission as well.

Six years would pass between the publication of Farnham's journals and the settlement of the Oregon Question by treaty that designated the Oregon Country as American rather than British. During that time, Farnham's words—first in newspaper serial form, later as a pamphlet —inspired thousands to leave all that was familiar and strike out for their own adventure en route to the Eden of the West.

LET'S INTERPRET

Discussion 1

"We [the United States] discovered the mouth of the Columbia and most of its branches; and that valley is ours as against the world. Ours, also, by purchase from Spain, the first discoverer and occupant of the coast. . . . We are the rightful and sole owner of all these parts of Oregon . . . Oregon Territory, for all these reasons and many others which will be found in the energy with which—if necessary—our citizens will defend it, is the rightful property of the United States."[80]

—THOMAS J. FARNHAM, 1839

"The Chinooks flatten their heads more. . . . There was one among the Dalles band who, it is said, resisted so obstinately the kind efforts of his parents to crush his skull into the aristocratic shape, that they abandoned him to the care of nature in this regard. Much to the scandal of his family, his head grew in the natural form. He was called 'Boston'; so-called because the form of his head resembles that of Americans, whom the

Indians call 'Boston' in order to distinguish them from 'King George men'—the Hudson Bay Company gentlemen."[81]

—THOMAS J. FARNHAM, October 13, 1839, at Bent's Fort

Farnham and most Americans of the time were convinced the Pacific Northwest should rightfully belong to the United States. Great Britain was just as convinced it should rightfully belong to Great Britain. Both countries maintained political outposts and forts there; both had developed commerce stations; both encouraged their missionaries and citizens to settle. Which country do you think had the strongest claim to the land in 1839, the year Farnham undertook his journey? Why? How did Great Britain and/or the United States view tribal claims to their home territories in this disputed—and coveted—area?

Discussion 2

"The utmost good faith shall always be observed towards the Indians; their land and property shall never be taken from them without their consent; and in their property, rights, and liberty, they shall never be invaded or disturbed . . . but laws founded in justice and humanity shall from time to time be made, for preventing wrongs being done to them, and for preserving the peace and friendship with them."[82]

—ORDINANCE FOR THE GOVERNMENT, 1789

"There are about 135,000 Indians inhabiting the Great Prairie Wilderness. The National Government has purchased from the indigenous tribes at specific prices; and under treaty stipulations, to pay them certain annuities in cash, and certain others in facilities for learning the useful arts, and for acquiring that knowledge of all kinds of truth, which will . . . in the end, excite the wants—create the industry—and confer upon [the Indians] the happiness of a civilized state."[83]

—THOMAS FARNHAM, July 6, 1839

"The indigenous, or native tribes of the Indian Territory are: the Osages, about 5,510; the Kauzaus or Caws, 1,720; the Omahas, 1,400; the Otoe and Missouri, 1,600; the Pawnee, 10,000; Puncah, 800; Quapaw, 600—making 21,600. The tribes that have emigrated [to the Territory] from the States are: the Choctaw, 15,600 (This estimate includes 200 white men, married to Choctaw women, and 600 Negro slaves.) The Chickasaws, 5,500; the Cherokees, 22,000 (This estimate includes 1,200 Negro slaves, owned by them.) The Creeks (including 900 slaves) 22,500; the Seneca and Shawnees, 461; the Seminoles, 1,600; the Pottawatamies, 1,650; the Weas, 206; the Piankashas, 157; the Peorias and Kaskaskias, 142; the Ottawas, 240; the Shawnees, 823; the Delawares, 921; the Kickapoos, 400; the Sauks, 600; the Iowas, 1,000. It is to be understood that the numbers assigned to the emigrant tribes regard only those portions of them that have actually removed to the Territory. . . . These . . . amount to 94,860 under the fostering care of the Federal Government."[84]

—THOMAS FARNHAM, July 6–9, 1839

[Note that Farnham lists Negro slaves owned by the Cherokees; likewise, he lists slaves (race not specified) owned by the Creeks.]

In fifty years, across an ever-westering national boundary, official policy toward Native Americans had gone from "in their property, rights, and liberty they shall never be invaded or disturbed," to that of trying to "confer upon [them] the happiness of a civilized state." Suppose you are a tribal member who has experienced this shift during your lifetime, perhaps even one who has been relocated to Indian Territory from your traditional homeland. What are your feelings about the words or actions of white men? Can treaties be trusted? What are some of the things you would consider while making the decision whether to abide by new treaties? Now suppose you are, like Farnham, one of the vanguard to Oregon Country. What are your feelings about the tribal peoples you encounter en route? What are your feelings about their sovereignty over the land? What would you consider necessary for them to achieve a civilized state?

Discussion 3

"The Indians want pay for being whipped, the same as they did for praying [which they said they did] to please the missionaries during the great revival of 1839. Some of the influential men in the tribe desired to know of what benefit this whipping system was going to be to them. They said they were willing it should continue, provided they were to receive shirts and pants and blankets as a reward for being whipped. They had been whipped a good many times and had got nothing for it, and it had done them no good. If this state of things was to continue [they said] it was all good for nothing."[85]

—INDIAN BUREAU REPORT from the Oregon Country to the Secretary of War, 1843

"We can never whip them into friendship . . . [whereas a treaty] can do no harm and the expense would be less than that of a six months' war."[86]

—SUPERINTENDENT'S REPORT to the Governor, Upper Missouri Indian Agency, 1849

Obviously some aspects of civilization were less successful than others. Some tribes were issued hand-farming implements and leather harnesses then expected to till the soil rather than hunt for their subsistence. Many of these items were never put to agricultural use. Instead, they were fashioned into thongs, belts, decorative pieces, and utensils—more in keeping with traditional tribal culture. Some were issued seed for planting but ate the seed instead when traditional food supplies ran out. What are some of the difficulties you can imagine in trying to effect radical change from one cultural orientation to another? Which do you think would be more effective: force or enticement? Why? Think of examples where this type of change might be taking place today.

Discussion 4

"These solitary [French trappers] were apparently very happy. Neither hunger nor thirst annoys them, so long as they have strength to travel and trap and sing. Their camps are always merry, and they cheer themselves along the weary march in the wilderness with the wild border songs of

'Old Canada.' The American trappers present a different . . . character. Habitual watchfulness destroys every frivolity of mind and action. They seldom smile; the expression of their countenances is watchful, solemn and determined. They ride and walk, like men whose breasts have so long been exposed to the bullet and arrow, that fear finds within them no resting place."[87]

—THOMAS FARNHAM, August 4, 1839

"When a white man is disposed to take unto himself [an Indian wife] among the Snakes [also called Shoshones], he must conform to the laws and customs of the tribe, that have been ordained and established for the regulation of all such matters. And, whether the color in any individual case be black or white, does not seem to be a question ever raised to take it out of the rules. The only difference is, that the property, beauty, etc., of the whites frequently gives them the preference on change and enables them to obtain the best [women] of the nation. These connections between the trappers and [Indian women], I am told, are the cause of so many of the [trappers] remaining [the rest of their lives] in these valleys of blood. They seem to love them as ardently as they would females of their own color."[88]

—THOMAS FARNHAM, August 12, 1839

The wilderness of this time was, if not a melting pot, then certainly a *mixing* pot of tribes, nationalities, and cultures. It is interesting to note that Farnham cites not only tolerance, but acceptance, of "individuals . . . black or white" by the Snake Indians in the marriage arena. In this, they were fundamentally different from American white society of the day. Review Thomas Farnham's chapter. From his descriptions of tribal peoples, list attributes or cultural characteristics about them you admire. Then, list things that you find surprising or unexpected about them. List things you disagree with or find distasteful. Do the same for Farnham and his traveling companions. Now, list things about your personal life style or cultural practices that might seem strange or unusual to someone from a different country or culture. How do you determine whose viewpoint is right?

1. Horace Greeley: editor, politician, founder of *The New York Tribune*. He also helped establish the Republican Party.

2. The official phrase for this way of thinking became Manifest Destiny. It eventually became government policy. In the thinking of the time, this destiny of claiming the land for America was the birthright of every (white, male) American citizen. However, it did not extend to those of other colors, ethnicities, or gender. Neither did it take into account that the lands were already populated, already home ground of many sovereign tribal nations.

3. England's Queen Victoria in 1839. She came to the throne in 1837.

4. Thomas Farnham, *An 1839 Wagon Train Journal: Travels in the Great Western Prairies . . . and in the Oregon Territory* (New York: Greeley and McElrath, 1843. Reprint, Northwest Interpretive Association, 1979). Journal entry for May 21, 1839.

5. Firearms of the day used gunpowder and lead balls. From Farnham's description, we know he used a percussion firearm on this trip. A tiny metal cap fit on what was called the nipple, the point upon which the gun's hammer struck when the trigger was pulled. Inside the cap was a chemical. When the hammer struck the cap, this chemical ignited, sending a shower of sparks through the nipple hole into the gun's chamber. Here, these sparks ignited the gunpowder, causing an explosion which fired the ball out of the weapon.

6. Farnham, 4, May 21.

7. *The States* denoted, to Oregon Trail emigrants, all of the United States that was civilized, anything that was populated primarily by white Americans.

8. A tributary of the Missouri River.

9. Farnham, 6, May 30.

10. A fortnight is two weeks.

11. Farnham, 6, May 30. It was common for parties traveling the Oregon Trail to designate officers, assign duties, and sign legal documents agreeing to certain terms of behavior and travel. This gave structure to the daily business of the wagon train minisociety. Typically, these Articles of Confederation were signed only by the men, but the terms applied to all.

12. Ibid., 6–7, June 4, 5, and 7.

13. Eating arrangements; a group of people that regularly takes its meals together.

14. Farnham, 6, June 5.

15. Ibid., 7, June 7.

16. *Game* was—and is—a generic term for nondomesticated animals killed as food.

17. Farnham, 7, June 9.

18. Marrow is the soft, fatty tissue that fills the cavities of most mammal bones. Commonly, cooked bones were broken open and the marrow sucked out. This innermost part was considered the choicest—and most nutritious—of treats.

19. Farnham, 9, June 10.

20. Ibid., 10, June 12.

21. Ibid., 12, June 17.

22. Also called by Farnham the Konzas and the Kauzas; most probably, the Kansas Indians.

23. Identified by Farnham as "on the Konzas River."

24. Farnham, 14, June 27.

25. Ibid., 60, August 12.

26. Farnham defines this term as "inscrutable and irresistible sources of evil" in his journal entry for June 27, 1839 (15). This is a nontribal definition of "Medicine," which may or may not accurately reflect the Caw's understanding and use of the word in this particular instance.

27. Farnham, 15, June 27.

28. Ibid.

29. Typically, these officers of the group (see endnote 11) were given rank similar to the hierarchy of the military, even though the men were civilians.

30. Farnham, 18, June 28.

31. Named for William, chief trader and one of the Bent brothers who built it, this

Fort William became better known as Bent's Fort.

32. Farnham, 20, July 5.

33. Ibid., 35, July 10.

34. Dresses.

35. Farnham, 36, July 10.

36. Ibid.

37. "Ute," "Utahs," and "Utahns" were used interchangeably in describing the same large, geographic tribal group by those not familiar with the finer points of band and tribe identification. Occasionally, the Paiute peoples were also lumped into this generic description.

38. Farnham's term, typical for the era.

39. Farnham, 36, July 10.

40. Ibid., 36, July 11.

41. A very hard, black variety of coal, commonly used for jewelry in the Victorian era.

42. Farnham, 36, July 11.

43. Ibid, 37.

44. Ibid. While Farnham wrote this as a factual event, it exemplifies the Noble Savage image that became wildly popular fifty years later. American society held a remarkably double standard when it came to tribal people. They were both elevated into the Noble Savage realm, and cast down into the miserable creature category, depending on the circumstance and context of experience.

45. Farnham, 41, July 18.

46. Ibid., 42.

47. Ibid., 43, July 20.

48. Ibid., 50, July 31.

49. Common sagebrush.

50. Farnham, 55, August 11.

51. In what is now Wyoming.

52. Farnham, 61, August 12–16. The Snake man was describing the hats worn by the expedition members, and their beards. As he had never seen white people before nor their modes of dress, he evidently thought the hats to be parts of the heads. To the beardless tribal members, beards could very well have been regarded as skin that was "loose and flowing, and of various colors."

53. Ibid., 62, August 17.

54. Ibid., 62, August 18.

55. Hudson's Bay Company

56. Holes dug into the ground in which to temporarily store supplies, goods, or furs. The holes were commonly lined with twigs or plant matter then, after the goods were deposited, were filled over again with earth and camouflaged.

57. A very popular resort of the day, located in New York State, where people could "take the waters" for their health.

58. Farnham, 67, August 29.

59. Ibid., 68, September 1.

60. Ibid., 70, September 4. Indeed, the features of flattened forehead described here were considered a mark of aristocracy and privileged class among some of the tribal peoples of the Columbia.

61. Bright red vermillion was highly prized among the tribes for decoration of their bodies. Lewis and Clark took a large supply of the mineral with them in 1804–6; apparently by Farnham's time, it came packaged in papers, specifically for trading.

62. Fort Boise. The area was named originally by the French *le bois*, the trees or woods.

63. Either of the two shafts between which a horse is hitched to a wagon.

64. Farnham, 73, September 14–15. This was what remained of the Whitman and Spalding wagon.

65. The Lone Tree Valley of northeastern Oregon, now called the Baker Valley. Farnham's journal cites September 19th, 1839, (73) as the day he "cooked dinner at L'Arbor Seul. . . ."

66. Farnham, 74, September 21.

67. Cayuse.

68. Farnham, 75, September 22. How Farnham knew that the hymn was in the Nez Perce language is not clear.

69. Now known as the Hawaiian Islands.

70. Farnham, 76, September 23.

71. In this date, Farnham was incorrect. The Whitmans established the mission in 1836–37. His journal entry for September 24, 1839, (77) expresses astonishment that so much could have been accomplished in only

five years. All he surveyed had actually been accomplished in barely three years.

72. Farnham, 77, September 24.

73. Ibid., 78, September 25–28.

74. Ibid., 80, October 2.

75. Ibid., 81, October 5.

76. American Protestant Episcopalian Methodist Church.

77. Farnham, 82, October 6–13.

78. Ibid., 84, October 15.

79. Ibid., 85, October 16.

80. Farnham, 3, introduction.

81. Ibid., 82.

82. Vine Deloria, Jr., ed., *Of Utmost Good Faith* (New York: Bantam Books, 1972), 1.

83. Farnham, 23, July 6, at Bent's Fort.

84. Ibid., 24, July 6–9.

85. Helen Hunt Jackson, *A Century of Dishonor* (1885; reprint, Norman: University of Oklahoma Press, 1995), 109.

86. Ibid., 70.

87. Farnham, 53, August 4, 1839.

88. Ibid., 57.

JESSE APPLEGATE
A Boy's Grand Adventure

1843

I WAS ONLY seven years old when my family left Missouri for the Oregon Country. For a long time before we started, the journey was talked about: whether to make it, whether to stay where we were. Mr. Shortess, a friend of my family who had already traveled to Oregon, wrote letters to my father, telling him of that Land of Milk and Honey, urging him to come. His letters were published in the newspapers and read by many. The excitement which followed was called the Oregon Fever.[1]

Now, this wasn't a sickness that could be cured by taking doses of Injin Fizic,[2] or tonics.

This was something that got into the men's blood—a confidence of greener pastures, abundance for everyone, a life of rich return . . . in the Oregon Country. Before I knew it, Mother, Father, my two brothers, uncles, aunts, and cousins were all bound for what the grownups had started calling the Promised Land. We knew if they were calling it names from the Bible, it must be something grand.

Oregon, in my mind, was a country a long way off . . . and I understood for us to get there, we would have to travel through lands swarming with wild Indians who would try to kill us with tomahawks or scalp us. At least, that's what my older brother said. I didn't know whether he was just trying to scare me or whether it was true, but lots of grownups believed it so I decided I would, too.[3]

Some of my girl cousins—older than I—often took their coffee cup after drinking the coffee and turned the mouth of the cup upside-down. After it had drained, they'd turn it aright and peer into the patterns made by the coffee grounds, trying to make out pictures of future scenes. We children thought we could see covered wagons and Indians scalping women and babes.[4] That's what we children talked about most, of course—the most gruesome and wildly terrible things we could imagine. Our imaginings never did come true, but we liked to terrify ourselves and each other wondering, *What if—?*

There were over a thousand people in the wagon train Father joined: men, women, and children of all ages. One hundred and twenty wagons were pulled by six-ox teams all yoked together, plus five thousand head of loose cattle, and another thousand or so head of loose horses and other live stock. We were quite a sight!

At first, everyone tried to travel together as one train. When we crossed the Missouri line from the United States into Indian Territory, one man pulled off his hat and waved it above his head toward the east, shouting, *Farewell to America!* We all felt we were embarking on an adventure equal to those of the ancient Greeks and Romans in the stories Father used to read to us.

The first Indians I remember seeing were Caws. We came up on the south side of the Caw River and camped near one of their camps. It was said they grew corn, beans, and pumpkins, which was much like our gardens at home. My brothers and I admired several of the Indian men we saw there. We weren't afraid, for we had seen Osage Indians before. But these Caws looked different. They were more than six feet tall, ramrod straight, and they moved with a proud step. They wore blankets drawn around their shoulders, and leggings. Their hair was shorn to the scalp, except something of a "rooster's tail" on top of their heads, which was colored red.[5] We boys thought they looked wonderfully exotic.

The men in our train said they had to make the wagons water-tight for crossing the Caw River. They soaked rags, cloth, and paper in pine tar or hot pitch and stuffed those between the wagon boards to seal them. They poked them in with sticks, or pounded them in with hammers and chisels. Then they smeared more pine tar on top of that. Most all the children thought the wagons made fine boats, and did not give a thought to the possible danger of capsizing or drowning. Some of the people traveling with us could not even swim.

Many were the times, back home, Mother had chastised us boys for running off to the swimming hole, but now I think our skills were a relief to her. Our little red wagon, as we called it, floated like a cork. The Indians helped us—and others—swim the cattle and horses across. I noticed they didn't swim like white men; they used an overhanded stroke; dog fashion, they said. They told us we would soon reach the country of the Cheyenne and Pawnee, and that they were bad Indians.[6]

About the second day after we had crossed the Caw River, we met a war party of about a hundred returning Caw warriors, marching afoot. They were painted and feathered for battle, armed with bows, spears, war clubs, tomahawks, and knives. But some were wounded and limping, some had blood on their faces, arms in slings, and bandages wound around their heads. They seemed to be tired and in a big hurry.

They told us they had been out buffalo hunting when they had been attacked by a war party of the Pawnee, and they had a fight with them. They said they had defeated the Pawnee and killed many of them. But when we reached the battle ground some days later, the only bodies we found there were Caws. We knew then, the Caws had been beaten back by the Pawnee; otherwise, they never would have left the bodies of their fallen warriors behind.

There was a Mexican man in our train who cut off a hand of one of those dead Indians at the wrist and hung it on a stake in our encampment. I saw it hanging there with my own eyes, and was afraid of it. A meeting was called immediately by the Council on the train. They were outraged that this Mexican had done such a thing. They voted him out, and he was forced to leave.[7] I don't know what happened to the hand.

The Council was a sort of high court. Usually it met on days when our caravan wasn't moving, to make decisions in arguments or disputes. Sometimes it revised the rules everybody had to obey or made new ones that all the men had to agree to. But sometimes—as in the case of the hand—the Council met right then and there, heard the case, made the judgment, and carried out the decision. I only saw men sit on the Council; nobody's mother or sister was ever allowed.[8]

At the crossing of the Blue River, we split apart into two columns that traveled close enough to one another to give protection from the danger of Indian attacks. We traveled like this all the way to Independence Rock on the Sweetwater River.

We were always fording rivers, it seemed. I remember one river running so wide and fast that it washed into the wagon boxes. A single team and wagon would have been simply swept away in the current, so the men formed the entire train into single file and attached the teams and wagons to a chain that ran the whole length of the train. The crossing was very dangerous. The men waded the river alongside their oxen, at times having to cling to the ox yokes and swim. In some of the deep places, the teams themselves swam, and the wagons floated, held up and in line only by the chain.

At one fording, Mother and all of us children were in our little red wagon, which was being drawn by one yoke of oxen. We were attached to the very back end of the train that day. Just as we were getting up the bank from the ford, our team broke loose, and the wagon and team rolled back into the river. We were swept away. The team swam and the wagon sank down. Water came rushing into the wagon box up to my waist, and we children had to scramble up onto the top of a trunk.[9] Mother shouted for us to stay there. We eventually drifted onto the sand and were rescued, but it certainly was a scare!

We children—the boys especially—tended to recover from such perils quite rapidly, and soon we were turning our attentions to the attractions around us. Particularly buffalo.

Buffalo and small game were everywhere on the prairies. Sometimes, buffalo were even found among our cattle in the mornings, quietly grazing! The men had great sport, hunting; we had an abundance of buffalo meat and venison all the time we traveled the plains.

One day as we were traveling on the bank of one of the rivers, we saw a lone buffalo swimming the river and coming in the direction of the train. Some of the men got their guns, and when the old bull came up the bank, they attacked him and finally killed him near the wagons. They had to shoot so many times to bring him down, though, the firing sounded like quite a battle. He had very large shoulders rising to a hump, which was covered with long dark hair, and he had a very ugly burly head. I thought him a very dangerous looking beast, indeed.[10]

Speaking of buffalo, we boys had quite an adventure gathering buffalo chips, which were the dried dung of the buffalo. Our mothers used these as fuel for their cooking fires, and it was our job to gather up as many as we could find. Several of us went out from camp a little distance, picking up the chips and throwing them into piles. Our group had a pile, and other groups had their piles. My brothers and I had claimed certain small districts, or territories, near our respective stacks of chips, and we warned the other boys not to trespass.

We were working hard when a boy about my size with yellow, sun-bleached hair and freckles on his face came over into our territory and tried to make off with a particularly large chip. I caught him in the act and threw another chip into his face so hard, it cut his face and made him bleed.[11] The older boys all laughed when the bleeding boy cried, but nobody tried to steal any of our buffalo chips again.

Simply making fire was quite an effort. Sometimes, a man would rub a cotton rag in gunpowder then shoot it out of a musket to get a flame, or put it in the pan of a flintlock gun and then explode the gunpowder in the pan. Often in camp, a flint steel and punk, or tinder, were used to create a spark.[12] I also saw my mother use a magnifying glass one time to focus sun-light onto dry grass, and then she coaxed that into a fire.[13] It seemed to me to be magic of the most marvelous kind, and I wanted to try my hand at it. But—under Mother's watchful eye—I soon found it took more skill and patience than I had.

It was far more interesting to spend my time watching the prairie dogs. These dogs were about the size of young puppy dogs, and lived together in groups. Their burrows were sometimes mounded up quite high, and there were hundreds of them. The population of some of their prairie-dog towns, I think, must have been as great as that of New York City! As we would pass through or near their settlements, they would come out of their holes and sit up straight on their hind quarters—always near their burrows—to yelp and squeak at us. Then, at the slightest alarm, they would drop into their holes. I sometimes saw tiny, burrowing owls sitting among them; some of the old folks said prairie dogs, owls, and rattlesnakes lived together in the same holes.[14]

SEEING THE ELEPHANT

Now and then, we sighted landmarks along the way. Chimney Rock, for instance. At first we could see only a pinnacle far, far off, looking much like a chimney flue or church steeple. But as we traveled closer, it appeared to change shape. Nearer, it seemed to me to touch the sky. We set camp at long last, not far from it. Or so we supposed. Some of the young men of the camp decided that evening to visit the rock. They returned very late at night, declaring it was ten miles away! As with so many other sights on the prairie, our eyes had been fooled into thinking it was much closer than it truly was because of its size.

Yet Fort Laramie, which loomed so large in the conversations of the grownups, didn't impress me much at all. What *did* impress me there was the great number of Sioux Indians I saw outside its walls. There were several pretty Indian women[15] with cheeks painted red, wearing beaded moccasins and beautiful red leggings, fringed along the outer seams. Some of them had papooses who appeared almost white and were very pretty. Some of these women were wives of white men at the fort, and some belonged to the great war party I saw there, gathering to fight the Blackfeet.

The Sioux warriors—both men and women[16]—were all painted about their faces. They were mounted on good horses, armed with bows and arrows sitting in quivers slung at the back. Some had spears; some had war clubs, but no guns—or if any, very few. This war party covered several acres of prairie. It was an exciting and savage-looking army. Sometimes when a squadron of those warriors would break away from the main body and come toward us, shouting their war whoop, urging their ponies forward at full speed, I thought it a grand display, indeed. I do admit, though, I could almost feel the hair rise on my head![17]

Several of these Amazons[18] visited our camp. They were dressed and painted and armed like the men. Some of them were very fine of figure, had pretty faces and eyes as soft and bright as the antelope on those wild plains. They were all young women. Their small, shapely hands and small feet clad in beaded moccasins were admired by our sisters, aunts, and mothers. To my astonishment, they even flirted with our young men with their eyes,[19] just as I had seen my older girl cousins do since we left Missouri! I wondered if their eyes flashed fire in the heat of battle.

The next landmark we came to was Independence Rock. We passed quite near it. It was a light gray color, about as high as a tall house in the middle, and it tapered down both ways, as long as a city block. It looked like an oval on top and, in the highest part, was quite smooth and slick. We boys talked about how fun it would be to slide right off it, right over all those names people had painted and chiseled there.[20] But we didn't dare, not even the oldest boys.

A man by the name of Lovejoy came to us somewhere in this part of the country. He told us he had been traveling the year before with some trappers, and they had camped in the neighborhood of Independence Rock. Mr. Lovejoy said he had gone to explore and examine it, and while he was marking his name on the rock—just as he was writing "j-o-y" on the end of his name—a party of Indians captured him. They took him to the trappers' encampment, and sold him back to his friends for ammunition and tobacco![21]

Mr. Lovejoy became a favorite amongst us boys, for he always had an exciting story to tell. Whether all was true or not, we didn't know. But that hardly dampened our enthusiasm for hearing what he had to say.

At Independence Rock, the grownups said the Indian danger was largely past, so the two columns of the train broke into even smaller parties, which proved better suited to the narrow mountain paths and small pastures. Finding enough grass for all our livestock in one area had become more and more difficult. So those families having only a few cattle, horses, or mules to look after, joined what they called the Light Column; those with more than four or five cows—like us—joined the larger and slower Cow Column.[22]

Our days then began at four o'clock in the morning! The sentinels on guard duty would discharge their rifles, signaling to us that our sleeping hours were over, even though the sun wasn't even up. While Mother and my older girl cousins saw to us children, Father and the other men would begin herding the loose stock toward their proper places. Sometimes, they had to go as far as two miles from camp, gathering in the strays. By six o'clock the cattle—all five thousand head of them—were milling around the circle of the wagons. Then, the men separated out their teams by running them inside the circle, which served as our corral.[23]

From six o'clock to seven was a busy time. We had to eat our breakfast, strike the tents, reload the wagons, yoke the teams, and get them attached to the wagons. Everyone knew when the trumpet sounded at seven o'clock, anyone not ready to take his proper place in the line would be sent to the dusty rear of the wagon train for the day.

There were sixty wagons in the Cow Column. These divided into groups of four wagons apiece. Each group—which the men called divisions or platoons—was entitled to lead the column in its turn. The leading platoon one day would be at the rear the next. This order would move up one position each day, unless some driver lost his place in line by laziness or some negligence. Then, his wagon would be assigned the very last place in line.[24] Nobody wanted to be last.

Usually, the men and older boys drove the wagons. The rest of us either rode inside the wagons or walked. It didn't take long for us to decide walking was far more comfortable than being bumped and jerked and jostled inside the wagons. Besides, inside the wagon, there was nothing to do but hang on. And outside . . . there were curiosities to see, adventures to discover, and games to play as we walked and ran. Outside the wagons, we children were *free!*

A pilot had been chosen for us when we split up the big wagon train. This man wasn't one of us—he had spent his life on the edge of the wilderness, Father said, and had been chosen for his knowledge of the Indians and of the land through which we had to travel. Our pilot always rode his horse in front of the wagons. Behind him followed fifteen to twenty young men on horseback, who served as hunters or scouts. They came and went during the day, sometimes riding as much as fifteen or twenty miles from the train to find game. Then came the wagons. Behind them ambled bands of loose horses under the watchful eyes of a group of men and boys. Lastly, the cow drivers goaded the remaining stock forward throughout the day.[25]

We formed a moving circus, almost three quarters of a mile long! And our motto was *Travel, travel, travel!*

As we traveled, I often wondered how places got their names. And I wondered why they were so different than how I expected them to be. I had been anxious to reach the Sweetwater River near Independence Rock, for I had fancied when we got to it, I would have all the sweet water I could drink. When we came to the river, I ran to the water's edge and, bending over, resting on my hands, took a long drink of the water. But I was greatly disappointed, for the water was very common indeed. Just plain water, not sweet at all.

South Pass, the backbone of the Rocky Mountains, was actually a very gradual ascent of hundreds of miles. As we traveled, it seemed almost level. When we reached the Divide, it was hardly worth mentioning.

Then there was the Green River. I was anxious to see that, too, convinced that it would be some marvelous dark green color. But when we came to it, the water was crystal clear, running across the country like a broad ribbon. Another disappointment.[26]

I began to wonder if Oregon, of which I had heard so many wonderful descriptions from Father and Mother, would be a disappointment, too, when we finally got there.

At least Soda Springs lived up to my expectations. We camped very near one of these springs, nearly a quarter mile from the Bear River. Here we met Mr. John C. Fremont with his party, and I thought their large tent—which was spread near our camp—was a very nice affair, indeed. There was a soda spring or pool between the camps, and Fremont's men were having a high time drinking the soda water. They were so noisy, I thought they must have had liquor mixed with what they were drinking.

After the men had been drinking from the spring nearly a whole day, one of our company fished out an enormous frog from the pool. It seemed to me to be about the size of a young papoose! And it was falling apart with rottenness. Soon after this discovery, we noticed that the hilarity at the Fremont tent suddenly stopped.[27]

Even more than the frog incident, I remember seeing my first cannon at Soda Springs. It was a six-pounder, Fremont said, made of shining brass. It rested on a low carriage that stood between his camp and ours, very near the spring. His men let me come up close to it and examine it several times. I discovered a touch hole near the breech and, looking in at the muzzle, could see the cannon ball . . . or thought I could.[28] Pretty exciting stuff for a seven-year-old boy from Missouri!

We stayed at the Soda Springs for two days. Some of the women took the opportunity to wash laundry in the hot water coming out of the ground. Some of the men explored the country surrounding our camp and discovered geysers spewing up hot columns of water and vents in the earth puffing hot clouds of steam. These were of the utmost fascination to us boys.

One vent, in particular, was too good to pass by. Some of the boys tried to keep it from puffing by closing it with clumps of sod and grass, but

SEEING THE ELEPHANT

whenever the spasm of steam came, the caulking would be thrown out. One young man had a wool hat which he placed over the hole and held there with his hands and knees planted firmly on the brim. This, I suppose, was generally regarded as a corker, but when the puff came, the hat crown stretched bigger and bigger then burst out at the top!

Father told me later this was called the Steamboat Spring, for it puffed like a steamboat.[29] There was also in the vicinity a rock that stood some six or seven feet above the ground. The men called it Bellowing Rock. It was shaped like a funnel, three feet across or more and nearly the same at the top as at the bottom. I think it must have been as hollow as a gun, for we were told at one time it bellowed like a bull. How long it had been since it had bellowed, no one could say, but I visited this rock twice while at our Soda Springs camp. I stood a long time near it, listening and thinking I might get to hear it bellow. But it never made a sound.[30]

Then we entered the Great Sage Plains, as we called them. They were thickly set with sagebrush and greasewood shrubs, growing nearly waist high to a man, and as we had no proper wagon road to follow, we had to break our own road through this stiff, scratchy stuff. It was hard work for the teams in the lead, so these had to be changed every day, even when we used the strongest teams. Part of the time, we followed game trails through the sage when we could find them; sometimes, we followed trails made by pack animals and horsemen who had gone before. We often had to travel until late at night to find water. Some camps were dry camps, with no water to be found at all.[31] The days were hot . . . dry . . . monotonous. Our parents wouldn't even let us play hide and seek, as the sage brush was so tall, they were afraid they would lose us. Soon, we were as grumbling as the grownups. When would we get to Oregon? When would we see the Land of Milk and Honey?

It was a relief when we reached Fort Hall. *Civilization at last!* cried Mother, even though it was really just a trading post. Here, we saw trappers, mountain men, and lots of Indians. Inside the fort, we found women and children living there. Mother said most of them were Snake Indians or mixed bloods. They wore very pretty moccasins and other garments of deer and antelope skins that had been tanned and dressed. These the women had ornamented with needlework, beads, and porcupine quills of different colors. The moccasins had red and blue instep pieces.

Although I had been taught not to stare, I did see many bracelets of gold or brass on these women's wrists, and broad rings of the same on their fingers. On their garments, they had sewn a profusion of brightly-colored ribbons that fluttered in the breeze. Most of the ribbons were red. I thought the bright colors looked beautiful against the brown skin and glossy black hair of the women; I even caught my older girl cousins admiring them.

Of course, conversation was very difficult between our women and the others, but by the use of hand signs and a few words, all parties seemed to make themselves agreeable.[32]

There had been no wagons beyond Fort Hall, and the people there were of the opinion we should leave ours there and take only pack animals forward. A special Council was held, the pros and cons were discussed, and in the end the Cow Column decided to move on with our wagons.

Before moving on, though, we slaughtered a very large, fat ox. Our camp was about one hundred yards from the fort. Here, the ox was killed and dressed. That afternoon, we boys happened upon the slaughter site, where we found the stomach, or paunch as we called it, lying there on the ground. The weather was warm; the stomach had swollen to the size of a large barrel. Boys being boys, we decided we would make a fine game with it. The object of the game was to run as fast as we could and butt our heads against the bloated paunch, thereby being bounced back by its elasticity. Now, we found this very exciting, but it wasn't long before a rivalry grew up between the boys as to who could butt the hardest.

Amongst us there was a boy named Andy Baker, who was much taller than I was; he had a long, slender neck, and his hair was cut very close to the scalp. Andy was ambitious to be the winner in this game, so he backed off a long way to have a strong run. He backed off much further than anyone had before. Then, lowering his small head, he charged the paunch at the top of his speed. Just a couple of yards short of the target, he leaped up from the ground and came down like a pile driver against the paunch . . . but he did not bounce back.

We gathered around him to see what the matter was and discovered that Andy had thrust his head *into* the stomach! It closed so tightly around his neck, he couldn't get his head out! We took hold of his legs and pulled and pulled. Andy struggled and struggled. Finally he popped free. The whole event became a favorite joke among the boys for the rest of our trip.[33] I don't remember Andy thinking it was all that funny.

We left Fort Hall and trudged through more of the Great Sage Plains. Walking behind the wagons now frequently necessitated pulling prickly pear cactus thorns out of our toes, as the spines went right through our shoes. The oxen's feet grew sore, and they coughed from the dust thrown up by their plodding and by the wagon wheels.

The flat plain gave way to great, abrupt grooves sliced into the earth where the rivers had cut through. At one camp, it was more than a quarter of a mile deep in the plain. The slope down to the river was very steep, but there was bunch grass in abundance, so after camp was set, our cattle freely grazed the slopes all the way down to the river.

Some of the boys were rolling big rocks down this slope to the river. They didn't seem to consider the danger to the cattle below them; they were just enjoying the sport of seeing the big stones rush and bound all the way down to the river and plunge with a tremendous splash into the water—sometimes throwing water twenty-five and thirty feet high.

I hadn't been invited to join their sport, so I just watched from a safe distance. One boy rolled a huge rock to the edge of the ravine and pushed it over the side. It gathered the speed of a cannon ball . . . in the exact direction of a yearling calf grazing at the foot of the slope. He yelled and yelled for the calf to get out of the way, but of course the rock hit it. That calf was killed as dead as if it had been struck by a bolt of lightning.[34]

I didn't stick around long enough to see whether the boy's father had anything to say about the matter.

Not far from there, we heard the roar of what sounded like distant thunder. As we grew closer to its source, the ground shook under our feet and wagons. This was the Salmon Falls of the Snake River. Many Indians gathered here, Snakes and Shoshones, Father said.[35] We could see long lines of something red, which I thought were clothes hung out to dry. But as we came nearer, I could see those lines were salmon which the Indians were drying in the sun.

When we halted, many of the Snakes visited our camp, bringing fish—both fresh and dried—that they exchanged for our old clothes. A number of them strutted around, dressed in their newly-acquired garments, seeming to enjoy their often absurd combinations as much as we did. When we would laugh, they would laugh, too. This was grand sport for us children, and the Snakes didn't seem to object to our fun at their expense. Our visit with them was very pleasant and entertaining.[36]

We reached Fort Boise with little trouble. While camping in the neighborhood of the fort, we children were very surprised and delighted to find small white beads in the ant hills. We picked up many of them but, while searching for more, came to a place where the ground was literally covered with them. We looked up, and discovered that the platform above our heads was thickly strewn with the decayed corpses of Indian dead. We knew then where the beads had come from. Many of the bodies were rolled up in blankets and robes. Some had been torn apart and scattered by scavenger birds.[37]

We fled to camp with the jackrabbit speed of barefoot, backwoods children to report our strange discovery and to exhibit our beads to the grownups. We were greatly disappointed that our report didn't create a sensation in camp. In fact, the old folks didn't admire our beads. They chastised us for taking the beads and made us throw them away.

I don't remember another time on the plains when I thought my parents as unreasonable as I did on this subject of the beads. I felt so wronged by it, I didn't sleep all that night, and almost made up my mind to run away and go back home to Missouri. I even decided on what I thought was an infallible argument: the Indians who owned the beads were dead, so they had no use for them any more. And the ants that collected the beads from the ground surely had plenty left to gather. So I should be allowed to keep what I had found.

But Mother and Father would have none of it. We children left that place, utterly beadless.[38]

We moved westward across a level country for days, where no trees were to be seen. But one day, looking ahead in the distance, I saw what I thought was a bush. As we moved toward it, it continued to grow . . . and grow . . . and grow. In two days' time it grew from looking like a small bush, to a very large tree. It was the famous Lone Pine. Its round, straight trunk towered up like a great column, supporting a massive spreading top. We camped nearby and marveled at it.[39] This, at least, lived up to its reputation.

Our family had a very strong wagon—in addition to our little red wagon—which we called the meat wagon. This was our provision wagon, heavily laden with foodstuffs. It was drawn by a team of two yoke of oxen and driven by a man by the name of George Beal, who was the dark-skinned, black-eyed son of a slave owner from Missouri. Mother had told me not to ride in this wagon, but one day as I was walking beside it, I decided to climb up into it and sit beside the driver. There was a skin-covered trunk up there which had been placed against the front of the wagon bed. The lid of the trunk was very slick, and it rose several inches above the foregate. Just the place to make a fine seat, I thought.

The day was warm, and the oxen were walking slowly. George Beal was drowsy and not paying too much attention to me. Somehow, I got hold of the ox whip. Now, this ox whip had a stock about five feet long, and a lash about six or seven feet long. Feeling now the full importance of my new job as teamster, I swung the whip around and then forward with all my strength to make it pop over the oxen's backs.

But the effort to jerk it back pulled me forward, and I slid off the trunk, over the foregate, and off the wagon. I fell down between the oxen's heels and the front wheels of the wagon, one of which ran over me. I tried to escape the hind wheel, but it then rolled over my legs. I could see the team just behind us approaching only a few feet away. I tried to escape but couldn't stand. Fortunately, the man driving the approaching team saw me. He stepped quickly forward, scooped me up, and put me into his wagon.

I knew I was hurt. Adding to my physical pain, though, was the mental pain, for I had disobeyed Mother and had gotten hurt because of it. I didn't relish having to face her and Father and 'fessing up.

When the wagons stopped that night, I saw Mother ahead, already sorting some things from the baggage that had been taken out of our wagon. I resolved to behave myself in such a way that she wouldn't suspect anything unusual had happened. The driver unhitched the team from his wagon, lifted me out, and put me down by one of the front wheels, which I caught for support. It was a shock to me that I couldn't yet stand alone.

Mother looked over at me, but I straightened up and made a great effort to look normal. When she took her eyes off me, I caught hold of the front of the wagon box and pulled myself forward. I managed to reach the wagon tongue and straighten up just as Mother looked at me again. My last desperate effort was to walk along the wagon tongue, using it for support. But my scheme failed, and I fell forward as I fainted. Mother cried out and ran to me, catching me in her arms.[40]

She didn't scold me until far later, after I was healed. She told me I was lucky—other children had been crippled for life, and even killed, by falling under the wheels of the wagons. Then she used me as an example in obedience for the other children.

I remember crossing the Blue Mountains very well. The trees grew so thick, they had to be cut down and thrown aside to make way for the wagons. The trees were cut just near enough to the ground to let the wagons pass over the stumps, and the road through the forest was only cleared wide enough to let a single wagon pass. Some of the trees still standing were scarred by the axles on the wagons' wheels as the passage was so narrow.

The men in our train greatly admired the abundance of timber. They even talked about the possibility of a railroad being built across the plains someday. The same man who had waved goodbye to America when we crossed the Missouri line pointed to a very fine grove of fir or pine and remarked, "When they go to building a railroad out here, I want the contract of making rails. I'll split the rails right there in that grove."[41]

Passing through the Blues, we were overtaken by a snow storm, which made our progress dismally slow through the mud and wet. But once we were on the other side of the mountains and down on the flats, the weather grew pleasant again. The Indians in that country were Cayuse, who had many horses and some cattle. They were friendly to us, sociable even. They brought late vegetables from their gardens, such as pumpkins and potatoes, to trade for clothes and trinkets, scraps of iron, and ammunition.[42]

We passed Whitman's Mission, which some called a station. There was nothing cheerful or inviting about the place; only a low and very modest house or two, the doctor in the yard, and one or two other persons could be seen. We didn't stop there, only passed by. The country continued the same to the Columbia River: drifts and hummocks of dry sand, sagebrush occasionally, and everything dry, dusty and dreary all the time.

By the time we reached the banks of the Columbia, our wagon train was down in number to ten families and twenty wagons. Others had split off before along the route and gone their own ways at different times. Father, himself, had done that once—just after the Devil's Backbone of the Snake

River Country. Now, at Fort Walla Walla,[43] our little train of wagons with their canvas bonnets all torn, grease-stained, and the color of dust presented a spectacle that had never been seen there before.

Our faithful oxen, sore-necked, sore-footed, and worn out from drawing the wagons from Missouri to the Columbia, were unhitched for the final time. Our plan was to float down the river to the Willamette country, so of course the wagons and stock had to be left behind. We branded them with H.B., the brand of the Hudson's Bay Company, and turned them out to roam at will for the rest of their days in the Oregon Country.[44]

We remained at Walla Walla for two weeks so that Father and the rest of the men could saw lumber and build boats from trees that had drifted there during high water. They called the boats skiffs, and they were big enough to carry a family of eight or ten.

I remember well our start down the great *River of the West*. It was the first of November when we shoved out from the canoe landing into the river. How I enjoyed riding in the boat! It felt like an old grapevine swing to me. Deep whirlpools lapped and splashed and rolled about us. Often when the current was strong, the men would rest on their oars and let the boats be carried along by the current.

We were several days into our river journey, when at camp one night my Aunt Cynthia, Uncle Jesse's wife, pointed up to a raven flying close overhead. "See that raven, there?" she asked. "There's going to be a death in the family."[45]

Now, I hadn't heard anyone complain of hardships yet on the Columbia nor express fear of dangers ahead. This business of reading the future from flights of birds was new to me, but reading the expression in my aunt's face . . . seeing her gesture . . . hearing her tone of voice, I could tell she believed it.

Nothing dangerous or scary happened the next morning, so I put the omen out of my mind. I was much more interested in our meeting of a group of Indians and a black man in a canoe. They crossed our bow with their own canoe, and the black man shouted *Smoke six!*, which meant *Tobacco, friend!*

This man was very large and stout, with obviously more black in his skin than a red man. His eyes looked like burnt holes in a blanket. He had an immense shock of grizzly, almost curly hair that grew down to his ears and to within an inch of his nose, making his head seem unnaturally large. Some of our party gave them a little tobacco, and they passed on.

Who was that man? we asked Father. We were told he was the son of a negro man who came to the coast with Lewis and Clark's expedition about forty years before, and who—because of his black skin, wooly head, large proportions, and thick lips—was so petted by the Indian women, that he sired many sons.[46]

The river grew wilder and the foam-crested waves began to slap us back and forth. I began to think this was no ordinary rapid. Our boat was about twenty yards from the right-hand shore. Looking across the river, I saw a smaller boat opposite us toward the south bank. In it were three men with my brothers Elisha and Warren and my cousin Edward.

Their boat should have followed us through the rapids. We had a pilot. He knew the way. Why was their boat over there? Couldn't they see it was too dangerous?

There was no time to think or yell. Suddenly, the boat I was watching disappeared in a whirlpool of white water. The men and boys were thrown out. They were struggling in the water. They were drowning! Father and Uncle Jesse sprang from their seats, threw down their oars, and were about to leap out of our boat and make a desperate attempt to swim out to them. Mother and Aunt Cynthia held them back. "Men," they pleaded, "don't quit the oars. If you do, we will *all* be lost."[47]

I could hear their words clearly above the rushing waters. I could hear the agony in their voices. It was madness to try to swim through the rapids to the other side. And what would happen to everyone in our boat, should they try? The men returned to the oars just in time. The rapids grew more ferocious, as if trying to devour us, too.

After what seemed an eternity, we were at last in calmer water. We rowed our boat ashore. Mr. Doke, who had been in the other boat, could not swim but had taken hold of a feather bedtick[48] which carried him safely to the foot of the rapids, where we picked him up.

Mr. Parker, a strong swimmer, also got hold of a feather bedtick and guided it to safety. My brother Elisha managed to get back into his boat after it spilled him out into the whirlpool, but then a second whirlpool seized it and gulped it down, end foremost. Elisha climbed to the uppermost end as the boat descended and leaped as far as he could, to avoid being sucked down with the boat. When he rose to the surface again, he discovered he had one foot thrust into a pocket of his coat; he sank and rolled repeatedly, trying to kick free. Mr. Parker overtook him near the shore, and both came to safety holding onto the bedtick.[49]

My brother Warren and my cousin Edward were never recovered. Warren disappeared when the boat went down the first time and did not resurface. Old Mr. McClellan—the last adult in their boat—was last seen in the water, trying to save Edward. He had placed my cousin on a couple of oars and was trying to swim toward shore. But being hampered with a heavy coat and boots, he fell short of safety; both he and Edward disappeared under the projecting cliffs and were seen no more.

We climbed up the river bank to a narrow plateau running parallel to the river. From there, we had a good view of the current below. An Indian footpath ran along this plateau, and we followed it down the river, very slowly, all the time searching the river with eager eyes. Now and then one would stop and point to the river and say, *I see someone's head there*, and we would all bunch up and strain our eyes to see. But it always turned out to be nothing.

Nobody said anything now about the raven we had seen the day before.

Mother and Aunt Cynthia wept and grieved openly for their lost sons. Then Mother said to Elisha, "You learned to swim in Missouri by disobeying my orders, and it saved your life. I will never object to you boys going swimming any more."[50]

That afternoon a windstorm with cold rain burst upon our wretched and broken-hearted families. It lasted into the night. Late that evening a man from Peter Burnette's camp nearby came to ours looking for a little negro girl who had not come back from the river. She had been sent down, he said, to fetch a bucket of water and hadn't returned.

By morning, she was still missing. Some thought the girl might have entered one of the boats beached on the rocks there, to dip up the water, and been thrown overboard by the storm and drowned. Others said maybe she had been taken by Indians. In any case, she was never found.[51]

The next dangerous part of the river we had to pass was The Dalles, which was also called the Devil's Gullet. The banks of the river approached to within a few yards of each other and were faced with overhanging cliffs of volcanic stone as black as pot metal. The river poured through them in a crooked channel the men called the Chute. A boat in the Chute was like a toboggan on ice.

Father said the river had claimed too many Applegates already. Most of us hiked around the rapids while four strong men took two boats through. While following the path down the river bank, we children discovered a thicket of wild rose bushes. We ate as many rose hips as our stomachs would allow then picked more to take back to camp. Poor as they were, they were still fruit, and the older girls carried a quart or two back to Aunt Melinda. She made a pudding of them, using what was left of some home-made starch in the recipe.[52]

Still following the path, we passed a few native huts and a storehouse containing, among other things, acorns which were sweet and quite palatable. We helped ourselves and ate many of them. Then we came to a place where the Wascopum Indians were drying fish eggs. The eggs were hanging in festoons on poles that were propped up by forks stuck into the ground. This sort of dry house held no attractions for us; we held our noses and fled.[53]

When we passed the Cascades, the river was at its lowest stage, and the water covered only a part of the riverbed. On the north side, the stone floor of the riverbed was covered with a soft green moss. I walked barefoot on this soft carpet and thought it fine, indeed. I was told in summer the waters rolled here fifty feet deep!

The men had to carry the boats over these same moss-covered rocks. Below this *Portage of the Cascades*, there was open water all the way to the sea. We began to see seals swimming in the river. Their heads would stick up out of the water for only an instant then vanish again before we could get near.

It was in this part of the country our party tried to buy a colt for food. We had been without flesh of bird or beast for a long time. There were no cattle with us anymore, no sheep or hogs in this part of the wilderness. True, we had learned from the Indians what was good to feed upon: berries, acorns, tender plants, the yampa and camas tubers, bulbs, and roots. We had drawn the line, though, at a few of the Wascopum luxuries of caterpillars, the larvae of yellow jackets, and fish eggs.

Emigrants were always hungry. Children seated in the boats could enjoy themselves for hours, gnawing off the fat coating from the dried salmon skins. An emigrant not hungry was thought to be sick. So we bargained for a sleek, fat colt. But we never did get him. I don't know why.[54]

Maybe it was because we were so close to Fort Vancouver, and the grownups knew there would be food there. What a glad day it was when we reached Vancouver! Our camp was near the river, and the fort was a little farther inland. Breakfast was being served when I opened my eyes, and the roast fish and potatoes were the first things I saw. I jumped from my bedroll, and puddles of water pooled off me. My bedding was as wet as if it had been dragged straight out of the river; I had slept soundly all night while a pouring rain had drenched everything in sight. But I didn't care, for we were almost at the end of our journey.

Dr. McLoughlin of the Hudson Bay Company had not known of our arrival until he visited our camp that morning. When he came near to where I was standing, he smiled and bowed to me. He won me over immediately. Then he was introduced to our young ladies and their mothers. Two of the young ladies were my cousins, Lucy and Rozelle, who were each about fourteen years old.

In those days, girls from age twelve to seventeen were called young ladies. Over that age, they were called old maids. Nobody wanted to be an old maid. There was even a ditty we used to tease our cousins with:

Old age is honorable, but
Old maids are abominable.[55]

Dr. McLaughlin invited us all visit him at the fort, and some did. But Father said we needed to push forward to the Willamette River and from there, a place called Tum-Chuck[56] in Mr. Shortess's letters. We left Vancouver in our big family boats, passing under the bow of a schooner that was at anchor there. As we passed, British sailor boys tossed big red apples to Cousin Lucy, the eldest of our young ladies. She tried to catch the apples in her apron, but they all bounded into the river and were lost.[57] She acted mortified.

We were several days reaching Tum-Chuck. When we got there, we saw fewer than a dozen houses, including a tin shop, blacksmith shop, saw mill, and what we took to be a grist mill. We spent only one night there. The next morning, two or three Kanakas[58] helped us launch our boats above the falls and clear the rapids. That evening, we landed at Champoeg and stayed that night in a long shed that housed a bin of peas.

The next day, while Father was meeting with some men in Champoeg, I waded around for hours in that large bin of peas. They were white and very hard. The Indians there seemed very fond of peas. They called them *lep-wah*, and used them in soup, which they called *liplip*.[59]

We left our boats at that camp, and I never saw them again.

From Champoeg, we traveled all day by land until we reached Dr. Elijah White's house. He had heard of our coming and left a light in the window to guide us. A crackling fire was in the fireplace, and supper was on the table when we arrived. The smell of frying pork made me forget how tired I was of traveling. After supper, Father said we must press on again—one more mile to a place Dr. White had called Old Mission.

Here, Jason Lee had founded the first Methodist mission in the Willamette Valley. The mission itself was abandoned now; there were three log cabins under one roof, standing empty. It was perfect for our families and our hired men. We moved in immediately. It was November 29th, 1843.

Most everything we had started out with from Missouri had been left behind or lost in the river. We had little to see us through the winter, yet Mother found a skillet lid in one of the cabins. She said she could cook on that. Father said he would find work for food instead of money.[60] Everything would be all right. After all, this was Oregon. This was the Promised Land.

My grand adventure, instead of being over, seemed to be just beginning.

SUMMARY

Ten years after making the trek from Missouri to Oregon, at age seventeen, Jesse A. Applegate became a soldier in Southern Oregon's Rogue River War. Later, he attended Bethel Institute, where he received an advanced education. He married at age twenty-two and fathered thirteen children—not an unusual number in those days. A family of only five or six children was considered small.[61] He taught school, and subsequently served as school superintendent in Polk County, Oregon. After that, he practiced law at Dallas and Salem for thirty years. He finally died in Jacksonville,

Oregon, at age eighty-three.[62] He was considered by many in Oregon to be the Prince of Pioneers.

Jesse Applegate's narrative of his family's journey to Oregon raises many interesting—and at times, conflicting—issues of his day. Consider: fascination and acceptance of certain aspects of encountered cultures yet prejudice toward others; thoughtless consuming of natural resources en route yet appreciation for tribal uses of the same resources; preconceived expectations of how the emigrant experience would be, then the realities that often proved far different.

When we think of prevailing prejudices existing in Applegate's time, we automatically think of those held by whites against tribal people. But there were far more: prejudices against Hispanics (called Mexicans), the Irish, the Chinese, and other ethnic groups; against Jews, Mormons, and followers of other religious doctrines; against the wealthy and the very poor; against certain classes or professions. The list goes on and on.

Apparent in Articles of Confederation of various wagon trains, these mobile microsocieties perpetuated some of those prejudices and concerns. Often, certain groups—by name—were specifically excluded. In other cases, they were singled out when the Articles mentioned codes of conduct that would be followed by them or by others when dealing with them. Indeed, Americans brought their prejudices with them when they emigrated to the Promised Land.

Yet, at the same time, the Trail seemed to create its own social reality. With every encounter at tribal camps, forts, and wayside supply stations, new cultural experiences bombarded the emigrants. Two thousand miles of shared physical and emotional tribulations threw together disparate groups as helpmates, rescuers, and—sometimes—friends. Some of these experiences showed immediate effect; some, effects that were more subtle and took longer to become apparent. While certain behaviors continued to be strictly enforced en route, other behaviors that would have been unthinkable—or, at the very least, discouraged—in the States, became tolerated. Was it any wonder, then, that the society forged at the end of the trail reflected a blending of all that had been experienced before?

Even so, some things were—and remained—outside the realm of consideration of most emigrants, such as the consuming of natural resources along the Trail. In the thinking of the day, the grass was simply there for the stock to eat. The wild game was simply there for the emigrants to kill and eat. Watering holes and springs were the logical places to camp. The only cause for concern might come when others had reached those same places before them; their stock had eaten the grass; their latrines had fouled the springs; their campfires had used the available fuel.

When we begin to count the number of hooves, heels, and wagon wheels that pounded the same route year after year, the results are predictable. More and more people found fewer and fewer resources at their disposal. Disease bred and flourished in the watering holes and springs. Wild game was over-hunted or deserted the route altogether.

But lest we lay the blame solely at the feet of the emigrants for all these changes, it is instructive to remember that many tribal peoples regularly set fire to the grasslands and certain forest lands to encourage new growth in future seasons. This had been a proven and accepted practice for generations by the time the pioneers arrived. (As early as 1632, this practice was recorded with the comment, "[the land] can be smelt before it is seen.")[63] Indeed, certain grasses and trees *require* fire to reproduce. But wildlife and domesticated stock cannot eat burned grass.

The tribes also used fire to change the landscape to benefit themselves: improving access to wildlife range and other resources; eliminating certain kinds of vegetation and encouraging others; and herding, driving, or encircling animals into specific areas.

With the advent of fur trading posts and forts along the route, tribal people quickly adapted to hunting for wholesale trade with whites rather than solely for their traditional uses. Beaver pelts; deer, elk, antelope, bear and mountain sheep hides; buffalo hides, tongues, horns—all these quickly translated into blankets, cooking pots, foodstuffs, and weapons for the tribes. This spurred even more harvesting of the available wildlife.

Buffalo drives had been recorded by Lewis and Clark on their overland trek of 1803-6 and were still in use during the emigrant era. Many of the Plains tribes seasonally stampeded herds of buffalo over high precipices so they could take advantage of the mass killing to obtain their winter meat. Tribes also routinely drove or lured buffalo into rivers, sloughs, cut banks, and mud wallows for more large-scale killings. These were highly effective techniques for providing thousands of pounds of meat with the least amount of individual effort.

Did any of the meat or hides go to waste? The answer depends upon your cultural viewpoint. Was every morsel of meat, every piece of hide, every bit of bone consumed, used, or traded by the tribes? No. Then, what became of that which was left behind? Scavenger animals eventually cleaned the carcasses.

To emigrant sensibilities, that would have constituted waste. To tribal thinking, they took what they could use, preserve, or trade; then the rest was consumed by others (four-legged or winged) who had the need. The bones of the slaughtered animals eventually returned to the earth to come up again, in some distant year, as grass. So nothing, in the end, was wasted.

With 20/20 hindsight, we can see today that all these uses had a lasting impact on the environment in which the tribes lived and over which the emigrant traveled. In 1843, the year Jesse Applegate and his family came West, one thousand emigrants traveled the Oregon Trail. It was only the beginning of massive change within both cultures and upon the land.

LET'S INTERPRET

Discussion 1

"Oregon, in my mind, was a long way off . . . and I understood for us to get there, we would have to travel through lands swarming with wild Indians who would try to kill us with tomahawks or scalp us. . . . I didn't know whether . . . it was true, but lots of grownups believed it, so I decided I would, too."

. . . .

"The Indians' tribal names were Cayuse, Nez Perces, and Walla Walla, and we had many visitors from all these tribes. I think there was no hostile feeling among these people against us, but some of the emigrants were prejudiced against Indians of whatever kind, and were annoyed by the familiarity assumed by them in their dealings with the whites."

. . . .

"This man was very large and stout, with obviously more black in his skin than a red man. . . . We were told he was the son of a negro man who came to the coast with Lewis and Clark's expedition about forty years before, and who—because of his black skin, wooly head, large proportions, and thick lips—was so petted by the Indian women, that he sired many sons."[64]

—JESSE APPLEGATE, *A Day with the Cow Column, 1843*

Many white emigrants had existing prejudices against tribal people and against black people when they started their journey from the States. (Indeed, a number of emigrants owned slaves and brought them on the overland trek). It is interesting to note in Applegate's description of this man "with more black in his skin than a red man" (see note 115) that York—the negro slave of Clark—had been much esteemed and sought after *because* of his skin color and ethnic attributes. In this, the tribal peoples seem to have been far more open than their white counterparts. Prejudices cut all ways, however. What are some of the preconceived ideas and prejudices tribal people may have held about white emigrants? Other religions? Other tribes? What were some of the prejudices—from both the white and tribal stances—regarding mixed-bloods? Hispanics? Support your answers from various chapters' text.

Discussion 2

"Today an extra session of the Council is being held to settle a dispute . . . between a proprietor and a young man who has undertaken to do a man's service on the journey in exchange for bed and board. The Council was a high court in the most exalted sense. It was a Senate composed of the ablest and most respected fathers of the emigration. It exercised both legislative and judicial powers. . . . [It] heard the case, made the judgment, and carried out the decision. I only saw men sit on the Council; nobody's mother or sister was ever allowed."

. . . .

"The Sioux warriors—both men and women—were all painted about their faces. . . . Several of these Amazons [women warriors] visited our camp. They were dressed and painted and armed like the men. Some of them were very fine of figure, had pretty faces, and eyes as soft and bright as the antelope on those wild plains. They were all young women. Their small, shapely hands and small feet clad in beaded moccasins were admired by our sisters, aunts, and mothers. To my astonishment, they even flirted with our young men with their eyes. . . ."[65]

—JESSE APPLEGATE, *A Day with the Cow Column, 1843*

Gender roles were sharply divided in both white and tribal culture; however, upon occasion, women were permitted choices in tribal society they never would have been allowed among the emigrants. Using chapter texts as your historical sources, list normal and accepted roles for emigrant men, women, boys, girls. (Include chores, privileges, types of work, and types of recreation, social habits, or games considered suitable for each. Don't forget smoking.) Now do the same from the tribal standpoint. Compare. Based upon its overall expectations of you, which culture would you have preferred to live in?

Discussion 3

"Some of my girl cousins . . . often took their coffee cup after drinking the coffee, and turned the mouth [of the cup] upside-down. After it had drained, they'd turn it aright and peer into the patterns made by the coffee grounds, trying to make out pictures of future scenes."

.   .   .   .

"Now . . . I will say that our people, for frontiersmen and women of those days, were unusually free from superstitious whims. But mother . . . sometimes spoke of a belief . . . that seeing the new moon over the right shoulder was an omen of good luck. And to be candid, I must admit that when I know the new moon is out, I sometimes put myself to a little trouble to get first sight of it over my right shoulder. "

.   .   .   .

"We were several days into our river journey, when at camp one night, my

Aunt Cynthia, Uncle Jesse's wife, pointed up to a raven flying close overhead. 'See that raven, there?' she asked. 'There's going to be a death in the family.'"[66]

—JESSE APPLEGATE, *A Day with the Cow Column, 1843*

While many emigrants were quick to dismiss many unfamiliar ethnic and cultural practices (tribal, African, Hispanic) as superstitious, they themselves hung horseshoes over the door for luck, looked at hog's fat to predict weather, read tea leaves to see the future, and more. By reviewing chapter texts, list beliefs and practices that you would label as superstitions. Now list beliefs, sayings, or practices you would consider superstitions that are still in evidence today. (Don't limit yourself to your own culture.) How many things on your list are considered superstitions by some, but real by others? Why?

Discussion 4:

"Finding enough grass for all our livestock in one area had become more and more difficult . . . so those families having only a few cattle, horses, or mules to look after, joined what they called the 'Light Column'; those with more than four or five cows—as we did—joined the larger and slower 'Cow Column.' . . . Father and the other men would begin herding the loose stock toward their proper places. Sometimes they had to go as far as two miles from camp, gathering in the strays. By six o'clock [in the morning] the stock—about five thousand head—were milling around the circle of the wagons."[67]

—JESSE APPLEGATE, *A Day with the Cow Column, 1843*

"This is my country, and my people's country. My father lived here and drank water from this river. My mother gathered wood on this land. The buffalo and elk came here to drink water and eat grass, but now they have been killed or driven out of our land. All the grass has been eaten off by the white man's horses and cattle. The timber has been burned. And now, when our young men have been hunting, and are tired and hungry, they come to the white man's camp and are ordered to get out. They are slapped, or kicked, and called 'damned Injuns.' Sometimes they have been so abused that they have threatened to kill all the white men they meet in our land."[68]

—WASHAKIE, Shoshone, 1863

Emigrants brought livestock of all description with them on their journey: cattle, horses, oxen, mules, sheep, pigs, goats, chickens, and turkeys. Each family that owned its own stock brought not only animals enough to transport their wagons and possessions, but enough to slaughter en route for food. Some even drove herds from Missouri to the Oregon Country to sell them at the end of the trail for an enormous profit. Consider the impact on the land of literally millions of hooves, tens of thousands of iron-rimmed wagon wheels, plus hundreds of thousands of emigrants' feet over essentially the same route year after year. Study the chapters' texts and answer the following: What did the emigrants use for fuel? Where did they go to the bathroom? Where did they acquire fresh meat and greens to supplement their diets? Now, list the changes you think their passage made in the landscape. In the natural springs and watering holes. In the rivers. List the impacts you think their passage made on the wildlife populations along the route. How would these impacts have affected the tribal peoples' traditional way of life? How would they have affected emigrants traveling in later years?

NOTES

1. Jesse Applegate, *A Day with the Cow Column in 1843* (Fairfield, WA: Ye Galleon Press, 1934; reprint 1990), 134.

2. Applegate's term and spelling. Physics were plant and root-based medicines most commonly used as cathartics (stomach or bowel evacuants) or tonics. Applegate labels Injin Fizic as epecaquane, whose usefulness, he says, was learned from the natives. It was given in the form of a tea.

3. Applegate, *A Day with the Cow Column*, 56. In point of fact, statisticians tell us overland emigrants were up to ten times as likely to die from physical accident or illness than

from Indian attack during their trek.

4. Ibid., 56.

5. Ibid., 57–58.

6. Ibid., 58.

7. Ibid., 59. While Applegate may have used the description "Mexican" simply to designate which man had done the deed, it is important to remember there was strong prejudice against Mexican people among many "white" Americans in this era. The cutting off of enemy body parts for display, while condemned by Applegate's train, was far from new, and not restricted to cultures other than Applegate's own. The practice was common

in ancient times, both in the Old World and the New World, and has survived to our present time. Combat trophies of war in the field during WWII, the Korean Conflict, and the Vietnam War included human ears, fingers, etc.

8. Ibid., 65–66.

9. Ibid.

10. Ibid., 64–65.

11. Ibid., 70.

12. Ibid., 71–72.

13. Stick matches, or lucifers as they were called, were not widely available until later.

14. Applegate, *A Day with the Cow Column*, 70. Then, as now, many old wives' tales prove inaccurate.

15. Ibid., 66. Applegate's term in this passage was "squaws."

16. Ibid., 67.

17. Ibid.

18. Ibid., 67. Applegate's term; fabled women warriors of extraordinary courage and ferocity.

19. Ibid., 68.

20. Ibid., 62–63.

21. Ibid., 63.

22. Ibid., 28.

23. Ibid., 28.

24. Ibid., 29.

25. Ibid., 32.

26. Ibid., 75.

27. Ibid., 77.

28. Ibid.

29. Ibid., 79.

30. Ibid.

31. Ibid., 73.

32. Ibid., 80.

33. Ibid., 81–82.

34. Ibid., 83–84.

35. Ibid., 85.

36. Ibid., 84–85.

37. Ibid., 93–94.

38. Ibid., 91–92.

39. Ibid., 68.

40. Ibid., 95–96.

41. Ibid., 98.

42. Ibid., 99.

43. Under the ownership of the Hudson's Bay Company.

44. Applegate, *A Day with the Cow Column*, 103.

45. Ibid., 115.

46. Ibid., 116–17. Applegate's citation of this event and the information related states that this son of York (William Clark's slave during the expedition of 1804-06) "left the expedition in the Walla Walla Country, and remained with the native daughters." We know from the Lewis and Clark journals that York did not remain behind with the tribes. He traveled to the Pacific Ocean with the others of the expedition and returned to St. Louis with William Clark in 1806. Ten more years passed before York was granted his freedom. Clark indicated in his personal papers that York did not return to the West. However, there is tribal oral tradition among the Blackfeet that states he did. Regardless, York was much admired by the tribal peoples and most probably did sire many children along the expedition route.

47. Ibid., 121.

48. The cloth casing for a feather mattress. In this passage, bedtick apparently means the mattress itself. The location is cited as being in the vicinity of the main Dalles.

49. Applegate, *A Day with the Cow Column*, 127-28.

50. Ibid., 124–28: Applegate's account of the drownings.

51. Ibid., 129. "Negro" was Applegate's term.

52. Ibid., 132.

53. Ibid., 133.

54. Ibid., 136.

55. Ibid., 139.

56. Now Oregon City, Oregon.

57. Applegate, *A Day with the Cow Column*, 140.

58. Men from the Sandwich (Hawaiian) Islands.

59. Jesse Applegate, *A Day with the Cow Column*, 146.

60. Ibid., 149.

61. Ibid., 139.

62. Ibid., 23.

63. Shepard Krech, *Ecological Indian* (New York: W.W. Norton and Company, 1997), 101.

64. Applegate, *A Day with the Cow Column*, 56, 104, 115.

65. Ibid., 65–68.

66. Ibid., 56, 114, 115.

67. Ibid., 28.

68. Russell Freedman, *Indian Chiefs* (New York: Scholastic, Inc., 1987), 78.

CATHERINE SAGER
Oregon Trail Orphan

1844

FATHER WAS what you might call a rolling stone; he was one of those restless men who was never content to stay in one place very long. Late in the fall of 1838, when I was not quite four years old, we moved from Ohio to Missouri. There, Father took a place on the Green River, but that fell through. Then the next year, we settled on a farmstead in Platte County. Farming and blacksmithing, that's what Father did. He had quite a reputation for his ingenuity. Anything anyone needed to be made or mended, he was the man to figure out how it could be done. But he never could take root.[1]

In 1843, the famous missionary doctor, Marcus Whitman, came to Missouri from his mission near Fort Walla Walla. He talked up the Oregon Country to anyone who would listen and made it sound almost like a heaven on earth. He said the climate was much more healthful than Missouri, which appealed a great deal to my mother. Dr. Whitman planted the seeds of change in both my parents, though Father hardly needed convincing. Moving to Oregon was the theme of their discussion all winter long. Then it was decided. Father sold his property on the Platte and moved the family to St. Joseph. As soon as there was enough grass growing on the prairie to feed our oxen, he told us, we would head overland. By the end of April, 1844, we were Oregon-bound.

There were four girls and two boys when we started out, plus Father and

Mother. We children ranged in age from thirteen to barely old enough to be any help at all. The two boys—John and Frank—were thirteen and twelve, respectively.[2] I was third in line at ten. The other girls were all younger. Mother would add another baby girl to our throng at the end of May, so altogether we were to be nine, which wasn't considered to be a large family at all in those days, just a normal size.

Our first encampments were a great pleasure to us children, as it seemed to us we were living within a traveling circus. The long lines of wagons stretched as far as we could see in front and as far as we could see behind. They were every shape and color. Those who could not afford the better wagons often brought their farm wagons and covered them as best they could with canvas cloth. Some were painted with slogans, some with animal designs. *Goin' to See The Elephant!* they read. All sought their proper places in line; nobody wanted to be last. The yokes of oxen strained and bellowed, the wagon wheels and beds creaked and jolted and groaned. People of all descriptions milled around us, speaking in ways peculiar to their place of birth. Everywhere, everywhere, there was the excitement known as Oregon Fever.

We waited several days at the Missouri River while more wagons congregated. Many friends and families came that far to say good-bye to the travelers, so it was a place of great happiness and optimism . . . and of great sorrow and many tears. For every person heading west to Oregon, there were many others staying behind. I thought then—as I do now—it was easier to be the one who was leaving than the one to be left.

The captain of our train signaled: *time to go*. And suddenly, a great fluttering of handkerchiefs and gruff farewells filled the bright spring morning. We were off!

Our train was divided into companies; as there were so many wagons, the men felt they had to break into smaller groups to keep discipline. Our company was commanded by Mr. Willis Shaw. All the men called him simply Captain.

Father had one wagon, two steady yoke of old cattle, and several head of young and not well-broken ones.[3] At first, we children rode in the wagon, but the motion of its swaying and jerking made all of us sick. It was weeks before we got used to that seasick motion. It helped some to tie up the canvas bonnet as we traveled, so fresh air could come through; but when the

Catherine Sager

rains came, we had to tie them down, and the close air was nearly suffocating.[4] It wasn't long before we chose to walk instead of ride, all except the littlest girls.

Soon after we started, our cattle broke away in the night and recrossed the Missouri River to their winter quarters. Father had to go back, then, to recover them. A delay right at the start was not a good sign, he said. The rest of the wagon train didn't wait for us, and it was a long, hard march to catch up.

After a while, though, everything began to settle into a routine. All went smoothly, and our train made steady headway. The weather was fine, and we enjoyed our journey immensely. There were several musical instruments among the emigrants, and often in the evening when camp was made, we would hear music, merry talk, and laughter resounding from the evening campfires.[5] As the eldest girl in the family, it fell to me to help keep the younger ones quiet, so sometimes we'd sing "Hot Cross Buns" together, or play "Button, Button" and other hand games[6] until Mother said it was time for sleep.

Father continued to have trouble with the oxen. He simply couldn't get them to mind! Finally, he called upon Captain Shaw. Captain got them going soon enough—he pelted them with rocks until they moved[7] their sorry hides the way Father wanted them to go. *That's all there is to it!* Captain told him. Thereafter, my brothers were always allowed to keep their pockets full of stones.

Once we reached buffalo country, though, Father arranged for someone else to drive the team. Many young men made their way to Oregon in just that way. They had no wagons of their own yet drove for others in exchange for money, provisions, or simply for a steady place to lay their bedrolls. Sometimes they drove for a day, sometimes for a month. It didn't matter to them how long, as long as they grew ever nearer the Oregon Country with each passing mile.

Father was much better suited to the hunt than to the wagon box. He not only killed the great bison[8] on many occasions but often brought home antelope, which is much harder to kill. The boys said anyone could bring down a buffalo; as there were so many of them, you just couldn't miss! But an antelope—exceptionally fleet of foot and keen of eye—an antelope called for a true marksman.

We plodded on, across the plains. I think the boys had more fun than we girls. They got to help Father with the animals. They got to run off and play hide-and-go-seek in the long grass when the fancy suited them, just as long as they kept up with the wagons. Sometimes they got to hunt. Sometimes they even helped drive the teams! I had to help Mother with the children. I had to sew, and launder, and cook, and clean up. I had to study *The American Frugal Housewife*, to learn about home remedies and cures.[9] It didn't seem fair. But I didn't dare complain.

"Every girl should know how to be useful,"[10] Mother told me. "You'll have a family of your own to look after, someday. You'll need to know what to do—and how."

I couldn't even imagine how quickly that time would come.

Just after crossing the South Platte, one of our unwieldy oxen ran on a bank and overturned our wagon. Mother, who was inside with the baby, was knocked unconscious. Father peered inside the wagon, and cried out. He ran to set up a tent in the shade and immediately laid Mother in it. But she was unconscious for a long time. We were all afraid she would die. I had never seen Father so worried; even my brothers cried. Fortunately, there was a Dutch doctor in our company, Dr. Dagon.[11] He tended to Mother, and eventually she came back to herself.

Father pulled me aside and told me I would have to take more of the responsibility in looking after the family. Mother needed her rest now, even more than she had before, and I would be expected to fill Mother's shoes. I promised him I would do my best.

August 1st, we nooned in a beautiful grove on the north side of the Platte. By this time, we had become quite adept at climbing in and out of the wagon, even while it was still in motion. That afternoon, I was doing just that when my dress caught on an axle helve,[12] and I was thrown under the wagon wheel. Before Father could get the team stopped, the wheel passed right over my leg and crushed it. Badly.[13]

When Father tried to pick me up from the ground, he saw how my leg dangled at an odd angle. *Oh my dear child, your leg is broken all to pieces!* he exclaimed. The news soon spread along the train, and Captain Shaw called a halt for everyone. The same Dutch doctor who had ministered to Mother, now set my leg. We were back on the move to Fort Laramie soon afterward, but this proved to be the last of my wheel-jumping days. My broken leg confined me to our wagon for the remainder of our long journey.[14]

After Laramie, we entered the Great American Desert, an inhospitable country that was very hard on our already-tired teams. Here, sickness became common. Father and the boys were all sick, and we were dependent upon Dr. Dagon to become our driver. He may have been an excellent surgeon, but he knew little about driving oxen. Often, Father or the boys would have to rise from their sickbeds to wade the streams and get the teams safely across.[15] It seemed they were always chilled, always tired. We didn't know then, Father had typhoid.[16]

One day, four buffalo ran between our wagon and the one behind us. Though feeble, Father seized his gun and gave chase to them. The doctor called his actions imprudent. In fact, they were fatal. When Father finally returned to camp, he lay down in the wagon, never to stand again. He knew he was dying. Yet his thoughts were not for himself.

"Poor child," he turned his head to look at me. "You are helpless. What will become of you?"[17]

Captain Shaw came to check on Father and found him weeping. Father said he knew his last hour had come, and his heart was filled with anguish for his family. Mother was ill, I was crippled, and the other children were not old enough to look after themselves, not even the boys. We had no relatives on the train, nor any nearby. A long journey lay ahead.

He begged Captain Shaw to take charge of us and see us through to Oregon. This, the captain promised. Then Father died.

They buried him the next day on the banks of Green River. His coffin was made from two troughs cut out of a tree.[18] Now Mother, as weak as she was, had to be the head of the family. She hired a young man to drive, as she was afraid to trust the doctor's driving skills. Even so, this kind-hearted man would not leave us and declared his intentions to see us safely to the Willamette Valley in Oregon.

At Fort Bridger, the stream was full of fish, and we made nets of wagon sheets to catch them. That evening, our new driver told Mother he would hunt for game if she would let him use Father's gun. He took it, and we never saw him again.

Some of the other men in our company said they thought the young man had a sweetheart in one of the trains some weeks ahead of us. They thought probably he was headed there. Regardless, we saw neither him nor the gun until at long last we reached Whitman's Mission Station.[19] He had left it there for us when he passed by, maybe in a pang of conscience. That certainly was no use to us now, though, along the Trail with no weapon! We struggled along as best we could, with the doctor's help.

Mother now planned to winter over at Whitman's Station and regain her health. She knew we had many weeks' travel yet to go before reaching their sanctuary, but it seemed our only reasonable hope. She tried to hang on.

The nights and mornings were very cold now, and she took cold from the unavoidable exposure. She fought bravely against fate for the sake of her children . . . to no avail. She failed by degrees under the continuing burden of her sorrows and became bedfast. With camp fever[20] and a sore mouth, she suffered terribly. Traveling in this condition over a road clouded with dust, she could not breathe. Her bones ached. Her innards rebelled. Her cries were delirious until at last she became mercifully unconscious.

Other women from the train came nightly to wash her face and to look after my baby sister. They tried to make Mother comfortable, propping her with quilts and bedticks, smoothing her brow, murmuring over her as they would their own family. This went on for several days.

Mother was clear of mind off and on. In one of her lucid moments, she gathered all of us children together around her and bade us each farewell. She told us to take care of one another, no matter what might happen in the future. Then she charged Dr. Dagon to look after us until we could reach the Whitmans' station. She made the same request of Captain Shaw. This done, she lapsed back into delirium.

We traveled a very rough road the day she died. She moaned piteously all the time. That night, one of the women came in as usual, but Mother made no sound. This kind-hearted woman thought Mother asleep, so she gently washed her face then took her hand. The pulse was nearly gone. Mother lived only a few minutes more. Her last words were to my dead father: "Oh Henry! If only you knew how we have suffered."[21] Then she was gone.

A tent was set up some little distance from the wagon, where Mother's body was properly laid out by the other women. We children were told we might come in and look one last time at our mother's face.

The grave they had prepared for her was near the wagon road. Willow brush was laid in the bottom. The women wrapped Mother's body in a quilt, and then the men placed her in the grave. More brush was placed on top. Then the earth was filled in. Her name was cut on a head-board. And the train moved on.[22]

It occurred to me then, in deepest grief and shock, that I was an orphan. We were all orphans, seven of us . . . and the youngest one, a baby. How would we ever get to Oregon?

Families of the train adopted us. The baby was taken by one of the women who had been caring for Mother. The rest of us were looked after by one and all. Captain Shaw and his wife were as careful and solicitous of us as if they were our real parents. When the flour in our own provisions gave out, Uncle Billy and Aunt Sally, as we began to call them, divided their last loaf of bread to share with us.[23] Dr. Dagon watched over us like an uncle. With the help of our extended train family, we children were able to stay together. John, fourteen now, and Frank divided the work normally done by Father; the little girls and I took the role of Mother.

At Snake River,[24] the company stayed over to make our wagon into a cart, as our team was wearing out. We loaded what we could onto it, packing only what Captain thought essential. Some of our things were sold, and some were left by the side of the trail.[25] We had seen many such abandoned articles on our journey: iron cookstoves, trunks of clothes, overstuffed chairs, and dressers. Each piece had a story. Each piece seemed to me to be a piece of someone's life. But after leaving both Father and Mother on the Trail, no possession seemed to us too dear to cast away.

The last of September, we passed through the valley of the Lone Tree Sentinel. But there were only scattered pieces of it, lying about the ground. It had been felled for firewood by some emigrant's axe. All that remained now was the stump.

It was not long after this, in the valley of the Grande Ronde, that Sister's clothes caught fire. There was already snow on the mountains lining the valley. We had long been building fires to keep warm when we laid by, as well as to cook on at night. And Sister got too close to the fire. The ever-present wind of the Grand Ronde whipped her clothes about her and fanned the sparks to flame. She went up like a candle, screaming and trying to run. If not for our good Dr. Dagon—who beat the flames out with his bare hands—Sister would have burned to death.

There were so many times I cried in my heart to Mother. How could I look after all of us? I should have been keeping closer watch on Sister. Hadn't Mother warned us girls—how many times!—to keep our skirts, our aprons, our bonnets, out of the way of the fire? She told us of grown women who had been caught unaware by the flames and horribly burned and disfigured. Why hadn't I been paying more attention? The girls were my responsibility now, even though I was only ten. No one blamed me for my carelessness out loud, but I blamed myself.

But try as I might, I couldn't keep my eye on the children well enough. One night Little Sister crawled out of the wagon in her bedclothes and wandered off into the cold night. If not for her cries in the darkness, Uncle Billy might not have found her.[26] She might have frozen to death in those mountains!

Another day, when we were making a fire of wet wood, Frank thought he would help get the flame going by holding his powder horn over the small blaze. Of course, the powder horn exploded in his face. He ran to a creek nearby and splashed water all over his face and hands. When next we saw him, his winkers[27] and eyebrows were gone, and his face was blackened beyond recognition. It's a wonder he was left alive.[28]

All through the rugged Blue Mountains, cattle had been giving out and were left lying by the side of the road. The sight was pitiful, and the stench was awful.

We had been out of flour for a long time, living only on meat. But this meager diet was taking its toll, so a few from our company were sent ahead to get supplies from Dr. Whitman, then return to the train. Since we Sagers had only the cart and could travel faster than the other teams, we went with Uncle Billy, Aunt Sally, and the advance party.

Dr. Whitman's Indians, as they called themselves, were returning from buffalo hunting, and often came into our camp. They were loud in their praise for the missionaries and seemed anxious to help us. They even sometimes drove up some poor beasts that had been left by the side of the trail and returned them to their owners.[29]

We reached Umatilla on October 15. My baby sister was very sick. She was so sick, many thought she would die. So Aunt Sally convinced us we should leave her with the rest of the company until they could catch up to us. The shaking of our little cart would only weaken her further. Dr. Dagon agreed.

On November 6, Uncle Billy took us ahead toward Whitman's station to see if the doctor could take care of us. He and Aunt Sally would return for us the next spring, he said, after they got settled in the Willamette and had a homestead built. Dr. Dagon went with us, keeping his promise to Mother.

My brothers and sisters faced forward, toward the mission. I looked back. Aunt Sally waved. She stood looking after us, as long as we were in sight.[30] I don't imagine there was a much more pitiful sight than our cart full of orphans going to find a home among strangers.[31]

We reached the station before noon. For weeks, this place had been the subject of our talk by day and our dreams by night. We expected to see log houses occupied by Indians and the kinds of people we had seen around the forts. Instead, we saw a large white house surrounded with palisades.[32] It looked like a mansion. A short distance from this was another large adobe house. That was the house used by emigrants who wintered over; in the summer, it was used as a granary. Nearby was a mill pond, and the grist mill was not far from that.[33] Between the two houses were the blacksmith shop and the corral. The garden lay between the mill and the house, and a large field was on the opposite side. A good-sized irrigation ditch passed in front of the house.

We drove up beside the mansion, and halted near the ditch. Uncle Billy went inside to talk with Mrs. Whitman. We could hear his voice plainly from our little cart. He glanced out the window at us then said to her, "Your children have come. Will you go out and see them?"[34]

Then he came outside. "Help the girls out," he told the boys, "and get their bonnets." It was easy to talk of bonnets, but not to find them![35] We hurried to dig them out of the goods in our cart. Certainly, we had been traveling like wild things, with niceties such as sunbonnets far from our minds. Our browned complexions were proof enough of that. But now, to meet Mrs. Whitman, we wanted to present ourselves as best we could. We finally discovered one or two by the time she came out of the house, but we didn't have time to tie them on.

Now here was the scene: in front stood the little cart; near it lay the tired oxen which Dr. Dagon had unyoked. Sitting in the front end of the cart was John, weeping bitterly; on the opposite site stood Frank, his arms on the

SEEING THE ELEPHANT

cart wheel and his head resting on his arms, sobbing aloud. On the near side of the cart, I huddled with the little girls, bareheaded and barefooted, looking first at the boys, then at the house, and back . . . dreading I knew not what. By the oxen stood our good Dr. Dagon, with his whip in his hand, trying to keep his emotions in check.[36]

Mrs. Whitman was a large, well-formed woman. She had very pale skin and beautiful auburn hair. I thought she had rather a large nose, but her big gray eyes drew me in. That morning she had on a dark calico dress and gingham sunbonnet. We children thought—as we shyly looked at her—she was the prettiest woman we had ever seen.[37] Besides Mother, maybe.

She spoke kindly to us as she came up to the cart, but like frightened things, we ran behind it, afraid to more than just peep at her in quick glances. Dr. Dagon and Uncle Billy began throwing things off the cart, and Mrs. Whitman arranged them on the ground. Then she directed the boys and the doctor where these things should be taken—inside the emigrants' house. Seeing my lameness, she kindly took me by the hand. With her other hand, she took my little sister. We all entered in.

As we reached the steps, Uncle Billy asked if she had children of her own. Mrs. Whitman pointed to a grave at the foot of a little hill, nearby. "All the child I ever had, sleeps yonder," she answered.[38] "It's a great comfort to me that I can see the grave from my door."

When Dr. Whitman came in from the mill, he looked surprised to see so many of us waiting there. We were a sight, indeed: dirty and sunburned until we looked more like Indians than white children. John had cropped our hair short so that it hung in uneven locks about our faces, only adding to our odd appearance. Mrs. Whitman said with a laugh, "Come in, Doctor, and see your children."[39]

Mother had begged Uncle Billy that we children not be separated from one another, so he urged the Whitmans to take charge of all of us. Doctor Whitman feared the Missionary Board might object, saying he was sent as a missionary to the Indians, not director of an orphanage. But Uncle Billy argued that a missionary's duty was to do good, and we children were certainly objects worthy of missionary charity.[40]

Doctor Whitman was finally convinced to keep us until spring. His wife didn't want to keep the boys, only the girls. And when she was told of our baby sister back with the company, she exclaimed she wanted the baby most of all. But the doctor said he wanted boys as well as girls. His word was law, so we were able to stay together.

Uncle Billy and our faithful friend, Dr. Dagon, left us at last in the care of our new family and returned to the rest of the wagon train. The written agreement Uncle Billy had signed with Dr. Whitman gave us over completely into the mission's charge. *You need not give yourself any further care concerning them*, he told Uncle Billy. It was a painful goodbye for us, being stripped, for a second time, from the only family we knew.

Baby sister was brought over to the mission a few days later. She was very, very sick, but under Mrs. Whitman's steadfast care, she did recover.

The first week or two, Mrs. Whitman was too busy to pay much attention to any of us, except the baby. Being a cripple, I wasn't able to join my brothers and sisters in their play with the other children at the mission or in exploring our new home. They were far too busy enjoying themselves to give much thought to me. So, seated by the cradle in the house, I sewed. And sewed. And sewed. I saw my brothers and younger sisters only at meal time.[41] Indians came and went at all hours.

I grew so shy, I burst out in tears whenever anyone spoke to me. I was sure I could never be happy where everything was so strange, where I felt so completely alone.

As so often happens in life, though, as the weeks and months wore on, our lives at the mission fell into a predictable routine. There were school lessons to learn, chores to do, disciplines to remember. We had been so long without restraint on the Trail, our habits tended to be wild and unmanageable. We were always getting into trouble. Finally, Mrs. Whitman gave each of us a string of beads to wear—just like the Indians wore—saying that anyone who had to be corrected or chastised for doing wrong, must return the beads to her. We guarded those beads jealously and tried to be as good as she and the doctor expected.[42]

The Whitmans were good to us even when we needed punishing. They would set out our faults before us, and speak of their own responsibility to bring us up correctly. They asked what we thought our parents would wish them to do at such times. And their punishments were strict but fair.[43]

We grew to respect and love them. The other children at the mission—children of mountain men, mixed bloods[44]—all called them Mother and

Father. We began to do that, too. For the next three years, we were no longer orphans in the Oregon Country.

SUMMARY

Catherine (or Katie, as she was called by her brothers and sisters) remained crippled. As it was very hard for her to move around, she was confined to the main house a great deal during the next three years. She became quite close to Mrs. Whitman, saying in her journal, "she could not get along without me." Brother Frank, however, did not respond as well to the missionaries' discipline and expectations. He ran away and joined a wagon train heading for the Willamette the spring following the children's arrival at *Waiilatpu*. He could not be persuaded to return until Dr. Whitman proposed, by letter, to help set up Frank and John with cattle and horses so the boys could acquire property when they were of legal age. This convinced Frank to return the following fall, so the family was once again reunited.

November 29, 1847, tore the family apart forever. John, Frank, and six-year-old Louisa died in what history books call The Whitman Massacre and its aftermath. To understand better the clash of cultures that led to this killing, one must remember that the Cayuse considered their homeland territory—some of the richest agricultural land in the Pacific Northwest—to be under their proprietorship alone. This was the tribal way. When Whitman established and operated his mission within that territory, he ignored the custom of officially—and repeatedly—giving gifts to the Cayuse for the privilege of settling, doctoring, and farming there. Indeed, it was widely known that Whitman considered the highest calling of their land to be that of white settlement.[45]

Instead, Whitman tended to their sick upon occasion, taught them his Protestant religious views, and tried to educate them in what he considered the ways of civilization. All the while, he encouraged more white emigrants to come across the Oregon Trail, using the Mission as a favored stopping, resting, and resupplying place.

As the number of white emigrants trekking through Cayuse territory grew from hundreds to thousands—and as the impact of those emigrants upon their land and lifeways grew ever more permanent—tribal attitude changed from welcoming and helpfulness to one of distrustful resistance. When the white man's diseases began to spread like wildfire through the region's tribes, killing most of the natives but sparing the Whitmans and their mission population, the Cayuse suspected they were being poisoned so that the whites could seize their lands once and for all.

Add to this volatile mix the fierce rivalry between the Protestant and Roman Catholic missionaries for the souls of the same tribal people. Some of the Cayuse became Catholic converts; some (through Whitman), Protestants; and some remained unconvinced that either outside system was necessary. Dissension and infighting were actively encouraged by the Whitmans in an effort to bring more of the native peoples to the Protestant side of the equation.[46] This helped divide the Cayuse into antagonistic factions and eroded the traditional control of the Tribal Council to keep peace.

According to tribal oral tradition, after the accidental drowning of the Whitman's two-year-old daughter in 1839 (their only biological offspring), the missionaries hardened their hearts and became increasingly inflexible to tribal ways—overly proud, even haughty. Whippings of tribal members at the mission school, and other corporal punishments that were unacceptable to the tribes, only convinced the Cayuse that the Whitmans were not their friends but their enemies.

In the autumn of 1847, another terrible epidemic struck the Cayuse. Before it was over, almost half of the remaining tribe had died. Again, few white people succumbed, as their immune systems were already accustomed to these "white man diseases." As the Cayuse lay dying at a rate of five or six per day, a mixed-blood man who worked at Whitman's mission reported to the Cayuse chiefs he had actually overheard Whitman plotting with other white men (including Spalding) to poison the remainder of the tribe so they could take what was left of their land.[47]

Had Whitman said this? Was the old, persistent rumor true? At least some of the Cayuse believed it. On November 29, a small group of them killed Marcus and Narcissa Whitman, three of the Sager children, and eight others who were inside the mission compound at the time. They took forty-seven additional people hostage. These were successfully ransomed by the Hudson's Bay Company agent, Peter Skene Ogden, almost a month later. Catherine Sager, her two younger sisters Elizabeth and Matilda Jane, and baby Henrietta (Rosanna) were among these survivors. They were taken by Mr. Ogden to Fort Vancouver and from there to the Willamette Valley, where they were adopted out to different families. They grew to adulthood, eventually married, and continued to be considered by other settlers as very notable Oregon pioneers.

Though the events at Whitman Mission horrified and outraged white society, they did little to stem the human tidal wave of emigrants who were determined to reach their Land of Milk and Honey by way of the Oregon Trail. If anything, in the 1949 words of a fellow missionary, "In meeting death the way [they] did, it might be said . . . that [the Whitmans] died martyr[s] to the progress of American civilization."[48]

LET'S INTERPRET

Discussion 1

"Calf's Foot Jelly – Boil four [calf's] feet in a gallon of water, till it is reduced to a quart. Strain it and let it stand till it is quite cool. Skim off the fat, and add to the jelly one pint of wine, half a pound of sugar, the whites of six eggs, and the juice of four large lemons. Boil all these together eight or ten minutes. Then strain into the glasses, or jars, in which you intend to keep it. Some [women] lay a few bits of lemon peel at the bottom, and let it be strained upon them."

.   .   .   .

"Ear-Wax. Nothing is better than ear-wax to prevent the painful effects resulting from a wound by a nail, skewer, etc. It should be put on [the wound] as soon as possible. Those who are troubled with cracked lips have found this [ear wax] remedy successful when others have failed. It is one of those sorts of cures which are very likely to be laughed at; but I know of its having produced beneficial results."[49]

—*The American Frugal Housewife,* 1829

"In the meantime, the Caw high chief visited our [gunshot] patient and administered some sort of pungent colored water made from the steeping of roots, then a salve of rendered fat and plant parts."[50]

—THOMAS FARNHAM, June 21, 1839

From the first settlement of Europeans on the North American continent, keen observers of tribal medicines and practices adopted these for their own usage. Herbalists were quite respected and sought after as settlement pushed ever westward from the Eastern seaboard. On the Oregon Trail, many accidents required doctoring. In fact, emigrants were ten times as likely to be hurt or killed by accidents as they were from skirmishes with Indians! Many trail illnesses and upsets were treated with a combination of familiar medicines—most of which were originally based on traditional herbs, roots, and barks. Tribal remedies that were observed or experienced en route were pressed into service when the tried and true remedies didn't work. Reviewing the various chapters' texts, list examples of emigrant accidents, injuries, and illnesses that required treatment. Now, list the treatments. How effective were they? Do the same for tribal injuries and illnesses listed in the texts. Now, list modern medicines and treatments that would be used for the same conditions today.

Discussion 2

"Father was buried the next day on the banks of Green River. His coffin was made of two troughs dug out of the body of a tree, but [the] next year, emigrants found his bleaching bones. . . ."

.   .   .   .

"A tent was set up some . . . distance from the wagon where Mother's body was properly laid out by the other women. We children were told we might come in, then, and look one last time at our mother's face. The grave they had prepared for her was near the wagon road. Willow brush was laid in the bottom. The women wrapped Mother's body in a quilt, then the men placed her in the grave. More brush was placed on top.

Then the earth was filled in. Her name was cut on a head-board. And the train moved on."[51]
—CATHERINE SAGER PRINGLE,
Across the Plains in 1844

"Mr. Lee pointed out the 'Island of Tombs' [in the Columbia River] where stood cedar board houses of the [Indian] dead. On them and about the houses were stacked the cooking utensils and other personal property of the deceased. Within were the dead bodies, wrapped in many thicknesses of deer and elk skins, tightly lashed with leather thongs and laid in a pile with their heads to the east. . . . Three or four of the tombs had gone to ruins and the . . . bones lay strewn upon the ground."[52]
—THOMAS FARNHAM, October 15, 1839

"We came to a place where the ground was literally covered with [small white beads]. We looked up, and discovered that the platform above our heads was thickly strewn with the decayed corpses of Indian dead. . . . Many of the bodies were rolled up in blankets and robes. Some had been torn apart and scattered by scavenger birds."
—JESSE APPLEGATE, *A Day with the Cow Column, 1843*

Burial practices were almost universally the same among the emigrants: women would lay out the body and wash and dress it for burial; then interment would take place in holes the men had dug. Usually these graves were covered over with brush and/or rocks and even campfires to deter wild animals or marauders from disturbing them. Some graves had headboards; most did not. Among the tribes, however, practices varied from region to region, tribal nation to tribal nation. When emigrants came upon opened tribal funerary bundles, or observed bones open to the elements, they were horrified. They pointed to this apparent state of disregard as savage. But to the tribal peoples, this was all part of the natural process and considered no less holy than the pioneers' own practices. How might these tribes have viewed emigrant burial of their dead in the ground? Review the chapters' texts. How might ignorance of local cultural customs lead to misunderstandings and confrontations? List different funerary and mortuary customs that are practiced today around the world.

Discussion 3

"At Snake River [the company stayed over] to make our wagon into a cart, as our team was wearing out. Into this was loaded what was necessary. Some things were sold [or] left on the plains.[54]

—CATHERINE SAGER PRINGLE, *Across the Plains in 1844*

"We'll start [the journey] with old clothes on. When we can't wear them any longer, will leave them on the road."[55]

—KATURAH BELKNAP, 1847

"Husband found a discarded cookstove near camp. [I] used it to prepare our meal this eve. First time I've had a proper cook fire since leaving Missouri."[56]

—LUCY HENDERSON, 1846

"What voice was first sounded on this land? The voice of the red people, who had but bows and arrows. What has been done in my country, I did not want. I did not ask for it. . . .When the white man comes [here], he leaves a trail . . . behind him."[57]

—MAHPIUA LUTA, Sioux, 1867

The Oregon Trail has been called a 2,000 mile long junkyard, as so many items were abandoned en route to lighten the wagon loads. It was common practice for emigrants to pile unwanted items by the side of the trail, with the understanding that the property became—from that point forward—free for the taking. How might you, as a tribal person, view these goods? How might you make use of some of the items? Where might you be able to trade some of them? Or would you view them simply as trash? How would you most likely view the goods if you were a passing emigrant? Support your viewpoints with passages from the book text. What do you suppose happened to all those goods as the years passed?

"There is no accomplishment of any kind more desirable for a woman, than neatness and skill in the use of a needle. . . . Every little girl, before she is twelve years old, should know how to cut and make a shirt with perfect accuracy and neatness."[58]

—*The Little Girl's Own Book*

"Some mothers will not make pockets in their boy's trousers because if boys have pockets they fill them so full of rocks, strings, dead beetles, dried fish worms, chewing wax, nails, tops, toys, toy pistols . . . fishing tackle, bullets, buttons, jew's harps, etc., that the strain on the suspenders often becomes too great."[59]

—JESSE APPLEGATE, *A Day with the Cow
Column, 1843*

"In this country, we are apt to let children romp away their existence, till they get to be thirteen or fourteen. This is not well. It has [the worst] effect on the morals and habits of children. *Begin early* is the great maxim for everything in education. Girls should begin mastering the art of needlework and other domestic arts as soon as they are able to receive instruction at Mother's knee. Boys, who by nature have a more tempestuous constitution, should be swiftly and firmly molded into accepted expressions of manly sensibility, so as to be welcomed into any level of society."[60]

—*The Lady's Home Magazine,* January 1860

Gender roles, as we discovered in Chapter 3, were far more structured in emigrant times than they are now. In the previous chapter, we examined the various gender expectations from both the emigrant and tribal standpoint. In this exercise, list normal or accepted roles for men, women, boys, and girls in America today. Now list roles or codes of behavior that are still considered unusual for each gender. (Don't forget to examine types of clothing, activities, rights and privileges, etc.) Do the same thing for countries other than the United States.

NOTES

1. Catherine Sager Pringle, *Across the Plains in 1844* (Reprint, Fairfield, WA: Ye Galleon Press, 1989), 5.

2. Mary Barmeyer O'Brien, *Toward the Setting Sun* (Helena, MT: Falcon Publishing, 1999), 58. Frank is also referred to as Francis in Sager's narrative. Apparently "Frank" was a nickname.

3. Oxen are simply male cattle that have been castrated, or "steered," at an early age and trained to work. Any breed can be used as oxen. Sager seems to use the terms "cattle" and "oxen" interchangeably throughout her account when she is referring to these draft animals.

4. Sager Pringle, *Across the Plains*, 6.

5. Ibid.

6. Maria Child, *The Little Girl's Own Book* (1834. Globe-Pequot Press, 1992), vix.

7. Sager Pringle, *Across the Plains*, 6.

8. Ibid. Bison is the correct scientific term for what the pioneers called buffalo. In this passage, Sager calls them bison.

9. Maria L. Child, *The American Frugal Housewife* (1833; reprint, Minneola, NY: Dover Press, 1999). First published in Boston in 1832, this very popular book contained cooking recipes, recipes, meat butchering guides, general housekeeping and childrearing hints, plus remedies for all sorts of common ills and complaints.

10. Child, *The Little Girl's Own Book*, iv.

11. O'Brien, *Toward the Setting Sun*, 58.

12. Kind of a handle or protrusion (Webster's dictionary).

13. Sager Pringle, *Across the Plains*, 7.

14. Ibid.

15. Ibid.

16. O'Brien, *Toward the Setting Sun*, 60.

17. Sager Pringle, *Across the Plains*, 7.

18. Ibid.

19. Ibid., 8. Whitman's Station was a well-established stopping place for Oregon Trail emigrants in what is today southeastern Washington State. By 1844, emigrants who could not make the rest of the journey to the Willamette Valley knew they would be welcome to stay the winter with the Whitmans at *Waiilatpu*.

20. Common name for cholera in this era. A sore mouth and high fever were symptomatic of the first stages of the sickness.

21. Sager Pringle, *Across the Plains*, 8.

22. Ibid.

23. Ibid., 9.

24. Fort Hall. This stop was often called by the emigrants *the place of Broken Dreams*, as many possessions had to be abandoned there.

25. Sager Pringle, *Across the Plains*, 8.

26. Ibid.

27. Eyelashes.

28. Sager Pringle, *Across the Plains*, 9.

29. Ibid. These Dr. Whitman's Indians were primarily the Cayuse. However, the Umatilla and Walla Walla also routinely traveled these lands.

30. Sager Pringle, *Across the Plains*, 9.

31. Ibid. Sager attributes this remark to Mrs. Shaw, saying it was spoken in later years as a reminiscence.

32. Protective walls.

33. Sager Pringle, *Across the Plains*, 10.

34. Ibid.

35. Ibid.

36. Ibid.

37. Ibid.

38. Ibid., 11.

39. Ibid.

40. Ibid.

41. Ibid., 12.

42. Ibid.

43. Ibid.

44. Ibid. Sager's term was "half-breed," which was commonly used at the time.

45. Marcus Whitman, letter of May 16, 1844, to his parents. "I have no doubt our greatest work is to be able to aid the white settlement of this country and help found its religious institutions." Thomas Jessett, *The Indian Side of the Whitman Massacre* (Fairfield, WA: Ye Galleon Press, 1985), 12.

46. Letter of Methodist Reverend

H. K. W. Perkins, October 19, 1849, to Narcissa's sister, Jane Prentiss, in response to Jane's request for details about her sister's death. Whitman College archives, Walla Walla, Washington, as cited in Thomas E. Jessett, *The Indian Side of the Whitman Massacre* (Fairfield, WA: Ye Galleon Press, 985), 10.

47. Alvin M. Josephy, Jr., *The Nez Perce Indians and the Opening of the Northwest* (New Haven, CT: Yale University Press, 1965), 47

48. Reverend H. K. W. Perkins, October 19, 1849, as cited in Jessett, *The Indian Side of the Whitman Massacre*, 10.

49. Child, *The American Frugal Housewife*, 31,116.

50. Thomas Farnham, *An 1839 Wagon Train Journal: Travels in the Great Western Prairies, The Anahuac and Rocky Mountains, and in the Oregon Territory* (1843; reprint, Northwest Interpretive Association, 1979), 16, June 21, 1839.

51. Pringle, *Across the Plains*, 7–8.

52. Farnham, *Journal*, October 15, 1839.

53. Jesse Applegate, *A Day with the Cow Column, 1848* (Fairfield, WA: Ye Galleon Press, 1990), 90.

54. Pringle, *Across the Plains*, 9.

55. Joyce Badgley Hunsaker, *Oregon Trail Center: The Story Behind the Scenery* (Las Vegas, NV: KC Publications, 1995), 23.

56. Ibid., 29.

57. Russell Freedman, *Indian Chiefs* (New York: Scholastic, Inc., 1987), 17.

58. Child, *The Little Girl's Own Book*, 203.

59. Applegate, *A Day with the Cow Column*, 105.

60. T. S. Arthur, ed., *The Lady's Home Magazine* (Philadelphia: T. S. Arthur and Company, 1860), Vol. XVI, January 1860, 15.

ABIGAIL SCOTT
Where Many Fond Hopes Have Been Laid

1852

M Y LAST NAME is Duniway now; I'm a married lady. When I crossed the Plains to Oregon with my family in 1852, though, my name was Scott. Abigail Jane Scott, but everyone who knew me well called me Jane or Jenny.[1] I was seventeen and a half years old.

We left our home in Illinois, left dear friends and family and all that was familiar behind us for the sweet promise of Oregon. Father had been laboring under the Oregon Fever since he first heard the missionary Jason Lee speak of the place when I was just a child. When Reverend Lee organized the Oregon Provisional Emigration Society and began publishing its magazine, Father signed on as its agent in Tazewell County where we lived. The magazine's name was *The Oregonian.* I'm sure Father felt that was a fair description of himself, as well. The fever to move west was further inflamed when Mr. Farnham and his Peoria Party made their trek to the Oregon Country in 1839. Father knew Mr. Farnham, you see, for he was from Tazewell County too.[2]

Father's brother was murdered, though, when I was seven years old, and Father became responsible for half his debts. This burden bankrupted us. We couldn't go to Oregon; we didn't have the funds. Fortunately, Father had a close association with the politician Edward Dickenson Baker and his friend, then-attorney Abraham Lincoln.[3] In time—with their discreet and generous influence—our family's accounts improved. Father was at last able to recoup his finances. Then, he made up his mind to go.

That's when the work began. All winter long, we women stitched, wove, knitted, and crocheted. Bedding and blankets, stockings and sunbonnets, shirts, aprons . . . any and every article of cloth that might be needed along the way, it fell to Mother, my sisters, and me to create.

Father and the boys sold off whatever could be spared and bought wagons. Gorgeous green and yellow wagons, with snowy-white canvases stretched across their stout hickory bows. Supplies of bacon and flour, rice and coffee, brown sugar and hardtack[4]—all the foodstuffs the guidebooks had recommended[5]—were purchased and packed with deliberation inside the wagons. Every space was filled. There was no room for impracticality.

Finally, on April 2, it was time to leave. Nineteen of us were spread out amongst five wagons. Our family alone counted for eleven of those: Mother, Father, and nine of us children. The cousins and their families made up the rest. Plus there were a couple of hired drivers, besides, who rounded out our company.

We attached names to the wagons, for ease in knowing which was which. The first one, we dubbed Mother's wagon. That's where she kept the smaller children, as best she could, with her. There was also the family wagon, the provisions wagon, the camp equipage wagon, and lastly, the miscellaneous wagon.[6]

We lined them up in the street, and climbed in. Our mood, which already had been subdued, now grew somber. The men tried to feign indifference. The women brushed back tears. The little ones sensed their parents' unspoken anguish and began to cry.

Then Father snapped his whip over the backs of the lead oxen. Our wagons groaned under their weight. The wheels began to turn. Goodbye! Goodbye!

Grandfather was standing at his gate. Goodbye, he waved with his bright red handkerchief. His thin gray hair was suddenly blown back by the April breezes and he tried to steady himself against the gate.[7] Then he wiped at his eyes and waved again, mouthing that terrible word, but no sound came out: Goodbye!

It began to snow.

Abigail Scott

Old Watch, our faithful watchdog, tried to follow. Father discovered him and sent him back with a stern, "Go home, dog!" Then, softer, "Go back home, Watch, and stay with Grandfather,"[8] I can still hear that dog howling after us, keening as if his heart were breaking, too.

The snow continued to fall. By the third day, new snow was four inches deep. A kind-hearted gentlemen whose house was not far from our camp offered us the use of one of his rooms until the storm had passed. It was a relief—even after these few days—to have all the niceties of a real home once again instead of just a campfire. Father had assigned me the duty of keeping a journal of our overland trek, so I took advantage of our forced delay to polish and refine the previous days' entries.

We left our comfortable lodgings the next morning and camped that night once again in the prairie. The place looked as if it were two miles west of nowhere in every direction.[9] But I did my best not to complain.

Mother became so sick she couldn't travel. Two others of our company came down with the ague and lung fever.[10] The rain came down in buckets; mud was as high as the tops of our shoes. We succeeded in buying hay for the oxen at the rate of twenty dollars a ton and were glad to get it, even at that exorbitant price.[11] It was not the auspicious beginning of which Father had so long dreamed.

It took a week's travel to reach the Mississippi. There, we boarded a ferry boat and crossed to the Missouri side. I noticed quite a contrast in the conditions between the different sides of the river. We saw farmers in Illinois near Quincy as we passed along, contentedly following the plough. On the Missouri side, though, we often saw slaves at work in the fields. They didn't seem to care how any part of their labor was performed. The contrast between the enterprising farming of Illinois and the dull, careless work of the negroes was so great, I could think of nothing else all day.[12]

We saw a man who said he owned seven slaves of good stock. He had raised them himself, he said, and two of them were worth one thousand dollars apiece. Then he told us he had not got enough work out of them yet, that in a few years, they would be worth even more. Imagine! I wrote in our journal that night: "May none of *us* ever be guilty of buying and selling the souls and bodies of our fellow creatures! Slavery is a withering blight upon the prospects, happiness, and freedom of our nation."[13]

Missouri was a strange place. One day, hay for the oxen was as plentiful as could be; we bought it at five dollars a ton and were well pleased. The next day, hay could not be found at any price. Corn could be purchased at fifty cents per bushel on a Monday, and by Wednesday the price had shot to seventy-six cents. A sharper tried to make us pay ten dollars for the privilege of grazing our cattle on a piece of prairie land near his house, but we were smarter than he thought us and saved our money.[14] It caused us constant consternation that so many were so eager to take unfair advantage.

It seemed the earth, as well, was conspiring to make our way difficult. Water was high; some streams were too swollen to get across, even when we raised our wagon bed some six inches or more. And of course, should we try crossing, the mud on both sides was so deep to completely mire every horse and ox in Missouri. In some places, it was a full two feet deep!

Once we got out onto drier ground, our moods improved considerably. There were wild flowers everywhere underfoot, and in the distance, blue-tinged timber and native shrubs. I took my leave of the wagons one afternoon and rode horseback far, far ahead. I finally halted to wait for them to catch up, only to discover they had stopped the teams for the night a full two miles back. Then I had the pleasure of riding back that distance in a hurry[15] before Father could get too agitated.

On May 5—just over a month since leaving home—we reached St. Joe.[16] It had rained very hard the night before. Everyone and everything in our camp looked as if it were just ready to swim off. We moved our wagons into the center of town and camped there. The provisions we had sent down by water from Illinois were waiting for us. We girls set to cooking all we could for the days ahead while Father and the other men packed the supplies.

We crossed the river without any difficulty five days later and traveled to a place where five men who were old acquaintances of Father's had been waiting two weeks for us to join them. My sister, Fanny, and I ascended to the summit of a nearby hill while the men were talking together and, with the aid of a spy-glass, took our last look at St. Joe and the United States.[17]

Almost immediately we encountered the Angel Death. During the day's travel, we passed seven new graves. Then, we came upon some folks who were just then consigning to a sorry grave the remains of a young man who had died of measles. The family had emigrated from Pennsylvania, they said. They had lost three of their company in St. Joe, but with a wish to overcome every obstacle, they had determined to push ahead. Little did they know they would be laying the remains of their son here in these ocean-like and boundless plains. They had become entirely discouraged with the idea of Oregon, they told us. When we left them, they were turning back, returning to Pennsylvania.[18]

We forged ahead, traveling even on the Sabbath when we heard reports of the Pawnees being numerous about us. They were said to be hostile and thievish,[19] so Father considered it best not to tarry in one place too long.

Even so, we stopped for small delights en route. There was one little stream I remember, called Ale Ness. But we renamed it Tadpole Sandy for our own memory. In many places, the sand was so much higher than the surface of the water, we could walk right across. And where there was water, it was literally filled with little tadpoles! We had to spade down two feet to reach good drinking water.[20] We thought our name for the place a great joke.

Not far from there, we met a large wagon train coming from Fort Laramie. It was loaded entirely with buffalo robes.[21] The men who drove the teams were a set of French and Indian half-breeds[22] who spoke a kind of French, Indian, and English jargon. When they talked to one another, their speech was mingled with a host of curses in English. It all sounded very strange to our ears.[23]

At Fort Kearny, we halted awhile to write letters and look at the curiosities. The fort itself was rather shabby looking but contained two very good houses. For those of us who had been traveling for three weeks without seeing a house or anything like civilization, it looked very fine, indeed.[24]

We didn't camp there, however. We pushed forward.

Our sick folks were all feeling better. In spite of all the obstacles which came our way—from dust so thick we could not see, to deep and dangerous river crossings—one hope inspired us all: that one day we would arrive at our destination. Where other folks had gone, *we* certainly could go. At least we thought so. But our resolve was tested when we met another company headed back to the States. They were from Springfield in our home state of Illinois. Giving up, they said, on account of sickness and death. They had buried one man the day before, and another that morning.[25] Better to turn back then, while they still could, before they got so far west there could be no retreat. That was their thinking.

Ahead of us, emigrants' wagons, cattle, and horses jammed the road as far as the eye could see. Behind us, it was the same. The plain was a living, moving mass, struggling toward Oregon.[26] We bade our disheartened countrymen farewell and doubled our determination to succeed.

As the weather grew hotter, the storms came. Rain fell in torrents, with thunder and lightning crashing all around us. After trying to push through only a few of these, we knew enough to halt thereafter whenever a storm would come up. We'd arrange our wagons beside each other as closely as we could then chain up the oxen and horses. We'd pitch our tents if there was time and gather as quick a supply of fuel—usually dry buffalo chips—as could be found.[27] Then we'd dig in and try to wait it out. Sometimes the wind blew in gales, upsetting the tents and making us wonder if the wagons themselves would stand steady.

One storm I particularly remember found us camped on a river bank with no buffalo chips nor wood at all except a few small sticks of cedar[28]— just enough to boil water. So our supper that night consisted of only hard-tack, or sea biscuits as Father called them. A fierce storm came up about six o'clock, and though it brought little rain, the wind blew so hard that the wagons rocked violently to and fro. One of the tents got blown over with some of our company in it, which struck us as terribly funny.[29] To watch them inside, struggling with the wet canvas, sent us into spasms of laughter and made us forget all about our fear. Of course, after only a few minutes, we helped them out of their predicament. All was tidied up, and on we traveled once again.

Of one thing we were especially glad on the plains, and that was the buffalo. The men were able to kill them, which thankfully changed the regular routine of our diet at supper time. We thought the meat tasted almost exactly like beef but had a coarser grain. They also killed a prairie dog one time and brought it to camp. They were curious-looking animals. I thought they resembled a rat, or squirrel, or even rabbit. They looked as though they might have been good eating, but we didn't want to be the first to try them.[30]

I entered into our journal the days we passed the famous landmarks: Nebraska Court House,[31] Chimney Rock, Scott's Bluffs. Father would read what I had written from time to time, and make corrections or additions of his own. He wanted the journal to be a complete account of our overland voyage. Many trail travelers had kept such accounts then published them, and they sold quite well. Ours was for our personal use alone, yet all of us had a sense we were helping make history. When I came down with the cholera, my sister Maggie and Father continued the journal till I was once again able.[32]

Little could I know while I was sick, that my first entry after my recovery would be to record the death of our beloved mother.

But it was so. Mother was taken about two o'clock in the morning with violent diarrhea and cramping—unmistakable signs of the camp cholera. She aroused no one, however, until daylight. We did everything for her that could be done, but it was too late. Her health had not been robust for many years, though her determination was strong. She struggled until supper time. Then her wearied spirit took flight.[33] You cannot imagine the knife edge of our grief.

In the camp just next to ours, another lady died. We wrapped Mother in a blanket, and buried the women next to one another so neither would be alone. The graves were situated on a high place overlooking a hollow ravine. Groves of small pine and cedar trees intersected it, making a little basin into which a spring of icy coldness, as clear as crystal, flowed. And around its rim, wild roses and other flowers grew in abundance. We heaped rocks over the graves, so animals wouldn't disturb them, then covered those cruel stones again with roses.[34]

Then we had to leave. It broke our hearts. Especially Father's.

The earth seemed steeped in sorrow, too, as we pushed ourselves forward. Gone now were the wild flowers; gone was the grass. Sagebrush became so thick, it was impossible for the grass to grow. Sage and thorny greasewood covering the sandy hills and hollows was all we could see. Rain became a welcome relief, except for the mosquitoes that swarmed about us after the storms had gone. Sometimes we were pelted with hail, while on the high buttes, we even saw snow.[35]

When we passed the buttes, rumors flew that gold had been discovered there. Some three hundred teams stopped to dig. Two from our party rode out on horseback to see whether the rumors could be true and returned with many specimens of mica. They said from what they had seen, they thought gold might be found in abundance along the creek below the buttes if it were properly explored.[36] But we didn't stop. Oregon Fever was bad enough without adding Gold Fever to it.

Two days later, we came to Independence Rock. Some wagons stopped, some didn't. Ours slowed but went by. Father said we older girls could stay to read the names carved upon it if we wanted to; we could catch up later. Fanny and Maggie immediately said yes. I agreed, and said we should take thirteen-year-old Kate with us, too. The rock was an immensity, about three hundred feet high, I would say, covering maybe ten acres. All four of us wanted to climb it. So up we went. We had only ascended about thirty feet when a heavy hail and wind storm suddenly whipped upon us, and we had to scramble down.

We started on toward the wagons, but before we reached them, they had all crossed the river except the last wagon in the train. We girls ran hard to overtake it. We climbed on just in time. But oh, the teasing we got! They had intended to let us wade the river, you see, to teach us not to lag so far behind.[37] Even though the river was waist deep at the crossing, I would have liked the fun of wading, I think. The teasing, however, I didn't like nearly so well.

On July the 2nd, a dispute arose amongst our company about whether the white substance on the summit of one of the Sweetwater hills to our left was snow or simply white granite. To settle the dispute and satisfy the curiosity, two riders went to see for themselves. It really was snow! Of course, we could plainly see a chain of the Wind River Mountains ahead of us, their lofty peaks capped with everlasting snow.[38] But we certainly didn't expect snow to be around South Pass at that time of year. That night, the temperatures fell low enough for frost.

The next night, we camped right in the snow! The way to our camp site had been exceedingly tedious and rocky. In many places the road was all uphill and perfectly smooth and hard, as it was made from tightly packed particles of sand and gravel. This—together with the large rocks—was very hard on our oxen's feet. We saw a great many abandoned, lame, and worn out cattle at the side of the trail. The air was literally filled with the stench of dead oxen. We passed one as often as every half-mile through the day.[39]

We couldn't help but think there was a great difference between the glorious Fourth of July festivities of only last year—in the States—and the dismal prospects we were seeing for the morrow. Indeed, the Fourth dawned bleak, cold, and cloudy, with the threat of more wind and snow. We did nothing to celebrate the day, save travel a few miles and wait out the storm.

Abigail Scott

Two days later, we passed through the continental divide. Both ascent and descent were very gradual; so gradual, in fact, it was impossible to say exactly where the very top was. The first accurate conclusion we could draw that we were, indeed, through South Pass, took place at the Pacific Springs. These springs flow toward the Pacific Ocean. The next stream we passed was called Pacific Creek. The water here ran west, while every other stream we had previously passed flowed either east or south.[40] This—though a seemingly small distinction—for us was cause for celebration.

To avoid the forty-mile desert between the Big Sandy and Green Rivers, we detoured into the Utah territory. We found the roads very good there and perceptibly downhill almost all the way to the Green River ferry.

The Green was a very swift and clear river, very difficult to cross. The ferrymen, however, were well prepared with two boats. We—as many others—camped there for the night near the ferry. There was a trading station there. Potatoes sold for ten cents per pound; butter, twenty-five cents; eggs, twenty-five cents per dozen; flour, six dollars per hundredweight, and other foodstuffs in much the same proportion as that. We had quite a spectacle that night with which to amuse ourselves, watching the various occupations of the world. Betting and the playing of cards was going on at one encampment, music and dancing at another, while at a third, people were singing religious hymns and psalms with apparent devotion. Indians of the Shoshone tribe were encamped near us in several wigwams. I thought them as loathsome a spectacle as I might ever wish to behold.[41]

We left in the morning. As we traveled from Green River, the weather was quite warm, but snow-capped mountains were in full view. Several miles in front of us, we could see spots of snow arranged one behind the other. They looked for all the world like our covered wagons, all in a line.[42]

The way grew more and more mountainous. The teams were obliged to go in a semicircle of about two miles to find a practical route for ascending the ridge known as Devil's Backbone. To save walking that extra distance, some of us decided to climb the mountain and strike the road in advance of the train. The ridge was much higher than we had thought. We ended up walking about two miles from its base to the summit, then another long way along the ridge top until we once again connected with the road.[43] We discovered once again—the hard way—how deceptive distances appeared out here in the West.

Then, of course, that afternoon the wagons had to descend that long, steep hill from the summit. We traveled two miles without even unlocking the wagon wheels. In many places the men themselves had to hold back the wagons with ropes, in addition to having both the back wheels locked.[44]

Not long after that, we met some Indians who were going to bury a man who had been thrown from his horse and had broken his neck. They were wailing most piteously. We gave them wide berth, but I could see the dead man was wrapped in a blanket and thrown across a pony. Another Indian rode behind him. When they passed us, the one who was riding directed our attention to the body then wailed again.[45] We were surprised and touched at his obvious show of grief. We hadn't seen anything of the kind before.

I continued to keep our journal up-to-date, noting the important landmarks: Soda Springs, Steamboat Springs, Bear River Valley. In the Bear River Valley, some of our oxen came down sick from drinking alkali water. We gave them each a dose of vinegar and molasses, which Father said would counteract the poisons. He was right. By nightfall, they were weak, but right as rain.

We laid by till noon the next day so the oxen would have time to rest. And what do you know, we met on the trail a mountaineer from Kentucky. He said had been in the mountains since 1839! Caldwell was his name, he told us. Then he and Father began talking, for there had been a Caldwell back home who was one of our nearest and most intimate neighbors. This man turned out to be our neighbor's nephew! He and Father grasped their hands together and talked like old friends.[46] But what a sight he was!

He stood about six feet three inches in height and weighed maybe two hundred pounds, all muscle. His broadcloth coat and silk neckerchief contrasted strangely with his buckskin pants and moccasins. He had long, flowing hair and whiskers, even though I didn't think him much over the age of thirty-five. All in all, he was the finest specimen of a backwoods man I ever saw.[47]

Unfortunately, he had to ride on, and so did we. But the memory of his appearance gave us girls much to talk about, all the way to Snake River.

Now the last of July in Snake River country was brutal. Oftentimes, we would have to travel late into the night, as we laid by longer during the heat of the day. This laying by gave our oxen much-needed rest, and us too, but we paid for the luxury.

I remember well one day's travel that had extended long into the darkness. Instead of walking—as we women usually did during the daylight—now we were jolting along in the wagons, anxious to reach a place where our bones weren't tumbled and tossed and bruised. The thirsty, lagging teams had been trudging for hours with their tongues hanging out. Yet they were urged on by their equally tired drivers. Children whimpered and cried. There wasn't a drop of water to be had. Tempers were very short.[48]

We came at last to a steep hill. The road sidled off into darkness, down over the ravine. Two men were pushed forward to see what was down there. When they returned, they reported, "Water! And a place to camp at the bottom."[49]

It was deemed prudent by the men for all women and children to get out of the wagons at that point and make their way to the camping place in the darkness on foot. We were not happy at the decision.[50]

The fat woman in our company, especially, was most vocal in resisting her husband's order. Her protests grew more sharp and loud with every utterance. Then, suddenly, everything went silent.[51]

Astonishment among us turned to dismay when something like two minutes of silence was followed by muffled shrieks, which seemed to come from the very bowels of the earth. They grew more distinct, however, as the poor woman caught her breath. An impromptu search with lanterns discovered her far down the mountainside, hanging onto a scrub juniper tree. Below her was only empty space and darkness.[52]

The voice of her husband had not been gentle before—when he had ordered her out of the wagon—but compared to what followed his tugging and straining to haul her up from her perch and tow her to camp, it was a summer zephyr to a howling Nor'easter![53]

He towed her into the bottom camp, left her at the wagon with a huff, and made his bed in the darkness. Her ire at him was placated only the next morning when she discovered her husband had inadvertently curled up all night next to a long-dead and very smelly gray mare.[54] The laughter from camp was deafening.

The smell of sulphur had been so strong on the night air, he stuttered, that he hadn't detected any other odor. It was certainly noticeable to the rest of us, however. And from that occasion forward, a suggestion from her husband that she go *take a tumble* was sufficient to quell any rising storm in the breast of that worthy and sorely-tried woman. Likewise, she did not hesitate to suggest upon occasion that maybe it was time for him to go sleep by himself again.[55]

It seemed good to laugh. Too often, the Trail brought us only sorrow and tears. It was not enough that Mother had been taken from us. Not enough that we had witnessed tragedy and deprivation of every kind since leaving Illinois. Now, in the Burnt River Canyon of Oregon Territory, the Trail took Willie. He was only four years old, the baby of the family. He took the cholera and died within two days.[56]

Father and the other men hollowed out the rocks on a high point, a hundred and fifty feet above the plain. A beautiful cedar waved its widespread branches over the spot. This was Willie's tomb. I couldn't tear myself away. Here lay the hope of his parents and the pride of his brothers and sisters. He was such a good child . . . . smart, kind, obedient. After Mother died, Willie had said repeatedly he wanted to die, too, and be with her.[57] Now, the only solace I could find was in the knowledge they were once again together.

I wrote a poem and read it aloud over that lonely spot. It was my requiem, not only for Willie, but for all that used to be . . . and never would be again:

I

Far away over deserts and mountains so wild
In our wearisome journey we've strayed
Towards a far distant land, a bright home in the West
Where many fond hopes have been laid.

II

The journey has been one of anguish and woe
Combined with some gladness and mirth
Yet we little thought when we started to go
That our hopes would lie low in the earth!

III

Yet He who provideth for children of men
Their pleasure, their grief and their woe

Abigail Scott

Has seen fit in His wisdom to enter our fold
And call one of our number to go.

IV

A bright little darling some four years of age
By afflictions' rude grasp has been laid
On a couch of deep suffering and he must soon go
Where grief will be ever allayed.

V

I'm watching him now, in the deep midnight hour
All nature is hushed in repose
No sound can be heard save the rivulet's fall
And the wind which most mournfully blows.

"Burnt River Mountains" a beautiful range,
Of these natural beauties of earth,
Their tops decked with cedar, their sides with fine grass
Which adds to their grandeur and worth.

The wind whistles through them with sad mournful sound
And the bright silver moon's shining clear,
Causing shadows of bushes to assume frightful forms,
Which have caused me to startle with fear.

In this wild retreat far away from our home
I'm watching a brother most dear,
Whose eyeballs are frightfully swimming in death,
And whose forehead looks glistening and clear.

Some ten weeks ago our dear Mother was called
To bid her dear children farewell,
And Willie will meet her beyond yon bright stars,
And together in Heaven they'll dwell.

Oh! God help us all to consider that this
Keen affliction is caused by thy hand!
And feeling it thus, may we cheerfully yield,
And not strive thy will to understand.[58]

Within three days, another of our company was dead. Young Mr. Clason, who had paid Father a hundred dollars in St. Joe for his passage to Oregon, finally succumbed to sickness. His land of bright promise proved to be only a shallow grave.

We traveled through what the emigrants used to call the Lone Tree Valley then directed our course over rolling hills and bluffs till we reached the brow of a mountain overlooking Grande Ronde. Beyond that, we came to a rocky ridge which had the longest and most difficult descent of any we had previously encountered. The dust would blow in clouds, hiding the wagons, teams, and road entirely until we had to stop. Then, a sudden gust of wind would blow the other way, clearing the dust enough for a few moments that we could proceed a bit. It was followed shortly by more dust . . . then more wind. The repetition was incessant. Rocks so filled the road, that anyone who had not begun to see the elephant would have been afraid to attempt the descent.[59] We, however, were well seasoned by this time and simply kept pushing.

When we reached the bottom, we were rewarded. The valley spread out nearly ten miles in width, covered with luxuriant-looking grasses, willow, birch, bitter cottonwood and alder. The high mountains surrounding it were densely timbered with pine, cedar, balsam fir, birch, and larch. The Indians there were very wealthy. They had huge herds of horses, and all manner of material goods. Contrary to our expectations, though, we found no provisions for sale here, except flour at the extravagant price of $40 per hundredweight.[60]

On September 3rd, we entered the Blues. The walls of the mountains were so steep and high, common conversations could be overheard a hundred and fifty yards away. Men speaking in loud voices to the cattle sounded loud enough to be mistaken for a war whoop. Echoes reverberated from hill to hill. A single rifle shot equaled a barrage of cannons as the sound bounced from mountain side to mountain side.[61]

We had no more than the usual trouble to speak of while crossing the mountains, save worn-out moccasins from the rocks and run-off cattle. While on the summit of the last mountain, we got our first view of the Cascade Mountains to our west. Mount Hood reared its snow-crowned summit in awful grandeur, so high it looked like a stationary white cloud.[62]

Abigail Scott

Directly below us, the Umatilla Valley rolled out in gentle beauty, an undulating prairie.

When we reached the Umatilla River, an Indian showed us where to water our cattle. The largest Indian village we had ever seen spread before us. I thought the inhabitants filthy-looking creatures. They had made some attempts to cultivate the soil but were too lazy to accomplish anything worth notice. There was a French trader, though; he sold us fresh beef at twelve and a half cents per pound.[63]

Two days beyond, we reached the Indian Agency. Though it was now unoccupied by the government, still there was a new-looking frame house. The sight of such a house lifted our spirits considerably, as it was the first we had seen since leaving Fort Kearny.[64] That seemed a lifetime ago. But it put our minds toward what waited for us in the Willamette Valley: houses, churches, office buildings. Civilization!

The thought of that goal sustained us, even when our the last of our food finally gave out. Then, as if sent by Providence, two of our relatives from the Willamette met up with us! They had come from that Garden of the World, they said, to greet us and see us safely through those last weeks to the end of our journey. They brought us beef, and flour, and a bottle of *Oh! Be Joyful!* that, of course, horrified the teetotalers among us. It was little wonder that one of our company—whom Father was bringing to Oregon to reform—got gloriously tipsy on the liquor, and engaged in a carnival of drunken songs . . . much to the enjoyment of the younger children who thought it was all very funny.[65]

Nearing The Dalles, we decided to send some of our outfit to Portland by way of the Columbia River and thence to Oregon City on the Willamette. Father accompanied two of our wagons to the town. There he bought shoes for us girls—the first we had had since Fort Hall. When our old shoes had given out, we just wore moccasins. Now it felt strange to have that stiffness on our feet once again.

But we were glad to have them when we started the last leg of our journey overland by way of Barlow's toll road. At the foot of the Cascades near Barlow's gate, we camped. The weather had turned menacing once again, and we were afraid to start in the storm. Father bought supplies, getting flour at forty cents per hundredweight, beef at fifty cents per pound, and

SEEING THE ELEPHANT

potatoes at nine dollars per bushel. We girls did the washing and prepared our provisions for the remainder of the trip.[66] Maggie agreed she would take over writing our family's journal, so I gave it to her and was glad to have one less duty.

The rain came thick and fast. It lasted for days. Finally, we *had* to begin. The mountains proved steep and dangerous. Laurel Hill was an almost perpendicular descent—over two miles of it! Fortunately, there were several little benches of soil where the oxen could stop and rest. Still, we had to chain the wagon wheels and slide the wagons down that rutted, rocky road.[67]

Rations grew shorter and shorter. We had used up all we bought before. A real relish was prepared for one meal by boiling an antiquated ham bone and adding a few scrapings from the dough pan into the liquid. This was our last measure of flour; it was musty and sour, at that. We still had coffee, so we made a huge pot of it. There we sat, at our last camp in the Cascade Mountains, sipping our nectar from rusty cups, and eating salal berries we had gathered during the day. It wasn't much, but it was something . . . and we pitied folks who had no coffee.[68]

Lean and hungry, we arrived at Mr. Foster's farm at the western base of the mountains. He sold us plenty of vegetables (though at quite a price), and we were off once again. Our destination lay one day's travel ahead; two at the most. We were oh, so anxious for this incredible journey to be over.

On September 30, we reached our far-famed and long-sought-after Oregon City. It was a hard-looking place—not how I had envisioned it at all— situated in a rocky canyon at the falls of the Willamette River. The roar of the falls was deafening. We stayed only an hour then moved six miles further and camped. None of us slept well, whether from the sound of the falls or our pent-up excitement, I can't say.

The next day, some twenty miles beyond and six months from leaving Illinois, we finally pulled our wagons up beside Uncle Johnson's place. They called this area French Prairie. Now, we called it home.

Abigail Scott, ever a hard-working and enterprising young woman, began almost immediately earning wages upon her arrival in the Oregon Territory. A letter from Abigail's younger sister Harriet to a friend states that "Fanny and Jane [Abigail] are sewing for the stores. They are making pantaloons and flannel shirts. They get two dollars for pantaloons, and five bits [62½ cents] for flannel shirts."[69] Her quick mind and immoveable determination gave her life a breadth and depth uncommon for women of that era. She became a wife, mother, teacher, poet, novelist, fashion hat designer, newspaper editor, and lecturer.[70] She founded and published her own newspaper, *The New Northwest*, whose opinions often conflicted with the ideas espoused in her brother's newspaper, *The Morning Oregonian*.

She was a tireless champion for women's property and voting rights throughout her long life and became nationally recognized as a leader in the suffrage movement. Most people recognize her by her married name, Abigail Scott Duniway, but it is clear from her journal and personal papers, the essential personality was well formed when she left Illinois in 1852 as Jenny.

In light of Abigail's championing of women's issues, it seems a bit of a paradox that her humanitarian stance did not extend to certain others. For someone so passionately against the institution of slavery, she seems—from her journal entries—to be disdainful of the slaves themselves. "Slavery is a withering blight upon the prospects, happiness, and freedom of our nation," she wrote. And yet, in the same breath, she criticized "the contrast between the enterprising farming of Illinois and the dull, careless work of the negroes [slaves]. . . . "[71] Likewise, Abigail spoke in her journals of the "filthy looking [tribal] creatures" of the Umatilla Valley, the "hostile and thievish" Pawnee, and the "loathsome" Shoshone.[72] As an adult, she spoke out pointedly on such varied subjects as politics, temperance, religion, child-rearing, marital obedience, economic theory, spiritualism, education, and divorce. But that same zeal did not carry over to the arena of prejudice and exploitation of tribal populations.

As the Duniway family crossed the western half of the continent, the Trail itself was changing. By 1852, tens of thousands of emigrants, their wagons, their livestock, and their diseases had made irrefutable impact on the land over which they traveled and the tribes they encountered on the way. After ten years of massive migration, natural resources were beginning to give out. Water holes were fouled to the point that emigrants were drinking slough water and were glad to have it. Communal campsites were barren of cooking fuels; even buffalo chips could be scarce. Supplies—when they could be found en route—were sold at exorbitant prices and were often of poor quality. There were more frequent and serious skirmishes with the Indians, more killings and retribution. Meanwhile, more murders, assaults, and robberies were noted within the wagon trains themselves.

And there was cholera. Measles. Smallpox. Graves marked the route from St. Joseph, Missouri, to Oregon's Willamette Valley like grim and melancholy mileposts.

The physical and emotional toll of traveling the Trail was becoming so high, more and more would-be Oregonians were turning back. Still others were discovering their real land of milk and honey was there, *beside* the Trail rather than *on* it, selling services and goods to those still determined to continue westward.

Guidebooks suddenly had competition. Journals and reminiscences of successful passages were being published with an eye toward turning a tidy profit. Some, heavily embellished and wildly fanciful, were factually misleading but wildly popular. Again, the brand of *Adventurer* was being applied to the overland traveler. It was a very effective marketing ploy, especially when one could ballyhoo the discovery of gold en route.

And what did the emigrant find at the end of the trail? Hardly a pristine country, overflowing with unbounded opportunity and promise. Quite the opposite. While there was always a niche for the enterprising entrepreneur, for the farmer and the homesteader, prospects were far slimmer. Many discovered the choice agricultural land already claimed when they arrived. Winter was coming on. Families had to be housed and fed by some means until land could be secured and cleared, then seed put into the ground. How were they to survive?

For many, this wasn't at all the *Garden of the World* they had pinned their futures on. But, like Abigail, their Trail experiences had only served to galvanize their resolve to triumph over the obstacles that still lay in their paths. What other choice did they have? They would do whatever it took to survive. And, indeed, they did.

Discussion 1

"Evenings after the weary stretches of travel [Abigail would sit] with the old book in her lap . . . while our father was giving her 'commands' to keep the 'Diary' correct! She was too weary . . . to write, but she always did her best."[73]

—ETTY SCOTT (Abigail's sister), reminiscing in 1925

"Palmer [in his guidebook] in speaking of [Chimney Rock] very truly says that it has the unpoetical appearance of a hay stack with a pole extending far above its top."[74]

—ABIGAIL SCOTT, June 14, 1852

Many emigrants had guidebooks as they made their trek. Some of these were factual, written by people who had actually traveled the route and knew the terrain. Others contained erroneous information; some were even written by people who had never set foot on the Trail! As the market grew back in the States for anything printed about the Trail, emigrants sometimes had their own personal diaries of their trip printed and sold for profit. If you were an emigrant starting out on the Trail, how would you decide which guidebooks or journals were accurate and true? If you knew you were going to have your own Trail journal printed for publication, what sorts of information would you record in it as you traveled along? Consider the social structure of the day. Which gender do you think wrote more for publication than for personal reasons? Why?

Discussion 2

"We passed four [more] new made graves. One was that of a man who was murdered, and found on the road by some passing emigrants. [He was] lying off a short distance from the road. Upon examination, it was found that he had been killed with buckshot and [stabs] with a Bowie knife. . . ."[75]

—ABIGAIL SCOTT, May 26, 1852

"The great cause of diarrhea, which has proven to be so fatal on the road, has been occasioned in most instances by drinking water from holes dug in the river bank and long marshes. Emigrants should be very careful about this."[76]

—ABIGAIL SCOTT, June 8, 1852

"A short time after this . . . two of the men got to playing cards for money. They got to quarrelling, and one of them took a shot at the other. The bullet went between the man's legs and through our fire where we were cooking dinner, and [it] scattered the coals and ashes all over the victuals."[77]

—JOHN KELSO, 1859

The Trail was changing. More and more emigrants meant more and more crime, death and disease on the trail. That Abigail did not attribute the murder of the man who was shot and stabbed to Indians tells us that she believed the murderer to be one of the emigrants. The diarrhea she mentions so often is one symptom of cholera, which rose to epidemic proportions during this time. Abigail herself contracted cholera, but survived. Today, we know that one of the main causes of that disease is poor sanitation. Consider the number of emigrants traveling, "cheek by jowl" over the same route, day in and day out. How would you, as a Trail traveler, ensure that you wouldn't contract contagious diseases? How would you ease tensions between emigrants before they escalated to violence? How would you punish crimes?

Discussion 3

"It is rumored that gold mines of considerable value have been discovered on the south side of a stream called Deer Creek, and that some three

Abigail Scott

City, Oregon (site of the emigrant's Lone Tree valley), was named in his honor. The Scotts—Abigail included—became close personal friends of both Edward Baker and the Lincoln family.

4. Catherine Scott (Coburn), Interview in *The Morning Oregonian* newspaper, June 17, 1890, regarding her experiences in 1852, as cited in Holmes and Duniway, 27. Original in the University of Oregon's Special Collections Library. Hardtack was a cross between a hard biscuit and a thick cracker. Originally created for long sea voyages, it was purposely baked so tough that it was virtually impervious to spoilage. Hence, it was ideal for Oregon Trail travel. Some journal accounts tell of having to soften the hardtack by holding it under the arm so it could eventually be chewed.

5. Abigail specifically lists the 1848 guidebook *Platts Guide* in her May 18 journal entry. Holmes and Duniway, 52, footnote 8, also list the following as having been studied by Abigail's father: Palmer's *Journal* (1847), Hastings' *Emigrants' Guide* (1845), Colton's maps, the Oregon Trail map of Charles Preuss (1846), John C. Fremont's *Report: Exploration of the Rocky Mountains* (1843), and his *Map of Oregon and Upper California*.

6. Scott (Coburn), *Covered Wagon Women*, Vol. 5, 32, 33, 35.

7. Ibid., 28.

8. Fanny Scott (Cook), 1925, in response to a questionnaire from Clyde Duniway, as cited in *Covered Wagon Women*, Vol. 5, 30. Fanny went on to say that after the Scotts arrived in Oregon, they received a letter from home telling them Old Watch had gone back to the family home as he had been ordered but, from that day forward, had refused food. A short time after the family's departure, the dog died.

9. Holmes and Duniway, 41, April 6.

10. Ibid., 43, April 7. Ague was a condition marked by alternate fever and chills. Lung fever was a congestive condition, complicated by fever. It often deteriorated into pneumonia.

11. Ibid., 41, April 7.

12. Ibid., 43, April 15. "Negroes" was Scott's term.

13. Ibid., 44.

14. Ibid., 65, April 26.

15. Ibid., 47, May 1.

16. St. Joseph, Missouri. The other principal jump-off point was Independence.

17. Holmes and Duniway, 49, May 10.

18. Ibid., 50, May 12.

19. Ibid., 53, May 20.

20. Ibid., 55, May 23.

21. Buffalo robes were the full-body, skinned hides of the bison.

22. Scott's term.

23. Holmes and Duniway, 55, May 25.

24. Ibid., 57, May 29.

25. Ibid., 59, June 1.

26. Ibid., 60, June 3.

27. Ibid., 61, June 5.

28. Emigrants commonly used the names cedar or mountain cedar for juniper.

29. Holmes and Duniway, 65, June 12.

30. Ibid., 60, June 3.

31. Also commonly called Courthouse Rock.

32. Holmes and Duniway, 66, journal entries from June 15 through June 19 are in the handwriting of both Margaret (Maggie or Mag) and John Tucker Scott.

33. Ibid., 71, June 20.

34. Ibid., 72, June 21.

35. Ibid., 76, June 26.

36. Ibid., 77, June 27.

37. Ibid., 78, June 29.

38. Ibid., 80, July 2.

39. Ibid., 81, July 3.

40. Ibid., 82, July 6.

41. Ibid., 84, July 9. The remainder of Scott's entry regarding the Shoshone tribal people she observed reads, "being as filthy and as far from every appearance of civilization as any set of dumb animals in the world." As with so many Anglo people of this era, Scott's willingness to see black slaves as human beings apparently did not always extend to seeing Indians in the same light.

42. Ibid., 84, July 10.

43. Ibid., 86, July 13.

44. Ibid. Wagon wheels were outfitted with friction brakes. By locking the wheels—preventing them from turning—momentum was diminished.

45. Ibid., 89, July 16.

46. Ibid., 93, July 21.

47. Ibid.

48. Ibid., 97–98, Scott (Coburn), Interview in *The Oregonian* newspaper, June 17, 1890.

49. Ibid., 98.

50. Ibid.

51. Ibid.

52. Ibid.

53. Ibid. A summer zephyr is a gentle, warm breeze. A howling nor'easter is a near-hurricane force storm.

54. Ibid.

55. Ibid.

56. Ibid., 115. Tucker Scott wrote the entry in Abigail's journal for August 25, 1852, when Willie was diagnosed. He called the illness Cholera Infantum and Dropsy of the Brain and said a doctor had advised him there was nothing that could be done; Willie would surely die.

57. Ibid., 117–18, Scott's journal, August 28.

58. Ibid., 154, Scott, from the back of her journal, verses I–V. Unnumbered verses from the 1853 revised version.

59. Ibid., 120, September 1.

60. Ibid., 121, September 1.

61. Ibid., 122, September 3.

62. Ibid., 124, September 6.

63. Ibid.

64. Ibid., 125, September 9.

65. Ibid., 128, Scott's journal, September 14, and in an interview appearing in *The Oregonian* newspaper on October 7, 1900.

66. Ibid., 131. Margaret Scott, Abigail's younger sister, wrote this journal entry for September 20.

67. Ibid., 133, Margaret Scott's journal entry, September 24–25.

68. Ibid., 134, Scott (Coburn), Interview in *The Oregonian* newspaper, June 17, 1890.

69. Holmes and Duniway, 160, Harriet Scott's letter, November 26, 1852.

70. Ibid., 21, Introduction.

71. Ibid., 44, April 15.

72. Ibid., 43, April 15.

73. Ibid., 24, June 12.

74. Ibid., 66, June 14.

75. Ibid., 56, May 26.

76. Ibid., 62, June 8.

77. Robert A. Bennett, *We'll All Go Home in the Spring* (Walla Walla, WA: Pioneer Press Books, 1984), 83.

78. Holmes and Duniway, 75, June 25.

79. Bennett, 147.

80. Russell Freedman, *Indian Chiefs* (New York: Scholastic, Inc., 1987), 9.

81. Holmes and Duniway, 50, May 12.

82. Ibid., 55, May 25.

83. Ibid., 59, June 1.

EZRA MEEKER
The Trail Was a Battlefield

1852

MOST FOLKS call me the Grandfather of the Oregon Trail. It's true I'm in my nineties now, and look like a skinny, bespectacled St. Nick. But my nickname has less to do with my appearance than with the fact I am the only man alive who has traveled the Oregon Trail by ox team and covered wagon, by automobile, by rail, and by aeroplane! I have traveled so many miles of the Oregon Trail throughout my lifetime, east to west and west to east, I could practically do it with my eyes shut now. My feet just instinctively know the way!

Of course, my mother always told me I was "the busiest young 'un" she ever saw, restless from the beginning.[1] I guess I was born so, for I never could stay still. When my family moved from Ohio to Indiana by wagon, I was just a chunk of a boy: nine years old. I walked every step of the way for nearly two hundred miles. Traveling by shank's pony, we called it, or shank's mare. That was probably the beginning of my wandering ways.

I wasn't cut out for sitting in a schoolroom, either. Book learning, to me, was a tedious chore. I played hooky so much, finally my mother gave up and let me stay on the home place as long as I worked to earn money. My whole life, my honest-to-goodness schoolboy days added up to less than six months.

It was, to say the least, a dangerous experiment.[2] Yet, the world around me offered a classroom as rich in learning as any schoolhouse. I loved to read. I even worked as a "printer's devil" in the printing office of the *Journal* when we moved to Indiana. The *Journal* published a Free Soil paper. The slogan of the Free Soil political party in those days was *Free Soil, Free Speech, Free Labor and Free Men.* You'd call it an antislavery party nowadays. And they supported free land for settlers.

All day long, leaflets and pamphlets and sideboards[3] were printed, stating their cause. My job was to take the printed sheets off the power press as they were finished. A big, strong negro man turned the crank of the press hour after hour, putting out the paper. He was the only power behind that power press.[4]

Sometimes, the *Journal* sent me delivering their papers. One of their subscribers at that time was the preacher, Henry Ward Beecher. His sister, Harriet, would later write the famous antislavery novel, *Uncle Tom's Cabin.*

Maybe those days formed my opinions more than I realized. Mostly, though, I was just trying to make money. By the time I was eleven years old, my biggest ambition was to get some land. I'd been working since I was eight, and managed to save thirty-seven dollars in those three years. I had heard there was a forty-acre tract in Hendrix County that had no claim on it. I was determined that as soon as I could get fifty dollars together, I was going to hunt up that land, lay my claim, and own it. The going rate then was $1.25 per acre.[5]

Of course, I didn't get that property. I was too young, and there were laws even then about how old a man had to be before he could own ground. But the pattern was set: I would place my mind on a goal and not give up until that goal was accomplished.

I was married before I was twenty-one. My wife and I moved to Iowa from Indiana in a covered wagon in October of 1851 and set up housekeeping. We didn't realize it at the time, but by the following spring, we'd be on our way to Oregon.

That winter in Iowa, I worked as a flagger in a surveyor's camp. It was bitterly cold and the wind just howled; I nearly froze to death. Well, it didn't take long for Oregon Fever to seize me and win me over. The Oregon Country in those days included the present states of Oregon, Washington, and Idaho, and parts of Montana and Wyoming. The northern boundary of the United States lay in dispute until 1846, when a treaty between America and Great Britain spelled out who owned the country north of the Columbia River. After the treaty was signed, settlers began to cross the Columbia in great numbers, and stories started coming back to the rest of us about the wonderful climate, the rich soil, and the fine stands of lumber.[6]

It was a special consideration to Wife and me that if we went to Oregon, the government would give us three hundred and twenty acres of land; whereas in Iowa, we would have to purchase it. The price would be low in Iowa, to be sure, but still the land must be bought and paid for on the spot. The Oregon Donation Land Claims Act, as they called it, granted 320 acres of land to any white or half-breed Indian[7] who staked a residence claim on the public lands in the Oregon Territory and cultivated it for a period of four years. I, as a married man, could claim land for myself and for my wife. I could even claim some land for my wife in her own name![8]

The inducement for moving was great. But Wife had an even more compelling reason for staying: she was expecting our first baby. After he is born, she said (and it *was* a boy), we'll talk about it further.

One month after the birth of our son, we were on the trail to Oregon. It was the first week of April, 1852. Our "train" consisted of our one wagon, two yoke of four-year-old green steers,[9] and one yoke of cows. We had one extra cow, but she strayed away in the river bottom before we crossed the Missouri and drowned.[10] I chose steers that had never been under the yoke because they had more spirit than those who were already well broken-in. Too often, broken-in meant broken in spirit, too. I was an oddity in a generation that felt oxen could not be driven without swearing at them and liberally using the whip.[11]

I knew that if I took care of these fine fellows properly, they would pull for me just by the sound of my voice. They would be far cheaper than horses or mules to look after, and once we were in Oregon, they would be far more useful in clearing and plowing my land. They would be my work companions for probably as long as fourteen years before they died, maybe as long as twenty-four years. I had heard of a team that old, once.[12] I named mine Buck and Dandy, and was well pleased.[13]

In the wagon, we had packed our butter in the center of the flour in double sacks; eggs, in corn meal or flour (enough to last us nearly five hundred miles). We had fruit in abundance, and dried pumpkins; a little jerked beef (not too salty);[14] and lastly, a large earthenware jug of brandy, for medicinal purposes only.[15] Wife had prepared homemade yeast cake to start off with, and we continued to have light bread to eat all the way across to Oregon. She baked it in a tin reflector, instead of the heavy Dutch ovens that most everyone else used on the plains.[16]

We had fresh milk every day and fresh butter that was churned in the can by the jostling of our wagon. We even had buttermilk. I shall never, as long as I live, forget the shortcakes and cornbread, the puddings and pumpkins pies Wife made on our journey. But above all, I shall remember the luxury of having buttermilk![17]

As we traveled our way down to the Missouri River, we were joined by other wagons and other families headed west. It was well into May before we reached the Mormon town of Kanesville, which later became Council Bluffs, just a few miles above the Missouri River ferry. Here, my brother Oliver joined us, having come from Indianapolis with old friends and comrades. Now, we were a train of five wagons.[18] In Kanesville, we made our last purchases and posted our last letters to anxious friends back home. We headed for the ferry landing. The road was cut to pieces from the huge numbers of wagons that had traveled the same ground.

"What on earth is that?" exclaimed one of the women traveling with us. "It looks for all the world like a great big white flatiron."[19]

We looked toward the ferry and saw wagons—several hundred of them—with their tongues all pointing to the landing. There seemed to be a center train with other parallel trains extending back in the rear, gradually covering a wider and wider space the farther back from the river one looked.[20] The white of the new wagon canvases did, indeed, give the whole scene the look of a gigantic white flatiron, pointing toward the Missouri River.

All around were camps of every kind. Some were bare, without covering of any kind. Some were clusters of comfortable tents. Nearly all seemed to be intent on merrymaking of some type or other. Yet, here and there, we could see a few small groups engaged in devotional services while they waited their turn to cross. We were told some of these pioneers had been there for two weeks!

The river was high and treacherous. Already it had swallowed two victims. I saw a third man drown on the first day we were there. His shrieking wife was standing right by me; we were helpless to save him.[21]

Ezra Meeker

Two scows—flat-bottomed boats with squared-off ends—continued to attempt crossing the wagons and teams. Too often, the cattle would become frightened and rush to one side of the boat or the other, tipping that side into the water and often capsizing everything into the water.

What should we do, we wondered. Finally, Margaret McAuley—a most determined maiden lady traveling with her younger brother and his family—said, "Why don't we build our own boat?"[22]

As Providence would have it, one of our party who had gone across the river in search of timber for oars discovered an abandoned scow almost completely buried in the sand opposite the ferry landing. We searched an entire day for its owner. When we finally found him—eleven miles downstream—he told us yes, we could have it, as long as we delivered the boat to him once we were safely across. My! Didn't we make the sand fly that night! By morning, we had a landing cut into the sandy bank on the Iowa side and the scow ready to bring us across.[23]

On May 17 and 18, we crossed the Missouri River and began our westward trek in earnest. As soon as a part of our outfits were landed on the right side of the river, however, our aggravations with the Indians began. Not in open hostilities, you understand, but in robbery and beggary. They were quite adept at stealing goods from around the wagons and, later, in extorting payment to cross bridges and ferries.[24] We did not, however, have much real trouble with them in 1852. The great waves of emigrants coming to Oregon at that time afforded us safety in numbers. We were all, as a rule, better armed than the Indians. And it must be remembered, this was before the treaty-making period, which was so often followed by bloodshed and war.[25]

Most of our early trouble came from other wagons on the trail. With many, the watchword seemed to be *Push ahead, push ahead! Make as many miles as you can in a day*. Nearly a thousand wagons thronged by us in those early days. These were the ones who eventually broke down their teams in their rush. These were the ones who wound up unloading piles of provisions in the first two-hundred-mile stretch. And these were the ones who fell such easy prey to the ravages of cholera.[26]

Night dances and violin music underneath the stars gave way to a more somber tone, even among the young people. The fatigue of a day's drive and the cares of a night watch were compounded by the great number who grew sick from overheating and the drinking of impure water.[27]

As we traveled, I saw things that would convert the most skeptical to the Presbyterian doctrine of total depravity—actions unbelievably brutal and selfish, to men and women and dumb brutes alike. Yet, there were also many instances of self-sacrifice, helpfulness, and unselfishness. It became a common saying that to *know* one's neighbors, they must be seen on the plains.[28] I will vouch for that. The trail brought out the best—and worst—in mankind.

We were beginning, as they say, to *See the Elephant*.

We kept apart as a separate unit as best we could—our little group of five wagons—but in reality we were all in one great train, never out of sight or hearing of the other wagons. In fact, at times the road would be so full of wagons, we couldn't travel single-file in one track and had to spread out where we could. In some places, we traveled side-by-side for miles.[29]

We were a moving mass of human beings and animals, mixed in complete confusion, a hundred feet wide or more. Sometimes two columns of wagons traveled near each other in parallel lines as a barrier to prevent loose stock from running afield, but usually there was a seething throng of cows, young cattle, horses, and men afoot moving along the outskirts. Here and there, the drivers of the loose stock "hupped" and "hiyahed." Some were on foot; some were on horseback. Boys and girls alike helped them drive the stock and often were sent after runaway cows when they wandered too far outside the general herd. The whole scene reminded me of a packed city street. No one looked right or left; no one paid attention to anyone else. All seemed bent only upon accomplishing the task immediately at hand.[30]

Of course, the farther we traveled, the louder the outcry became against the heavy loads and unnecessary goods some people had packed in their outfits. There was no chance to sell anything and no sense in destroying it. So, abandoned property at the side of the trail became common. First it was a cupboard or a table, then a bedstead or cast-iron cookstove. Then bedding, feather beds, blankets, quilts, pillows, trunks. Stacks of provisions followed—flour and bacon were seen the most. We even saw wagons, themselves, standing by the side of the road for anyone to claim. Hundreds of wagons were left this way, and hundreds of tons of goods. It was a case of *Help Yourself*; no one would interfere.[31] In fact, in some places signs were posted inviting all to take whatever they needed.[32]

As the months rolled by and teams became weaker, even more wagons were abandoned. Drivers often lost their heads and ruined their teams by running them too hard. There seemed on many days to be a stampede in the attempt to rule the road, to get ahead. It was against the rules to pass the team ahead of you. A wagon that had withdrawn from the line and stopped beside the trail could get into line again, but while we were moving, it could not cut ahead of the wagon in front of it. Now, though, whole trains would try to outrun others in front of them, and their poor, exhausted teams would simply give out.[33]

In one place, we laid by for four days. Sixteen hundred wagons passed us, with nearly ten thousand beasts of burden, and thirty thousand loose stock. As eight thousand people—men, women, and children—passed by us, I thought many surely were going to their graves.[34]

One event that made a profound impression upon me was meeting eleven wagons returning—traveling west to east. There was not a single man left in that entire train. All the men had died, we were told, and been buried on the way. Now, the women and children were determined to return to their homes, alone. The difficulties of their return trip east were only multiplied by the incredible numbers of emigrants now going westward, against them. How those women fared in their attempt or whatever became of them, we never knew.[35]

When we stopped at Independence Rock, we calculated by the dates inscribed upon it that there were wagons stretching three hundred miles ahead of us. We knew that the throng had continued to pass the Missouri River more than a month after we had crossed. It didn't require any stretch of the imagination to realize this great white snake of emigrant wagons must have been a full five hundred miles long . . . and that the column itself was made up of some fifty thousand people.[36]

Graves became commonplace. For awhile we tallied them in our journals: passed four graves today, passed eleven graves today, passed twenty-one. We stopped remarking on them when we began to see them laid in rows of fifties and in groups of seventies.[37] Forty people of one train died of cholera in one day and two nights; a family of seven all died within hours of one another and were buried in the same grave. While camped above Grand Island, we estimated sixteen hundred wagons passed by in three days. From those, a neighboring burial place grew from just a few graves, to fifty-two.[38] How many died all told that year? We didn't know. Some said ten percent. I think the number was more. Far more.

Our little group was determined not to become one of the fallen. We boiled our drinking water, refusing to dig little wells beside the rivers as many others did. We took our water from the free-flowing current always, even when it was as thick as mud.[39] We escaped unharmed.

The fortitude of our women cannot be overstated. Embarrassed at the start by the follies of fashion, they soon cast false modesty aside and abandoned their long dresses for bloomers. Elderly matrons, girls, even young women accepted the inevitable and fell into the habit of wearing them, without any comment at all.[40]

Some of them soon went barefoot, partly from choice and in other cases from necessity. The same could be said of the men as shoe leather began to grind out from the sand and dry heat. Patches became visible upon the clothing of rich and poor alike. The grandmother's cap was soon replaced by just a handkerchief or bit of cloth. Grandfather's high-crowned hat disappeared as if by magic. Completely hatless and bootless men became a common sight. Women without bonnets were seen on all sides. Yet some of the ladies wore their richest, finest dresses as they had no others left.[41] The other dresses had been left by the side of the trail as they wore out. Men did the same until scarcely a new suit of clothes was left. You never knew what kind of costume, or "get up" you'd see from day to day. It took an expert's ingenuity to discover either texture or original color of anyone's clothing, owing to the patchwork and the ground-in particles of sand and dust.[42]

Ah yes, the dust would settle. Dust, dust, everywhere dust! Until the cloudbursts. Then there wouldn't be a dry thread on anyone or anything. In one such storm, my boots were suddenly filled as full of rain as if I had been wading in water over my boot-tops! Water ran through my hat as if it had been a sieve. I was almost blinded by the fury of the wind and water. Tents were leveled, goods washed away, wagons were at peril of being swamped by the flooding torrent that came from nowhere.[43] Such were the gully washers on the plains.

I often thought William Thomas had a good idea with that Wind

Wagon of his. A true prairie schooner, that: a wagon outfitted with a sail! Let the prairie winds lend the power, not oxen, not mules. But last I heard, Thomas's invention was still coming to naught. His wagons keep ending up crashed and capsized in some ravine.[44] Too bad, too bad.

Oxen may have been slow, but they were reliable. Through every hardship we ever encountered, my oxen persevered. Buck and Dandy never gave up. I had chosen these two four-year-olds for their intelligent eyes as well as for their muscles, and had made no mistake. We camped together and slept together, with me curled up against Dandy's back.[45]

I trusted them, and I knew they trusted me. When they became lame or tender-footed, we tied cowhide shoes on their unshod feet.[46] When they were ill, we'd dose them with lard and vinegar and sugar.[47] I often said Buck understood English better than some people, for he always obeyed me to the letter.[48] I could pack them, drive them by only a word, and count on their affection in any situation. They never failed me.

I have never understood the expression *dumb as an ox*. In my mind, it should be a compliment to be compared to so noble and faithful an animal. I'd like to think there is a Heaven for all oxen that perished under the yoke in humble, uncomplaining servitude.

Of course, animals have their likes and dislikes just as people do. And, as our train was one that allowed dogs,[49] it was only a matter of time before some of the oxen and dogs tangled. Early in our trip, I had seen two become mortal enemies. The dog's name was Jim, and the ox's name was Dave.[50]

Usually Jim would trot beside his master as he walked beside the oxen and pay little attention to them. He would run after birds, jackrabbits, squirrels, coyotes, or anything else that could get into motion. When he'd get too hot, he'd dig the top off the dirt or sand and lie in the cool hollow he'd built for himself.[51]

But let the master get inside the wagon to drive the team, and Jim would make a beeline to the ox Dave, and the quarrel would begin. Sometimes, if the yoke kept him from getting at Jim with his horn, Dave would throw his nose and snort in disgust, just like a horse. But once, Jim came too close. Dave caught him under the ribs with his right horn and tossed him right over some sagebrush nearby.[52]

Jim managed to get even, however. When the master would put loose

SEEING THE ELEPHANT

hay under the wagon to keep it out of the storm, Jim would make a bed on it. Woe be to Dave if he tried to take any of it to eat! Jim would catch Dave by the nose and draw blood until he was shaken off. And the whole thing would begin again. This war kept up for more than a thousand miles of the trip. Their feud eventually settled down, but the two never did become what you could call friends.[53]

We were now nearing the crest of the continent. The climb was so gradual, though, we hardly realized it. Through South Pass, the summit of the Rocky Mountains, the country fell away in a wide, open, undulating country. Shortly after Big Sandy Creek, we left the Salt Lake Trail—called by some the Mormon Trail—and took the Sublette Cut-off over to Bear River and the Soda Springs. There, our little company of friends parted. The McAuleys and William Buck took the trail to California while the rest of us went northwest to Oregon.[54] It was very hard to say goodbye, after all we'd come through together; it was almost like saying farewell to family. We wondered what new challenges waited for us down the trail.

In 1852, there were only a few ferries. Where they did happen to be found, the charges were exorbitant. All my funds had been spent putting together my outfit in Iowa. I never dreamed there would be a need for money on the Plains, where there were neither supplies nor people. But I soon discovered my mistake. I had to keep my eye out, as they said, for opportunities to make some money. The crossing of the Snake River, though late in the trip, was one of those opportunities to remember.[55]

About thirty miles below Salmon Falls, we faced a hard choice: let our teams starve as we made our way down the river on the south bank or try to get our wagons across the river and swim the stock across. Some ahead of us had caulked three wagon beds and lashed them together. They had crossed all right but wouldn't help others for anything less than three to five dollars a wagon, and then the party had to swim their own stock. If others had crossed in wagon beds, I thought, why couldn't I? Out came all the old clothes we could spare, out came the tar buckets, old chisels and broken knives. We commenced caulking to turn our wagons into boats! We christened ours the *Mary Jane*.[56]

My boyhood pranks of paddling old leaky skiffs or logs in the waters of the White River now served me well. My first venture across the Snake was with the whole of the wagon gear run over the wagon box, gradually work-

Ezra Meeker

[163]

ing it out into deep water. The load was so heavy, water sometimes broke over the sides, but I got over safely. Then I was ready to do it again, this time with lighter loads.

We had no trouble crossing the cattle. Dandy would do almost anything I asked of him, so with a little coaxing, I got him into water deep enough for him to swim and guided him across with the wagon bed. The others all followed.[57]

We hadn't even finished crossing when tempting offers came from other wagons, saying they would pay for our service. But all of our party said no. Travel, travel, travel. That was the watchword. Yet, what about the lower river crossing? Those who had crossed over the Snake here must somehow or another, get back. It was less than 150 miles to where all would again have to cross to the south side of the river. I could walk that in three days, I thought, while it would take our ox teams at least ten. Why not walk ahead, outfit a wagon box as I had here, and start a ferry till our company caught up?[58]

Everyone in our little party agreed. So with a bit of food and a small blanket, I accomplished the trip to the lower crossing. When I reached my destination, some were disposing of their teams and starting to float down the river. A trader there had convinced them to sell him their teams "for a song,"[59] and embark in their wagon beds for a river voyage. Needless to say, all of them lost everything—some even their lives.

Others were trying to ford, a dangerous undertaking but more successful than the first group. It didn't take me long to get a wagon bed, and shorter still, to put it into operation as a ferry. I worked every daylight hour of those long summer days, ferrying wagons. By the time my own party came up, seven days later, I had one hundred ten dollars in my pocket.[60] I left the ferrying business in high spirits, not realizing the last leg of our journey would take all but $2.75 of my hard-earned cash.

But Wife was failing. We had to place her and the baby in a small wagon and take them overland that way. She was no longer strong enough to walk. It was one of the worst stretches of the entire trek. From the lower crossing of the Snake River to The Dalles was almost three hundred and fifty miles over mountains and deserts. It became a serious question whether there would be enough provisions left to keep us from starvation and whether the teams could muster strength enough to take the wagons on. Everything

SEEING THE ELEPHANT

that could possibly be spared was put by the wayside. Provisions—and only provisions—were kept back.[61]

The dust got deeper every day. Often it would lie in the road six inches deep, and so fine that a person wading through it would leave barely a track. Every disturbance threw it up in suffocating clouds.[62] We thought it a cruel joke that the worst to be endured came last.

Yet, at last—in September—we reached The Dalles. There, we joined a great crowd of travel-worn people. Every few hours more sweat-stained stragglers trudged in from the dusty road. Some were buoyant and hopeful in their anticipation of meeting friends they knew were waiting for them at journey's end. Others were downcast and depressed as their thoughts went back to the old homes they left behind. Some had buried friends and loved ones in shallow graves along the trail.[63] Some wore the look of dazed amazement at the struggle behind them and the unknown future ahead. But all were now ready to go down the Columbia River to find their homes in this long-desired Land of Promise.

We who took passage on the river—rather than taking Sam Barlow's overland road—felt our journey was now ended. The cattle had been unyoked for the last time; the wagons had been rolled to the last camp. The embers of the last campfire had died out, and the last words of gossip had been spoken.[64] This was an ending. We hadn't yet realized it was also a beginning.

There must have been a dozen families or more—mostly women and children—traveling with us. Many of their young men had chosen to struggle over the mountain road to get their teams through the Cascade Mountains. But Wife and Baby were both sick now, and I felt it my duty to stay with them. River travel would be much easier on all of us.

The deck of the scow on which we took passage provided a simple, smooth surface upon which to pile our meager belongings. The entire deck was covered with the remnants of the emigrants' outfits, which in turn were covered by their owners, either sitting or reclining against them. There was barely room enough to change positions or move about in any way.[65]

We were like a great army that had burned its bridges behind it as it marched, with little knowledge of what lay in the track ahead. Here we were, more than two thousand miles from home, separated from all that was dear or familiar by a trackless, uninhabited waste of a country, and it was impossible for us to turn back. Some were sick; some were both physically and emotionally wasted away. Many were on the verge of collapse.[66]

In our company, a party of three—a young married couple and an unmarried sister—lounged on their belongings, listlessly watching the ripples on the water. Little conversation passed between them. It was easy to understand why: the young husband was dying. He wouldn't live reach Portland. He wouldn't live to see the end of the Trail. This knowledge weighed so heavily upon the two women, they could barely conceal their sorrow and grief. Finally, to cheer up the dying man, the ladies began to sing. In soft, subdued voices, they sang:

> *Mid pleasures and palaces, though we may roam,*
> *Be it ever so humble, there's no place like home! . . .*

By the time they reached the chorus, all on the deck had joined in:

> *Home! Home! Sweet, sweet home!*
> *There's no place like home. There's no place like home.* [67]

As the echoes died away against the rugged basalt cliffs and the scow slipped into shadow, the second verse was begun but never finished:

> *An exile from home . . .*

It was as if an electric shock went through every one of us. We couldn't even get the words past our lips. Instead, sobs and outcries of grief split the air. Despair poured forth without restraint: for all we had endured, all we had lost, all we would never know again. The humble hymn had laid us bare. Even the rugged boatmen rested upon their oars, and soon there wasn't a dry eye to be seen.[68] But our aching hearts were relieved. And soon, the tears of sorrow gave way to tears of relief. Then laughter. We had survived. We *had* survived!

On the first day of October, 1852, at about nine o'clock at night and with a bright moon shining, we reached Portland. My brother Oliver, who had gone ahead by land, met us at the end of our Oregon Trail. I had to carry

SEEING THE ELEPHANT

Wife in my arms from our landing on the Willamette River to a lodging house three blocks away.

The door was opened by the colored man who kept the house, and he welcomed us.[69] It was the first house we had been in for five months.

Some might have refused to stay there, seeing who ran it, but the situation suited us just fine. Slavery had been outlawed in Oregon. Yes, I had heard of the Territory's exclusion laws and knew of its trying to keep negroes out, but the infamous Lash Law of '44 had eventually given way to forced labor and then just expulsion. Finally, the worst of those laws had been repealed. Now, there was simply a law forbidding any negroes from settling within the Territorial borders.[70]

It would take time, and it would take effort, but I had seen liberty work before. I remembered my Free Soil days. There would come a time in this new Oregon—God willing, in my lifetime—when such laws would be banished, and the prejudices that spawned them would die away.[71]

We had brought our battlefield with us. Our struggles were only beginning.

SUMMARY

Ezra Meeker was an uncommon pioneer. He was recognized in his own lifetime as adventurer, merchant, community leader, civic builder, world traveler, successful writer, and fierce, tireless champion of what he called the Old Oregon Trail. (Not bad, for a man with less than six months formal schooling!) At age seventy-five, it became Meeker's vision to memorialize and mark the route over which hundreds of thousands of emigrants traveled to claim their homes in the Far West. In his own words, "I longed to go back over the Old Oregon Trail and mark it for all time, for the children of the pioneers who blazed it, and for the world."[72]

Meeker considered the Trail experience as the epitome of the classical Hero's Journey, in which the Hero was white, Anglo-Saxon American civilization at large, symbolized by the westering emigrant. Tribal people, in his viewpoint, served only as foils in his Hero's epic: obstacles to be overcome. "The savage has neither past, nor aspiration for the future," he wrote.[73] In this tightly restrictive and ethnocentric view, he was completely representative of his time and culture. It was not until the last years of his life that he conceded certain tribal people had been wronged "by irresponsible white men." See Chapter Discussion Points.

Blacks (free and slave alike) fared better in Meeker's sense of the *Heroic Struggle*. He was outspoken against slavery at an early age and professed to hold abhorrent the Lash Laws and Exclusion Laws that were being enforced in the Oregon Country at the time of his arrival. Still, Meeker's definition of the Trail as battlefield allowed only one anointed victor, and that was the white, Anglo-Saxon pioneer.

But, because Meeker's active pioneering experience spans over seventy-five years and because he brought national legislative notoriety to the Oregon Trail, his own place in Trail history is unique.

His first passage on the Oregon Trail was in 1852. He was 23 years old. Fifty-four years later—in 1906—he set out from his home in Puyallup, Washington (a town he had founded), in a covered wagon pulled by oxen and began to travel west to east, retracing his 1852 route to his boyhood Indiana home. From there, he, wagon, and oxen continued to Washington, D.C. On the way, Meeker placed stone markers along what remained of the Trail, made speeches, sold postcards and books, and in general, called attention to his glorified vision for the Oregon Trail.

In Washington, D.C., he met with President Theodore Roosevelt. Meeker was determined to convince the President that the Oregon Trail had earned a singular place in American history. At the same time, he wanted to discuss with the President the possibility of a transcontinental highway that would join the Old Oregon Trail route with the Cumberland Highway. Meeker called it the Pioneer Way.

In Meeker's words: "Mr. Roosevelt . . . did not need to be told that the trail was a battlefield, or that the Oregon pioneers who moved out and occupied the Oregon Country while it was yet in dispute . . . were heroes. When I suggested that they were 'the winners of the Farther West,' he fairly snatched those words from my lips."[74]

President Roosevelt recognized marketable legislative packaging when he heard it. Roosevelt himself was considered by some—himself included—as being larger than life. It is no surprise, then, that Meeker's heroic vision appealed to him. He promised to further the Trail's cause.

Four years later, Meeker put his wagon and oxen back on the Trail at

The Dalles, Oregon, with a plan to uncover, mark, and map places that had been obliterated by civilization in the fifty-eight years since his first trek west.

Then, after successfully completing that trip, he formally retired his wagon and his oxen. When the oxen died, he had them taxidermied and offered them—with his wagon—to the Smithsonian Institution in 1915; the Smithsonian turned him down. Meeker then donated the display to the Washington State Historical Society, on the condition that the whole outfit be permanently enclosed in a glass case as a memorial to his glorious Trail.

By that time, the old pioneer was nearly eighty-six, but his Oregon Trail work was far from finished. In 1916, he was back in Washington, D.C. with his Pathfinder automobile to prove the viability of his Pioneer Way transcontinental highway plan. The Pathfinder was outfitted with a cooking stove and canopied rear chassis where Meeker could sleep. Painted with signs and slogans about the Old Oregon Trail, it could best be described as the descendant of the old covered wagon and the precursor to today's RV.

On September 30, 1924, as a publicity stunt for the Trail, he flew the route from Vancouver, Washington, to Dayton, Ohio, as a passenger in an open cockpit, two-seat U.S. Army transport plane. He flew at one hundred miles per hour what he had traveled by ox team at two miles per hour some seventy-two years before. From Dayton, he went on to Washington, D.C. to meet with President Calvin Coolidge and buttonhole Congressmen in the interest of his work.[75] Meeker was then ninety-four years old.

In 1925 and 1926, Meeker appeared with the J. G. Miller Wild West Show, demonstrating to new generations how ox teams had been driven on the Old Oregon Trail during the Great Migration. At age ninety-five, he founded and became the first president of the Oregon Trail Memorial Association. OTMA, as it was known, persuaded Congress to authorize the minting of an Oregon Trail commemorative coin. Sales of the coin (at one dollar apiece) would help finance the placing of more monuments along the trail route. Six million were sold.

Incredibly, the Grandfather of the Oregon Trail (as the press called him) was still not ready to quit. He made a cross-country Oregon Trail trip by rail to promote his cause this time, and celebrated his ninety-sixth birthday in New York City, surrounded by the famous and influential.

One of the famous men touched by Meeker's zeal was Henry Ford.

Knowing a publicist's dream when he saw one, Ford offered to help Meeker custom build what he termed an Oxmobile.[76] If Meeker would consent to drive the specially outfitted automobile/prairie schooner across the Oregon Trail once more, Ford Motor Company would be his official sponsor. Meeker agreed. This time, though, he couldn't fulfill his promise. Ezra Meeker died twenty-six days short of his ninety-eighth birthday, before he could embark one last time on the Trail.

It may be tempting to mythologize Meeker the same way he tended to mythologize the Trail. But it is important to remember that his vision was very restrictive. If we look at the Trail from the tribal point of view, from the point of view of the slaves, the Chinese, or any other of the minority groups who did not share in the Hero's perspective, we often find a different vision altogether.

Yet, Meeker's work on behalf of the Oregon Trail eventually led to its being designated a National Historic Trail by the U.S. Government. Because of this designation, ruts, traces, and historic sites along the route have become protected. Because he beat the drum so loudly and for so long, archives of Trail diaries, copies of era newspapers, and transcripts of tribal treaties and oral histories were established and are now preserved. We are able today to study and reflect upon *all* the truths of the Trail, as a direct result of Ezra Meeker and his passion.

LET'S INTERPRET

Discussion 1

"When we set foot upon the right bank of the Missouri River, we were outside the pale of civil law. We were within Indian country where no organized civil government existed. Some people and some writers have assumed that each man was a 'law unto himself' and free to do his own will. . . . Nothing could be further from the facts."

.   .   .   .

"A murder had been committed . . . and it was clear the motive was robbery. The suspect had a large family and was traveling along with the moving column. A council of twelve men was called. [They] deliberated until the second day, meanwhile holding the murderer in their grip. What were they to do? Here was a wife and four little children dependent upon this man for their lives. What would become of this man's family if justice was meted out to him? Soon there came an undercurrent of what might be termed 'public opinion' that it was probably better to forego punishment than to endanger the lives of [his] family [by not having him to look after them]. But the council would not be swerved from their decision. At sundown of the third day, the criminal was hung in the presence of the whole camp—including the family—but not until ample provisions had been made to insure the safety of the family by providing a river to finish their journey. I [saw] the ends of the wagon tongues in the air and the rope dangling."[77]

—EZRA MEEKER, recalling 1852

Consider the social rules of the time. How do you feel about the trail justice that was carried out? Why were there no women on the jury? Compare the process undertaken by the emigrants to accuse, try, and execute the murderer. How does that compare to our judicial system today? Study the Articles of Agreement given in this book. Is there any mention of how crimes will be handled? Give reasons that the emigrants would have been justified in doing what they did. Give reasons why you think they were not justified. What other sentence could have been given to the murderer?

Discussion 2

"The Oregon Donation Land Claims Act . . . granted 320 acres of land to any white or half-breed Indian who staked a residence claim on the public lands in the Oregon Territory and cultivated it for a period of four years. . . ."[78]

—OREGON DONATION LAND CLAIM ACT OF 1850

"In 1853 my owners decided to come to Oregon. A merchant, hearing that my master was to go to Oregon Territory, where slaves could not be held, came to [him] and said, 'I will give you $1200 for Amanda. You can't own her where you are going, so you might as well get what you can out of her. . . . [My master then] asked me if I wanted to be given my freedom . . . but I was afraid to accept my liberty. . . . The word of a Negro, even if a free Negro, was of no value in court. Any bad white man could claim that I had been stolen from him and could swear me into jail. Then, in place of keeping me in jail, he could buy my services for the time I was sentenced for; and by the time I had served my time for him, he could bring up some other false charge and buy my services again, and do whatever he wanted with me, for Negroes were the same as cows and horses and were not supposed to have morals or souls."[79]

—AMANDA GARDENER JOHNSON, recalling 1853

Though slavery had been declared illegal in the Oregon Country, the Oregon Donation Land Claim Act specifically excluded blacks and other ethnic groups. (Anyone with tribal heritage had to be at least half white to qualify.) Any blacks over age eighteen had to leave the region. The Lash Law of 1844 subjected those found in violation to whippings until they left. This law was later modified, substituting forced labor for the whippings, until the person left the region. Yet another exclusion law was passed in 1849 that forbade blacks from settling at all in Oregon Territory. Any in residence at that time, however, were allowed to stay. Take the stance of a freed black man or woman. How would these laws make you feel about the Oregon Country? How would you meet the letter of the law? Where might you go if you couldn't stay in the Territory? Take the stance of a slave-owner who has come to Oregon to settle with slaves. What would you do in order to meet the law's requirements? How would you feel about the law since you consider the slaves your property?

For more information about Oregon's slavery and exclusion laws, see End of the Oregon Trail internet home page: "Black History in the Northwest" link, and William Katz's book, *Black People Who Made the Old West* (New York: T. Y. Crowell, 1977).

Discussion 3

"The savage has neither past, nor aspiration for the future. On this trail heroic men and women have fought a veritable battle—a battle that wrested half a continent from the native race and from another mighty nation contending for mastery [of the] West."[80]

—EZRA MEEKER, April 11, 1906

"The [Indian] War [of 1855–56] was brought on by the fact that the Indians had been wronged. This seems certain. They were robbed of their lands by the treaties made in 1854, and there have been atrocious murders of Indians by irresponsible white men. The result was suffering and trouble for all of us."[81]

—EZRA MEEKER, *Ox-Team Days on the Oregon Trail*

Meeker's opinion regarding at least some Indians seems to have changed over the years. Examine this book's text for passages supporting both ways of thinking. What might have changed Meeker's mind? In some journal passages, tribal people are described as interesting and intriguing to watch, even pretty; in others, they are described as dirty, conniving, and loathsome. Why did emigrants have differing views of various tribes? Did these descriptions and views of specific tribes change over the course of the Great Migration? If so, why? Find passages in the book text to support your answers.

Discussion 4

"[These troubles] were brought upon us by the children of the Great Father [President] who came to take our land from us without price, and who, in our land, do a great many evil things. The Great Father and his children [the whites] are to blame for this trouble. It has been our wish to live here in our country peaceably, and do such things as may be for the welfare and good of our people, but the Great Father has filled it with [those] who think only of our death."[82]

—SPOTTED TAIL, Sioux, 1865

"I was ten years old when I saw large boats bringing white people over the Missouri River. I saw a great many of the white people killed by the Sioux when they came up the river in small boats. It was not until I was about twenty years old that . . . emigrant wagons going west [were] driving large herds of cattle. The Indians killed the white people as they came . . . because we felt they were driving away our game. They had guns and powder and knives, which we did not have. We wanted what they had . . . and we did not like to see them go through our country. When I first saw the [white] people moving through our country . . . I began to be afraid."[83]

—PRETTY VOICE EAGLE, Sioux, recalling 1850s

Some tribes were friendly to the whites; some were not. Some changed their acceptance of whites as the years passed. Name as many reasons as you can as to why these differing attitudes might have caused hostility between various tribes. Keep in mind that far before the white man came, tribes warred with one another over territorial issues, hunting boundaries, etc. How might the influx of emigrants have affected traditional bad blood between tribes?

NOTES

1. Ezra Meeker, *Ox-Team Days on the Oregon Trail* (Yonkers-on-Hudson, NY: World Book Company, 1922), 2.

2. Ezra Meeker, *The Ox Team or The Oregon Trail 1852–1906* (Mt. Vernon, IN: Windmill Publications, Inc. for the Ezra Meeker Historical Society of Puyallup, WA. Reproduction of the 1906 Original, 2000), 234.

3. Sideboards were large posters that typically would be placed on the sideboards of buildings.

4. Meeker, *Ox-Team Days*, 11. "Negro" is Meeker's term, not capitalized in the passage cited. Though Meeker doesn't state this, one assumes—given the employer—this man was hired labor rather than forced labor.

5. Meeker, *The Ox Team*, 234.

6. Meeker, *Ox-Team Days*, 20.

7. Note that the language of the Oregon Donation Land Claim Act designated "white and half-breed Indians" to be qualified settlers. Blacks (African Americans) and other ethnic groups were specifically excluded.

8. During this time, it was most unusual for a woman to own land in her own name unless she had been given the land by a man through inheritance or outright gift.

9. Green steers, meaning castrated cattle that had not yet been trained to work. Green generally referred to anything (or anyone) that was inexperienced, unfinished, or unproven.

10. Meeker, *The Ox Team*, 22.

11. Meeker, *Ox-Team Days*, 10.

12. Ibid., 23.

13. Meeker, *The Ox Team*, 60.

14. Jerked beef is smoked and dried with salt. The resulting jerky is tough and chewy

but lasts a long time and is not easily perishable.

15. Meeker, *The Ox Team*, 23.

16. This tin reflector (appearing in a line drawing in *Ox-Team Days On the Oregon Trail*, 23) was a two-tiered, fold-up model similar to what backpackers, river runners, and mountain climbers use today.

17. Meeker, *The Ox Team*, 24.

18. Meeker, *Ox-Team Days*, 24–25.

19. Meeker, *The Ox-Team*, 28. A flatiron was the forerunner of our clothes irons. It was shaped roughly like a triangle.

20. Ibid.

21. Ibid., 29.

22. Ibid., 30.

23. Ibid.

24. It must be kept in mind that a decade of heavy emigrant travel had seriously disrupted and altered traditional tribal lifeways along the route of the Oregon Trail. By 1852, natural resources such as wild game, plant material, watering holes, etc. were seriously impacted by the sheer numbers of emigrants themselves, their wagons, and their hundreds of thousands head of livestock. Tribal people adapted in whatever ways they could, which included sometimes raiding emigrant supplies and charging money for services or access. Of course, from Meeker's point of view, this was stealing and extorting.

25. Meeker, *The Ox-Team*, 33.

26. Ibid., 35.

27. Ibid., 34–35.

28. Ibid., 37.

29. Meeker, *Ox-Team Days*, 32.

30. Ibid., 39.

31. Ibid., 34.

32. Meeker, *The Ox-Team*, 63.

33 Ibid., 64.

34. Ibid., 39.

35. Meeker, *Ox-Team Days*, 42.

36. Meeker, *The Ox-Team*, 39.

37. Ibid., 40.

38. Ibid., 81.

39. Ibid., 64. Dismal sanitation—including human-polluted drinking water—was the single most contributing factor to epidemic cholera along the trail.

40. Ibid., 69. Named for Amelia Bloomer, a women's rights activist of the time, these full, loose-fitting trousers (much like our sweatpants) with their knee-length overskirts were considered absolutely radical when first created. They showed the form of the female leg, which was strictly against acceptable moral codes of the day. Bloomers were routinely booed and ridiculed in the cities by men and women alike. Political cartoonists lampooned them. On the trail, however, they proved more practical than women's long, cumbersome, always-in-the-way dresses. Even so, not all wagon trains endorsed bloomers as acceptable wear. Some journal entries recount how bloomer-wearing women caused such shock and dismay among their fellow trail travelers, they were forced to reclaim their traditional dresses—upon threat of being put off the train! Though Meeker says the practice of wearing bloomers was widespread in his train, it is unlikely it was "without comment" as he tells us, as they were always controversial.

41. Ibid., 70.

42. Ibid., 98.

43. Ibid., 72.

44. In 1846, William Thomas of Independence, Missouri, built a true wind wagon that was 25 feet long and 12 feet high, with a 20-foot sail mast mounted on it. The hubs were the size of barrels. When it caught the wind on its maiden (trial) run, the contraption went careening across the countryside and crashed into a ravine. Not to be daunted, Thomas continued trying to refine his invention until 1859 when, faced with failure after failure, he gave up. His original idea may have come from the experiences of Lewis and Clark some forty years before, when they hoisted a sail in a canoe that was being transported over dry land on trucks (wheels). Their journals recorded the canoe went faster on dry land than it had ever gone on water.

45. Meeker, *Ox-Team Days*, 46.

46. Ibid., 109.

47. Ibid., 204.

48. Meeker, *The Ox-Team*, 86.

49. Some trains expressly forbade dogs, as they ran the stock afield.

50. These were Meeker's dog and ox from the 1906 Oregon Trail journey. The story is used here—within the 1852 context—to illustrate what was common behavior among the animals.

51. Meeker, *The Ox-Team*, 195–96.

52. Ibid., 194.

53. Ibid., 195.

54. Meeker, *Ox Team Days*, 49–50.

55. Meeker, *The Ox-Team*, 74.

56. Ibid., 75.

57. Ibid., 76.

58. Ibid., 77.

59. Meaning for little to nothing.

60. Meeker, *The Ox-Team*, 78.

61. Meeker, *Ox-Team Days*, 57.

62. Ibid., 57–59.

63. Meeker, *The Ox-Team*, 98–99.

64. Ibid., 101.

65. Ibid., 102.

66 Ibid.,103.

67. Ibid., 104-5. Meeker simply states they sang "the old familiar song of 'Home Sweet Home.'" Most music historians count this song as among the most popular and beloved of the entire nineteenth century. It was written in 1823 by the British composer and lyricist, Henry Rowley Bishop, who was knighted for his resulting fame. The song quickly swept the United States, and remains in use today. Dorothy, in the movie *The Wizard of Oz*, mouthed the last lines of this song's refrain as her memorable verbal key that transported her back to Kansas and Auntie Em.

68. Ibid., 105.

69. Meeker, *Ox-Team Days*, 69. "Colored" is Meeker's term in the passage cited.

70. In June 1844, the Provisional Government of Oregon enacted its first laws regarding the status of slaves (therefore blacks). Slavery was declared to be illegal, and settlers who currently owned slaves were required to free them within three years. Any free blacks, aged eighteen or older, had to leave the area; men within two years, women within three. Black children were permitted to stay in the Oregon Country until they reached age eighteen.

71. Meeker, as many other of his contemporaries, seemed to have defined prejudice strictly as it applied to slavery and blacks. Native Americans were not included in his humanitarian view during these early years. See Chapter Discussion Points.

72. Meeker, *Ezra Meeker, Compiled from His Own Writings* (Puyallup, WA: The Ezra Meeker Historical Society, 1972), 16.

73. Meeker expressed this opinion again and again in his lectures, speeches, and published works. Though over the years he changed the word *savage* to *uncivilized* and *untutored*, his meaning remained the same. This specific quote is from Meeker's speech at a dedication ceremony for one of his Old Oregon Trail markers, as cited in the *La Grande (Oregon) Evening Observer*, 11 April 1906, 3.

74. Meeker, *Ox-Team Days*, 220.

75. Ezra Meeker, *Ezra Meeker, A Brief Resume of His Life and Adventures* (Puyallup, WA: Ezra Meeker Historical Society, 1972), 19–29

76. Sometimes called the Schoonermobile.

77. Ezra Meeker, *Ventures and Adventures of Ezra Meeker* (Seattle, WA: Rainier Printing Co., 1908), 49, 50–51.

78. Tompkins, 60.

79. Fred Lockley, *Conversations with Pioneer Women* (Eugene, OR: Rainy Day Press, 1981), 209–10.

80. Meeker, *La Grande (Oregon) Evening Observer*, 11 April 1906, 3.

81. Meeker, *Ox Team Days*, 179

82. Dee Brown, *Bury My Heart at Wounded Knee* (New York: Holt, Rinehart, and Winston, 1974), 89.

83. Jos. K. Dixon, *The Vanishing Race* (1913; reprint, New York: Bonanza Books, 1975), 73.

HELEN STEWART
Oh Dear, Oh Dear! This Is Going to Oregon

1853

M Y JOURNEY on the Oregon Trail began not in a wagon, but in a boat. We took passage on the steamer *Arctic* in Pittsburgh, bound for St. Louis, Missouri, on April 6. My sisters and I enjoyed ourselves very much, as the people on the steamship were all very agreeable, and we—as young ladies of marriageable age[1]— found much to amuse our time. I, especially, was very sorry when I had to leave our new friends at St. Louis and transfer to the steamer *Honduras*, for St. Joseph. It was not nearly so pleasant as the *Arctic*.[2]

Besides, I had grown homesick for our old home in Pennsylvania, where I had spent the happiest days of my life.[3] I missed the neighborhood parties, the congregating with my friends, and the prospect of playing croquet under the big shade trees in summer. Mother said never mind, we would make new friends in Oregon as we had on the steamer, but it just didn't feel the same to me.

It had been very nice making our way on the Missouri River, though it looked strange compared to the clear waters of the Ohio. There were such romantic-looking rocks, towering way up, it reminded me of some old, ruined castles that I had read about. One evening as we passed, there was a wildfire in the woods, and it went winding and spreading up the sides of the hills like a dragon's tongue. When the moon shone bright upon it, it made a picture I shall long remember.[4]

We arrived safely at last in St. Joseph and were glad to see our friends and relatives again. All had agreed to meet here—to *rendezvous*—at Black Snake Creek so that we could travel together across the prairies to Oregon. We had to be early enough on the plains that there would be grass and water enough for the stock, yet not tarry too long en route so as to be caught by snow in the mountains. We all had heard stories about getting snow-bound: snow up to a man's armpits, so deep nothing could move, neither man nor beast. People freezing to death as they clung to one another for warmth, being found days later with their arms entwined, stiff as a board.

There was even a story of a father and son who became lost from the others while driving their outfit through a blizzard. The father finally had to cut the wagon loose and use a whip on the team and on the boy to keep them moving. They trudged ahead all night to the whip so they wouldn't freeze to death. It was the only way.[5]

The moral of the story, Pa said, was that one had to be self-reliant out here, or one would not survive. Yes, sir, we all nodded. *Yes, sir!*

It took a while for everybody to get outfitted and organized. Our first Sabbath in this strange land was spent with everybody wrapped up in their own imaginations. Some wrote letters home; some read; some strolled about. The whippoorwills chirped and chirped, making me lonesome. I think I would have enjoyed my solitude far better if I had had about a dozen of my friends there to enjoy it with me.[6]

Even my sisters were deserting me. One announced she had joined her hand with one Frederick Warner on the eve of our leaving St. Joseph! She had actually married him! They had kept it a secret until now, for they knew Pa would holler. But she showed us their wedding daguerreotype. And there they were—Frederick in a fringed buckskin suit and wearing a big brim hat, his dark hair curling about his ears as he sat stiffly gazing out, and Sister, standing slightly behind him with one hand on his shoulder, the other hand anchoring a beautiful paisley wedding shawl that was draped around her shoulders—a wedding gift from her new husband.[7]

It all looked pretty grand to me, especially that shawl. And after Pa settled down and Mother stopped crying, there were hugs and handshakes all around. Sister was sent off with great hoopla to take her place on her husband's wagon. We gave them a real shivaree.[8] It got me to thinking . . . I was seventeen. Maybe I should start looking for a beau myself!

We finally got started May 3 on our long, tiresome journey to the West—only a few days short of one month since leaving Pennsylvania. The road was awful. The stormy weather made a mud bog of the roads. We were forever getting stuck in mud holes and having to double our teams. Some of the wagons in our company broke down and had to wait behind to be mended. We finally got within three miles of the ferry when it sank and drowned three men. One of them was an immigrant whose wife and children were in our company.[9]

We, however, made our crossing safely. On the other side, there was nothing for the eye to see but far spreading hills and prairies, droves of cattle, and wagons, wagons, wagons. Groves of trees wound among the hills, and clear water murmured in the fragrant shade. It was quite beautiful, a stark contrast to the number of graves laid by the roadside.[10]

A little boy belonging to our train died there and was left in that traveling graveyard surrounded by strangers. We all mourned his loss.

As we pressed westward, we had to cross more streams. Some had bridges and were guarded by Indians who demanded we pay a toll to cross. A few of the men in our train said they wouldn't pay and crossed their animals anyway. The Indians followed them for two days and stole some of their horses and cattle in payment.[11] It would have been far better simply to have paid the toll in the first place, Pa said.

The storms continued to assault us. It was disagreeable to the worst degree—raining and blowing and no fires to dry out our clothes. In the mornings, the sun usually shone in false promise. Then my sister Agnes and I would get out of the wagon and walk, easily passing the wagons.[12] One time while walking, I found a pocket book with some friendship cards, some poetry and other things in it. No doubt the owner of it was shot.[13] Agnes and I looked the things over then tossed it away for someone else to find.

By the middle of most afternoons, storms would blow up all around us, lasting well into the night. Between the shrieking of the wind, the howling of the wolves, and the uneasy moaning of the cattle, the storm made us very nervous. Thunder rolled and crashed. Sometimes hail the size of hens' eggs slammed down from the sky! Why, it even killed some livestock, hitting them on their heads. Brained them dead as a doornail, that's for sure.

Three wagons passed us one morning after such a storm, and two had their tops torn completely torn off.[14] The canvas of the third hung pathetically from its bows. "Whatever blows away now, will most certainly blow back later!" Pa joked.[15]

It was no joking matter to me. Many was the time we girls had to huddle together in the wagon for protection, with the lantern tied to the ridge pole to provide a bit of light. Every minute—with the lightning dancing round and round and the black clouds flying in terrifying grandeur—we were sure the covers would be torn off our wagons or the wagons themselves would be upset. I despaired, while trying desperately to hold the door flap shut, of ever seeing the sun rise again.[16]

Meanwhile, in the tent outside, the fellows tried to sleep through the storm. Now that was laughable. More times than not, the tent would blow over. They'd crawl out from under it and stand against the wind, trying to hold on . . . but failing. It was a wonder we all didn't come down with consumption[17] or pneumonia, as it was wet and wickedly cold all the time.

Some days we even had to stay where we were, not travel at all because the rain was so fierce. The roads would become too slick and the hills too treacherous to go up and down. At the bases of some hills lay pieces of wagons already—testimonies to foolishness.

We continued to pass graves. So many that we became numbed to the sight: two graves one morning, five graves that afternoon. Three graves near the road; two died the same day and were buried in the same hole. Then we came across a woman's grave, and the bones had been dug up. Her head was just lying there.[18] We didn't even stop to re-bury the bones. We just turned our faces and pushed on.

We had to think about the dangers at hand: Indians, river crossings, finding enough game so we wouldn't starve.

I never was so afraid of Indians as I was on the prairies, but it never kept me from sleeping.[19] River crossings, though, absolutely terrified me. We came to one dreadful creek with four separate crossings. I thought my heart would break through my dress front, it was beating so hard.

We could see there was one wagon already stuck in a hole before us and another that had just got out but had upset and broken. Captain directed us to a place that was supposed to be the best place to cross, but Oh Dear! Oh Dear! The wagons went down to their hubs and would not move. The cattle got discouraged and got all tangled up; one fell down. They had to be unhitched before they drowned, and new ones put in their places.[20]

All was chaos!

Our poor fellows had an awful time, wading up to their necks and turning around in some places, having to tug at the lead cattle with ropes around their heads—a very dangerous job. And sometimes the river was so deep, the oxen would have to swim, trailing the men behind them from their yokes and horns.[21]

Two of the men lost their footing and drifted down under the cattle. They might have been stunned with the oxen striking with their feet, but thankfully they came through the other side, missing only a hat.[22] One dog got caught up in the confusion, though, and drowned.

A man behind us decided to try crossing the river with his drove of sheep. He put in thirty thousand head, and he got out only five thousand on the other side![23] Everything and everybody looked like drowned rats when they got out of the water.

We girls had the job of running down to the river bank and wrapping blankets around the men as they came out of the water. Then we drenched them all—on the inside—with ginger tea and boiled coffee.[24] The river was so swift and swollen from the rains, it's a wonder we all weren't swept away.

Then, when we were on solid ground again and feeling safe, an accident happened to Mother. She fell as she was getting into the wagon, and the wheel ran over her leg. Luckily, no bones were broken; she was badly bruised but not hurt. Where she had fallen, the ground was sandy.[25] Otherwise, that heavy iron-rimmed wheel surely would have crushed her leg to pieces. I had seen that happen before with my very own eyes.

Pa said we were beginning to *see the elephant*.

When we finally got to Fort Kearny,[26] a soldier came out and tallied all of us: people, wagons, and all the live stock. He told us there were thirteen thousand head of people, three thousand wagons, and ninety thousand head of stock. He said we were the largest emigration that had ever passed the fort, to date.[27]

Pa bought another yoke of oxen there at the fort. They cost us eighty dollars![28] But Pa said we needed some fresh blood for our draft animals,[29] and he could alternate these with our dear old hardworking teams who had pulled us every mile from St. Joseph. Though we girls hadn't thought much of the oxen when we started out—they were stock, that was all—now we realized their importance. If they didn't stay strong and healthy, we couldn't go forward. Was there enough grass for the oxen? Enough water? Were they pulling too heavy a load? We dosed them with medicine about as often as we did ourselves! (And they disliked it equally well.) Many people gave their oxen names; some treated them almost like pets. We were too sensible for that, but we did grow quite fond of our steady, plodding companions.

The first Sabbath after passing Fort Kearny, we did not lay by, but traveled. Then, we stopped mid-day, and instead of worshiping, we took everything out of our wagons to give it air. It was good we did, for we discovered our flour was damp. Then we baked, and boiled, and washed our clothes. The land was strewn with flour, biscuits, meat, rice, oatmeal, clothes, and things too numerous to mention. Oh Dear, Oh Dear! I didn't know we could abuse the Sabbath in such a manner! It certainly was not our intent to do so when we started.[30] But many things were different on the Trail than how we had imagined them back in Pennsylvania.

The days passed. For a while we saw fewer graves than we had grown accustomed to and fewer dead cattle by the side of the road. But we saw plenty of buffalo heads from previous butcherings, strewn about.[31] The hot sun set up quite a stench, and flies buzzed everywhere.

On one of these summer days, Brother brought to camp two living antelope babies. They were the dearest little things I ever saw! Of course, as soon as he set them down, off they went. They were gone in the blink of an eye, but oh, how fine and beautiful they were![32]

When we laid by that day for nooning, Brother and five other boys went swimming in the creek. I wished I could, too, but that was considered improper for young ladies. Especially in mixed company. No, the best diversion I could manage was to walk ahead, over the bluffs, to see what I could discover. I never saw such a place for flowers: all kinds, colors, and sizes. And little prairie dog towns. What fun it was to watch their inhabitants sit up on top of the roofs to their houses and bark at me![33]

Sometimes, our wagon company would split in two, and camp on either side of some creek. Those were the nights I was most uneasy. There's safety in numbers, everyone knows that. But with the men asleep outside in the tents and we girls with the children alone in the outside wagon, it was scary. We were afraid to go to sleep, so we got a notion to read. But then we thought no, the light would attract some Indians' attention. So we put the out the lantern and tried to bed down. But the gallinippers were so bad, I couldn't keep my eyes shut. I fancied I heard wolves howling, Indians screaming, and all sorts of things.[34]

In the broad light of day, however, our terrors grew less . . . for a while, anyway. There was nothing to meet the eye but wagons. Cattle and wagons, wagons and cattle, spreading as wide as ten miles to our side and as long before and behind us as we could see. We, ourselves, were inching forward slowly in the general throng. The sand through which we traveled reflected back the searing heat of the sun in our faces, and the sweat trickled down. When there was not sandy soil, there was dust. Around us, children played, grumbled, cried, laughed, and shouted—adding to the incessant din. Sisters and I nodded to one another in silent understanding: Oh Dear! Oh Dear! This was going to Oregon![35]

One morning, just after we had finished our breakfast, the boys went out to gather cattle. Charles, one of the older ones, was riding as fast as his beast would go, and it stepped on something—or maybe stepped in a hole—and pitched him off. The horse turned clear over on him. When we got to him, Charles's senses were gone, and he ranted nonsensically about running on the mare all the time. The poor fellow! He was a very nice, quiet, sturdy young man. If it had happened to a wild, careless, lazy fellow, I wouldn't have cared a bit. But I feared Charles was worse off than we knew.[36]

We waited about an hour to make sure he was going to be all right and then started on. But the riding made him worse, so we stopped again. Pa sent for a doctor who was seven or eight miles ahead of us, but that doctor came to look at Charles with such an ill temper, I think we would have been better off without him. He took one look, and said he could not do any more for him than was already being done. Then he left.[37]

It took a number of days for Charles to get right in the head again. But after that, all the boys were more careful about running headlong across the prairies.

The memorable day we nooned at Courthouse Rock, we had great word of the Indians. They said there were five hundred of them and they were going to fight! There was among us one old bachelor—poor old John—who was dreadfully frightened at the news. He looked as if he wished his eyes might go ahead a piece and see if it were really true. He thought the emigrants should be stopped until more could come up and said it would be best to leave enough men with the wagons to defend them and send the rest to kill every Indian man, woman, and child—even suckling babes. For if babies could not fight now, he said, they would when they got older.[38] He swore all the time at a great rate, that the only good Indians were dead ones.

The great Indian army that had so frightened him, though, proved to be very friendly. One came first and shook hands with us and showed us a piece of paper that had the names of all the stuff on it that he wanted from us: tobacco, flour, coffee, and a lot of other things. He told us that his family was the best among his people and that he had ten children. It was true, his daughters were some of the prettiest girls . . . and they were dressed very nicely, after their own fashion. I don't know whether old John ever fully got over his panic or not.[39] But these Indians certainly didn't give us any trouble.

With the exception of a few exciting times like that, most all the glamour had gone out of our travels. I consulted our guidebook daily, wondering, *Oh dear, aren't we there yet?* and calculating how much further we had to go.

The day before my eighteenth birthday was so hot, the oxen were traveling with their tongues hanging out. The dust was flying in every direction and getting everywhere—eyes, ears, noses, mouths. The oxen coughed and coughed. They shook their big heads and narrowed their eyes till they matted over with dirt and flies. I wished we had goggles for them as we did for ourselves. We passed three dead oxen a close distance apart. What a death they must have died. And the day just kept getting hotter.

But the next day—June 22—it snowed! What an unexpected birthday present! We laid by and did not travel, as it was so suddenly bleak and cold. Besides, the oxen needed rest. There were lots of camps all around us. Some were moving, and others catching up.[40] Some of the children tried to play "Fox and Geese" before the snow melted.[41] Our family used the day to do our washing, to do some baking, and to fix many things including the tongue of our rattly old wagon. I wrote in my diary, "I can feel myself getting older, but not any wiser."[42] Sometimes I felt like a woman, full-grown.

Yet other times, I wanted nothing else than to run with the children at their games, play tag or hopscotch without a worry. I wondered what new adventure might find us on the very first day of my new year, tomorrow.

As luck would have it, my sisters Mary and Agnes came with me as I took a walk upon some of the high hills. Below, the rest of our company got situated to ford the river. As we were coming back, we met two Indians. One of them was dressed very handsomely. He had a broad strip of beads sewed down the middle of his blanket, and his shoulders were just covered with them. He had two pieces of fur fastened to the back of his head, and where they attached, there was a real black bird. But the bird was dead, of course. He had a small looking glass set in wood, swung around his neck, along with something that had a very pleasant odor. I cannot begin to describe the splendid fixings he had on.[43]

The other Indian had nothing nice on except his leggings and moccasins, which were just covered with beads. The well-dressed one was very talkative and made it known he wanted me to get on the horse behind him and ride back to the wagons.[44] I declined, saying my sisters and I had to stay together. I don't know how much of what I said he understood, but clearly he saw my intent. I figured we could set up a commotion that would be heard at the wagon, if need be. I wasn't about to become an Indian brave's[45] trophy! Mary was scared and wanted to run, but we didn't dare. Agnes held onto her, and we stood our ground. Finally, these Indians gave up and wheeled their horses away. Now *that's* what I call adventure!

We passed old Fort Laramie later that day and its graveyard, which was in ruins. The fence around it was all broken down, and cattle—anything— could get in and tramp all over it. The names had been cut on wooden headboards, but a great many of them were already worn away and unreadable. For so many big, tall, able fellows lounging around the fort, this place looked a disgrace. We crossed the ford nearby then came up a long hill and camped in the middle of a cactus bed, for there was nothing better there.[46] I could remember the times we had gathered cactus blossoms, as we thought them so pretty. That was when we first started out. Now, they were just a nuisance.

As we went deeper into the hill and bluff country, another huge train with its droves of cattle passed us. It was here I realized Agnes must be made of lodestone, for all the fellows in the new train stopped to see her, as if drawn by some invisible magnetic force.[47] They rarely did that with me. I wondered if I was going to wind up an old maid, having to watch all my sisters find husbands while I wound up a pathetic old Auntie in the Oregon Country.

On the Fourth of July, we came to a bridge by which stood a store and a blacksmith shop and several houses. There were a great many Spaniards there, all with their Indian wives.[48] One of these was making a beaded bonnet for her baby, which was very beautiful in her eyes. She put a fringe of dimes around the front of it. I counted eleven gold dollars on it, besides the many other pieces. We had to pay five dollars for each wagon and its four yoke of oxen and driver, a bit for each odd man,[49] and a dime a head for loose cattle. But the ladies went over the bridge free of charge.

In the States, a great many people were no doubt enjoying many patriotic pleasures on that day. We, on the other hand, celebrated by traveling in sand and dust. At day's end, though, we had a great dance. Agnes and I went up on the hill overlooking camp and talked over old times. Then, we came down and danced until nearly one o'clock in the morning. It was a beautiful night, and the stars were shining brightly. We thought it suited us very well since there wasn't any better fun to be had.[50]

The next excitement that presented itself was several days later. We had been ascending hill after barren hill and descending the other side. Over and over and over, with no grass for the oxen, no wood to burn. It was very different from what we remembered from the other side of the Platte. We traveled over dreadful, sandy roads; our oxen had to pull and pull. Many mornings, they had not one bite of grass to eat and had to pull anyway.

Then, suddenly, there it was! Independence Rock! There were a great many names written on it—some in pine tar, some cut into the rock itself. Many of our company made their marks as well. The men were keen on leaving some sign. The children and I were keen to climb up on it. I may have been eighteen, but this young lady couldn't resist the temptation to scramble up and view the world from the very top. Then, when I came down, Sister and I got up our spirits and mounted two good saddle horses. Astride! Most unladylike. We galloped all around that big rock and back before Mother saw us. Oh, she shot those brown eyes at us and clucked her tongue. But when she pursed her lips in that *certain* disapproving way, we knew we'd getter stop.

SEEING THE ELEPHANT

In our minds, at least, it had done no harm. And it had certainly helped our morale.

There were two trading posts at the rock as well, offering goods to trail-worn travelers. But Pa said the prices they wanted for even simple goods were beyond reason. So we pushed on across the Sweetwater, just past Devil's Gate, and camped there.[51]

Some of the wagons left us here. They were Saints, as some called them, or Mormons heading for their land of Zion. Mother said she had known of some Mormons, back in the States. Some called them foolish; some called them mad. But one of Mother's own cousins had been befriended by them in a time of dire need. And this cousin had named her next son Moroni after their Archangel, even though she wasn't of their faith.[52] These who had traveled with our train had kept mostly to themselves all the trip and not mixed with the rest of us, so it was not a hardship to have them go.

Yet, everyone's tempers were growing short. Quarrels among the leaders were more commonplace now, though there had only been three of any account since we left St. Joseph. The way grew more treacherous. We were all feeling the strain.

Even the ground conspired against us. The slow-going sands grew ever heavier, and the alkali lay thick upon them in a crust. In some places, the ground was like a sponge, heaving up and down when we passed over it. Then the alkali turned to dust. Oxen struggled and died. Nine or ten at a time, that was common. There was hardly a spear of grass, almost as little sage, and no water.[53] Sometimes we even had to travel at night. Oh *this* was going to Oregon!

Packers from California crossed our trail just on the edge of Oregon Country,[54] heading north and east. They had started from Sacramento City, they said, on the 7th of June—more than a month before. They looked very rough and weather-beaten to me. I don't believe even one of them had had his beard shaved since he left home.[55] But they were interesting to listen to, with their tales of gold and wealth just waiting. After they had gone their way, California was suddenly on the lips of many in our train.

We traveled all night by the light of the moon before reaching the Green River ferry. The hills were dreadfully slick going down, so we had to lock both wheels and the men used ropes to slow us.[56] Fortunately, all arrived safely . . . only to be "held up" to the tune of six dollars per horse and seventy-five cents per head of cattle for the ferry. We decided to swim ours across, instead.[57] And nobody followed us this time to steal back payment, as happened early on with the Indians.

Later, though, in the Bear River Valley,[58] we did run into some Indians whose looks gave us the shivers. They were the filthiest creatures I ever saw. Their clothes were horribly dirty. They would pick the lice out of their heads and eat them! We stayed not far from their village all morning and washed our clothes. Then, when we were ready to cross their little bridge, they wanted to charge fifty cents per wagon and something more for the cattle to cross. We turned and went out of our way a little, thereby avoiding that cost as well.[59]

Before we completely departed the country, however, these same Indians offered Frederick eighteen dollars for one of his oxen that was giving out. He didn't sell.

I think we were all starting to give out by then. Then novelty of wagon travel had certainly worn off: the same diet, the same clothing, the same routine day after day. We were tired. *I* was tired. We passed the grave of one Diana Stephenson, whose name was still distinct on her wooden headboard,[60] and I wondered to myself how many unmarked graves must we have gone by, unaware. I pitied all those souls who did truly give out before reaching their destinations. What a sorrow it must have been to come this far, to have sacrificed this much, then have it all end . . . for naught.

We camped at the Soda Springs to give our cattle rest. Our guidebook had given quite a description of the springs themselves, and I wanted to see them. I walked ahead some distance but never found the great spring the book spoke about. There were several smaller ones, which were interesting, but I was, in truth, disappointed. Afterward, we traveled on till we reached the Steam Boat Spring. I don't know why they ever gave it that name, as it looked to me more like a great caldron, boiling as it rises. We camped nearby that night, and I went to see it three times. It seemed much warmer after nightfall than in the daytime.[61]

Two days later, our wagon train divided. Some went to California via what they were calling the California Trail. The remainder of us continued toward the Willamette Valley on the Oregon Trail, as we had done since St. Joseph. The jumping-off place where the two ways separated was plainly evident. We had heard rumors there would be a signpost saying *Oregon*

SEEING THE ELEPHANT

pointing in one direction and a plain arrow pointing the other way, to California. Below that arrow would be a bucket of rocks, painted gold. It was said, *Those who can read, go to Oregon.* Of course, the Californians didn't think that was the least bit funny.

We never saw any such signposts.

We simply waved them all fare thee well, and urged our oxen onward. Onward, onward. *This* was going to Oregon!

SUMMARY

Here the diary of Helen Stewart ends. She made a notation in her journal some time later about those emigrants who continued on to the Willamette Valley: "Some, hearing of a shorter route through the hills and Cascade Mountains, decided to take that road. This road finally ended in a cattle trail, and they had to make a road to go farther. Their cattle were worn out and their provisions were almost gone. One of their number went ahead to get assistance and was nearly given out and starved when he arrived at the settlement which is now Lowell [Oregon]. . . ." (undated entry at the end of the journal).

The character of the Oregon Trail experience was changing, and changing fast. Helen described her journey more than once as dull, with only a few high points. Emigrants were so numbed to the ever-present graves of the Trail dead—even to the sight of scattered, disinterred skulls and bones—that Helen simply said, *We turned our faces and pushed on* (see note 18).

Severed heads of dead bison (slaughtered for their meat and hides) littered the route, as did the rotting carcasses of played-out oxen and other livestock. In one flood crossing alone, Stewart recorded that twenty-five thousand sheep—from a single herd—perished! The stench of decay was pervasive . . . and so commonplace, it barely merited mention.

The dangers of the Trail were counted as only three: "Indians, river crossings, [and] finding enough game so we wouldn't starve."[62]

By this time, certain tribes were charging emigrants money to cross the rivers by bridge or ferry. Others routinely traded, or swapped, with the travelers as they crossed their tribal lands. Still others—their traditional resources cut off, run off, or decimated by a decade of emigrant mass passage—had taken to outright begging or stealing. Though statistics tell us now that emigrants were nearly ten times more likely to die from physical accident than from tribal attack on the Oregon Trail, the fact is they were still convinced Indians were the Number One threat to their lives while traveling.

(Most Hollywood-type depictions of wagon train attacks never happened. Tribal people in need of foodstuffs and supplies knew that the trade routes—rather than the emigrant routes—were more fruitful targets. Were emigrants killed by Indians? Yes. Were Indians killed by emigrants? Yes. Were there terrible massacres on both sides of the ethnic and cultural fence? Yes, some. But the worst Indian fears of the great majority of emigrants never came to pass.)

The U.S. Secretary of the Interior, in making his official report for 1851, stated,

> It cannot be denied that most of the depredations committed by the Indians on our frontiers are the offspring of dire necessity. The advance of our population compels them to relinquish their fertile lands, and seek refuge in sterile regions which furnish neither corn nor game. Impelled by hunger, they seize the horses, mules, and cattle of the pioneers . . . [for which] they are immediately pursued and, when overtaken, severely punished. This creates a feeling of revenge and wrong among them [and] the whole country then becomes excited, and . . . a sacrifice of blood and treasure ensues.[63]

That being said, forts along the Trail that had originally been established as trading centers and political anchors now began to increase their contingents of soldiers to protect American citizens en route to Oregon and California and the settlers who had become permanent residents.

Traditional blood feuds and rivalries between various tribes were now being subjected to treaties to keep the peace. The Fort Laramie Treaty of 1851, for instance, mandated seven mountain and prairie tribes to cease warring with one another (as they had done as far back as there was tribal memory) and to keep good will toward the white emigrants pouring through their country. In effect, this treaty was for a peaceable travel-corridor easement across what the U.S. Government still recognized as

Indian ground. In return, tribal members received a dollar a year, apiece, in goods and animals.

The great Wagon Road itself now had established offshoots: to California, to the Great Salt Lake, and other destinations. The difference between the Oregon Trail of the early 1840s and the Oregon Trail of the mid-1850s was like the difference between a foot path and a freeway.

Helen Stewart, herself, never made it to the Willamette Valley. Her family got as far as the Lone Pine Valley in northeastern Oregon before deciding to settle. Though by 1853 there was no longer the signature Lone Pine, there was wild grass growing as high as a man's waist, fertile farm ground, plentiful water, and an abundance of wild game. The tribal people of the region were, for the most part, helpful and friendly. The Stewarts decided this was the end of their Oregon Trail journey, and they put down roots. Their descendants live there still.

LET'S INTERPRET

Discussion 1

"Besides, I had grown homesick for our old home in Pennsylvania, where I had spent the happiest days of my life. I missed the neighborhood parties, the congregating with my friends, and the prospect of playing croquet under the big shade trees in summer."[64]
—HELEN STEWART, April 6, 1853

"Ah, the tears that fell upon these garments, fashioned with trembling fingers by the flaring light of tallow candles; the heartaches that were stitched and knitted and woven into them through the brief winter afternoons, as relatives that were left behind and friends of a lifetime dropped in to lend a hand in the awesome undertaking of getting ready for a journey that promised no return."[65]
—CATHERINE SCOTT (COBURN), recalling 1852.

From what we read in the journals, women seem to express more heartache at leaving their homes for Oregon Country—and more homesickness once on the Trail—than men. Why do you suppose this is true? Were men more likely than women to take big risks (like uprooting from one place, and traveling two thousand miles to a new place they'd never seen)? Why? Keep in mind the socially accepted roles for men and women in those days. How might those roles have affected how each gender could have felt about making the move?

Discussion 2

"Everyone is in bed but Agnes and I, and we would be, too, but being the oldest we have to wait until the apples are stewed enough. The [night] watchers are walking about [the camp] to see if everything is all right."[66]
—HELEN STEWART, May 2, 1853

"It has been raining all forenoon, but has cleared up now and the boys are having game of ball, and have had a fine game of leap frog, a game of which I have often heard, but have never seen before. I really never was so excited in my life!"[67]
—HELEN STEWART, May 23, 1853

"When we laid by that day for nooning, Brother and five other boys went swimming in the creek. I wished I could too, but that was considered improper for young ladies especially in mixed company."[68]
—HELEN STEWART, June 9, 1853

Even though certain codes of socially accepted behavior were beginning to change for men and women by 1853, there were still very strict expectations as to what was proper for young ladies. Children to the age of nine or ten were far less constrained; boys, until the age of about fifteen, were also far freer than girls. Using this book's text, find examples of acceptable and unacceptable behavior for males. Now do the same for females. Why do you suppose these gender roles and behaviors were so strictly enforced? List any differences you may find between accepted behaviors on the Trail and those accepted back home or even at the end of the trail. Based on expectations of each gender, which would you rather have been in 1853 while traveling the Trail—a male, or a female? A child or a teenager?

Discussion 3

"We do not see as many Indians as we did, but we see plenty of Mexicans, which is a great deal worse."[69]
—HELEN STEWART, June 27, 1853

"Two or three squalid Mexicans, with their broad hats, and their vile faces overgrown with hair, were lounging about the bank of the river."[70]
—FRANCIS PARKMAN, recalling 1846

Why were Hispanic people (often called Spaniards or Mexicans in the journals) targeted for prejudice and disdain by the emigrants? Study political boundaries of the day. Were there territorial disputes around this time between the U.S. and Mexico that could have made emigrants feel that Hispanic people were the enemy? How do these views of Hispanic people compare to descriptions of Native Americans in the journals? Find other instances of prejudice in the text that are aimed at a group that is not tribal.

Discussion 4

"We pass Plum Creek. There [are] wagons standing in place of a grog shop, and they have two signs up."[71]
—HELEN STEWART, June 8, 1853

"There were two trading posts at [Independence Rock] as well, offering goods to trail-worn travelers, but . . . the prices they wanted for even simple goods were beyond reason."[72]
—HELEN STEWART, July 6, 1853

"The [whites] came, and they made little islands [of land] for us to live upon, and little islands [of land] for the four-leggeds, and always these islands became smaller and smaller, for around them surged the gnawing flood of the [white man] and it was dirty with lies and greed."[73]

—BLACK ELK, Sioux, recalling 1850s

The nature of trail travel was changing with the passing years. By 1853, there were supply stations and even grog shops along the way. If you were an emigrant, what might induce you to change your mind about going all the way to Oregon, and instead set up a supply stop for other emigrants? What sorts of supplies or services would you offer? If you offered supplies, how would you get them to your station? How would you set your prices? How would you support yourself during the months when few wagons passed (winter)?

NOTES

1. Helen Stewart, Diary of Crossing the Plains, 1853. Unpublished. Private collection of her family, by permission.

2. Ibid., April 6.

3. Ibid., April 29.

4. Ibid., April 6–28.

5. Margaret Comstock Dalton, A Lady from the Golden West. Unpublished. Private collection of her family, 21.

6. Stewart, May 1.

7. Dalton, A Lady from the Golden West, 1. Description of James Hervey Lemmon and his bride, Elizabeth, 1851. A daguerreotype was an early-day photograph made on chemically treated metal (also called a tintype) or on glass. This method supplied the first photographs that were available to common people. Even so, they were expensive. Only trained photographers in studios had the equipment and knowledge to make a daguerreotype. So, during this time period, people tended to reserve daguerreotypes for very special occasions.

8. A loud parade with kettles, horns, and all manner of noise makers, usually accompanying newlyweds to their new home. The custom comes from Europe in ancient times when the noise was thought to scare away evil and mischievous spirits from the new couple's

dwelling. This practice still goes on in some rural parts of America. Typically, the bride is pulled to her new home by the groom in a cart or pushed in a wheelbarrow.

9. Stewart, May 3. It is not clear from the context whether Stewart means "immigrant" (one who migrated from outside the U.S.) or "emigrant," another term for the pioneer who was traveling to the Oregon country within the borders of the United States.

10. Ibid., May 9.

11. Ibid., May 14.

12. Wagon travel averaged about two miles per hour.

13. Stewart, May 29. No explanation is given for why Stewart was so certain the owner of the pocket book had been shot. Unless there was a hole shot through the pocket book or the remnants of a ball still embedded in it (not recorded in Stewart's diary), there is no reason to believe the book could not simply have been lost or thrown away.

14. Ibid., May 17.

15. Dalton, A Lady from the Golden West, 17.

16. Stewart, May 21.

17. Tuberculosis of the lungs, characterized by an unrelenting, fluid-filled cough. The

term was also used in this era as a general reference to many lung ailments.

18. Stewart, May 23. Most likely, these remains were dug up by animals. The pioneers often voiced opinions that Indians might unearth burials to steal clothing, but there is little evidence to support this.

19. Ibid., May 29.

20. Ibid., May 28.

21. Ibid., June 10.

22. Ibid., June 11.

23. Ibid., May 31.

24. Ibid., June 11.

25. Ibid., May 28.

26. Pronounced "CAR-nee" in present-day Nebraska.

27. Stewart, May 31. The notation for number of wagons appears in different handwriting than Stewart's. It is not known when—or by whom—the notation was made.

28. Ibid., June 1.

29. Meaning newer, stronger animals.

30. Stewart, June 5.

31. Ibid., June 8.

32. Ibid., June 9.

33. Ibid.

34. Ibid., June 10. Gallinippers are large mosquitoes or other insects that deliver a painful bite. This term was also sometimes used as period slang to mean disturbing thoughts.

35. Stewart, June 15.

36. Ibid., June 16.

37. Ibid.

38. Ibid., June 17.

39. Ibid.

40. Ibid., 22.

41. Dalton, A Lady from the Golden West, 37. "Fox and Geese" is a running/tag game with boundaries trampled out in the snow.

42. Stewart, June 22.

43. Ibid., June 23.

44. Ibid.

45. Brave was a term commonly used by nontribal people in this era for an adult Indian man, more specifically one perceived by the pioneers to be a warrior.

46. Stewart, June 23.

47. Ibid., June 25. Lode stone is a strongly magnetic variety of the mineral magnetite; here, the term is used to mean something (some*one*) inexplicably attractive.

48. Stewart, July 3–4. Stewart's term was "squaws."

49. A "bit" was 12½ cents. Two bits equaled 25 cents; four bits, 50 cents; six bits, 75 cents.

50. Stewart, July 3–4.

51. Ibid., July 6.

52. Dalton, A Lady from the Golden West, 3. The child's name was Maroni Lemmon.

53. Stewart, July 9.

54. Ibid. From Stewart's journal notations, she seems to be near the Green River in present-day Wyoming.

55. Ibid., July 11.

56. Ibid., July 17. Though wagons were outfitted with friction brakes, it was often additionally necessary for men to attach long ropes to the backs of the wagon and keep those ropes taut by using their own bodies as drags and braces to slow the wagon's momentum. Oxen cannot set their back legs as mules and horses can, so they were not as much help in helping slow the wagons on a decline.

57. Ibid., July 17.

58. There is a Bear Valley in current-day Utah, also one in Idaho. This reference seems to be referring to the one in Utah.

59. Stewart, July 24.

60. Ibid., July 27.

61. Ibid., July 31.

62. Stewart, June 8.

63. Report from the U.S. Secretary of the Interior to the President, 1851, as cited in Jackson's *A Century of Dishonor*, 74.

64. Stewart, April 6.

65. Kenneth L. Holmes and David C. Duniway, eds., *Covered Wagon Women: Diaries and Letters from the Western Trails, 1840–1890*, Vol. V. (Spokane, WA: The Arthur H. Clark Comapny, 1991), 27.

66. Stewart, May 2.

67. Ibid., May 23.

68. Ibid., June 9.

69. Ibid., June 27.

70. Francis Parkman, (E. N. Feltskog, ed.) *The Oregon Trail* (1872; reprint, Lincoln, NE: Bison Books, 1994), 328.

71. Stewart, June 8.

72. Ibid., July 6.

73. T. C. McLuhan, *Touch the Earth* (San Francisco, CA: Promontory Press, 1970), 53.

SEEING THE ELEPHANT

FINCELIUS G. BURNETT
Army Indian Fighter on the Overland Trail

1865

I WAS DIFFERENT than most. I had no intention of breaking sod or
building a homestead. I was a soldier. An Indian fighter. I traveled the
Trail for adventure. And I ended up getting more than I bargained for.

Guess you could say I was a second-generation Trail traveler. Two of
Mother's brothers, George and William, decided they'd emigrate out to
California by way of the Overland Trail in the early 1850s, when I was just
a tad.[1] They took Mother's cousin and several other men with them. It was
a large wagon train they joined, with an average of six to seven yoke of oxen
on each wagon. Some had cows and oxen both, as the cows were broken to
work, too.[2]

Uncle George and Uncle William started out from our house on Fourth
Street in Canton, Missouri, armed with muzzleloading rifles and pistols.
Their pistols were the first revolvers that there were. Uncle George was
one of the handsomest men I ever knew—tall and dark, like Mother's side
of the family. I thought he looked mighty dashing, all armed and ready for
California. I sure hated to see him go.[3]

But he said Missouri was getting too civilized for him. Oregon country
sounded too dull, filling up with homesteaders. *Sod busters.* The way he said
the term, you knew his opinion of that. Nope, California was for him; California was for those yet untamed.

Being just a boy, I couldn't see it. Why, wasn't there enough adventure right here on the Mississippi? I surely thought so.

My Uncle David had his own steamboat called the *Lucy Bertram*, which he ran up and down the river for the St. Louis and Keokuk Packet Line. Sometimes he'd let me come along. The *Lucy Bertram* hauled passengers, freight, meat goods—Uncle David carried it all. They always packed the bacon in sacks in those days; a certain number of pounds to each sack. It was stacked on the levee in tiers probably five sacks high, just tons and tons of it,[4] to be sold to folks outfitting to head west.

Uncle David's second clerk, Sam Clemens, used to count the sacks as the deck hands loaded them onto the boat. Then he'd count the barrels of lard as they'd come aboard. That's right, Samuel Clemens. Mr. Mark Twain, himself. Of course, that's before he was famous. I remember him being a rather spare-made man, quick-motioned, and spry. And in those days he was young. History made him out a river pilot, but I never knew him as such.[5] To me, he was just Uncle David's clerk.

Imagine my surprise when he went west himself and wrote all those books! Everybody started calling him by the steamboat order, Mark Twain, for that's how he signed his stories. My own life on the river was very similar to his character Huckleberry Finn. Why, I wouldn't be surprised if Twain didn't get part of that story from my own life![6] After all, Finn is what they called me, short for my baptismal name, Fincelius. And I never had much schooling, just off and on. I wasn't a good scholar. I only wanted to run off and play down by the levee. Doesn't that sound like Huck?

Maybe that's what led me to the West at last—always wanting to discover what's around that next bend in the river. I'd wager some of those pioneers felt the same, too. Don't you think they'd have to? How else could they just pull up stakes and head into the unknown, leaving everything familiar behind?

But my time was yet to come. I was still just a boy, wet behind the ears. I had all the adventure I could stand, having the Mississippi River for a front door. People from all over the country came and went on the river all the time, more every year who had their eyes set on the Far West. Most of them were common folks, but some were businessmen or gamblers, and some were even famous.

One time Miss Jenny Lind rode on my Uncle David's steamboat, and I

SEEING THE ELEPHANT

heard her sing. She was known as the Swedish Nightingale then, and every-one in the nation hummed or sang her melodies . . . even the pioneers. The *Lucy Bertram* was crowded with passengers, more than half of whom had gone to St. Louis to hear Miss Lind sing but had been unable to get seats, due to the smallness of the buildings.[7] Her concerts were always sold out, you know.

They did everything they could, these passengers, to get Miss Lind to sing for them on the boat—offering to pay her and everything—but her manager refused to let her do it.

Well, the deck hands were all negroes[8] who normally sang while they worked at handling the freight for each landing. The first landing we made after St. Louis, these negroes—as usual—began to sing. Miss Lind was up walking on the hurricane deck of the steamboat at the time. It was a beauti-ful moon-lit night, and she appeared to be fascinated with the negro songs.[9]

As we proceeded up the river, she called down and asked them to sing for her again. Someone put the deck hands up to telling her they would sing for her if she would sing for them. So that's how it happened. After they had sung a number of songs for her, she complimented them. Then, as she stood near the railing on the hurricane roof, she sang what she said was her favorite song: Stephen Foster's "Way Down upon the Swanee River."[10]

I was sitting on old Nate's lap at the time. He belonged to Middleton Smoot, who lived on a fine estate about a mile south of Canton. At the end of Miss Lind's song, old Nate was crying. Big tears ran down his cheeks, and he kept murmuring, "Des lissen at dat, des lissen at that!"[11] Her singing was one of the most beautiful things I ever heard in my life, then or now.

Before and during the War—like many Missourians—we owned a fami-ly of negroes. Quite a few of those pioneers going to Oregon did, too. We used to see them, headed west, taking their slaves with them.

Uncle Ike and Aunt Stasia were great-grandmother and great-grandfa-ther to almost all of our family's slaves. Uncle Ike and Aunt Stasia had nursed Father and his brothers and sisters as far back as anybody could remember. Everybody knew them, and they were loved and respected by the whole community. Always in speaking of Mother or Father or any of our relations, they called them by their first names. They, in return, were always addressed by all our family as Uncle Ike and Aunt Stasia.[12] They were practically free.[13]

One night in 1861,[14] we received the *St. Louis Republican* newspaper. In it was printed the Emancipation Proclamation. Uncle David told me to go to Uncle Ike's quarters and have him come in. There was something he wanted to read to him. Now, Uncle Ike was a stately old gentleman. He always dressed in broadcloth and wore a silk plug hat. On this night, he came into the house as usual, with his hat under his arm. Uncle David read the Proclamation aloud. Uncle Ike listened attentively until the end, then jumped out of his chair, very indignant.[15]

"Davey, what damn nonsense is dese white folks up to now? Tryin' to set a lot of lazy negroes free? It's foolishness! Here is one negro they are not gwine to set free, and that is your Uncle Isaac, is dey?"[16]

Uncle Ike was always very indignant when you talked to him of being freed. Until the time of his death, he never admitted that he was a free negro. He was one colored man the Emancipation Proclamation never affected.[17] After Uncle Ike became too old to work, Uncle David took him and Aunt Stasia to his home in Canton and took care of them until they died.[18]

You might say that the Methodist Church—North Methodist and South Methodist—was the cause of the Civil War, the War Between the States. Any day, you could hear a Northern Methodist preacher telling you he could prove that slavery was the greatest sin against everything . . . and then the Southern Methodist preacher would preach that he could prove to you by the Bible and the Scriptures that slavery was an institution that was favored by the Almighty.[19]

When I was old enough, Father allowed me to enlist in the Monticello Grays, a regiment raised in Lewis County, Missouri, as part of the Southern Army.[20] We got into a scrape with a regiment of German soldiers[21] from the North and ended up killing some. When an Illinois regiment of infantry came down to investigate the battle, we expected they'd burn our town up and destroy everything.[22]

Instead, the Colonel told his soldiers to leave the town be. But he conscripted all of us fellows into the Union Army! Enlisted us right then and there. Well, I wasn't about to turn fire on my own friends and relations by fighting as a Union soldier. No sir! I deserted as soon as I was able. So did my friend, Joe. So did everyone else who was conscripted that day. We all simply deserted. I just jumped out of the frying pan into the fire, though, for that's when I made up my mind to head out West.[23] It was January, 1865.

Father and the father of my friend Joe rigged up a team. They gave us two boys an outfit of wagon and farm implements: a plow, rake and harrow, and such. Then they let it be known around town that we were going up into Iowa to farm. There were miles and miles of land then in Iowa to settle and homestead. Saying that's what we aimed to do was the only way a man of military age could get out of the state, you see. Joe was eighteen or nineteen at the time. I was twenty.[24]

We had no trouble until we arrived in Davis County, Iowa, where it rained until the roads became so muddy, the horses couldn't pull the wagon. We couldn't use a wagon if we couldn't move it, so we sold it—with the farm implements—and bought saddles with the proceeds. We started across the state on horseback, avoiding towns and sleeping out on the prairies. We were deserters, after all. We had nothing to eat for a long time,[25] for my pistol couldn't seem to bring anything down no matter how deliberate my aim. Not even a prairie chicken.

Finally, one night we saw the lights of a lone house in the darkness. I said to Joe, *Let's go there and see if we can get something to eat.* When we rode up to the house, we found a widow lady living there. She had two sons in the Union Army, she said, and her husband had been killed.[26]

We asked her if we could have food for ourselves and some feed for our horses. She evidently suspicioned that we were refugees on the run, for she asked me—real careful—where we were from. I told her we were from Missouri and then broke down and told her the whole truth. And for some reason, she took pity on us. She kept us overnight and fed our horses and gave us breakfast in the morning. Then she filled our pockets full of cornbread and meat and sent us on the road. She was a good-hearted old woman.[27] We never even knew her name.

Joe and I lived on what she had given us until we got to Council Bluffs on the Oregon Trail. We had no more trouble then and got across the river to Omaha. At that time, Omaha was a place of about 10,000 steady population, with a floating population of at least 5,000 men looking for work; men who—like us—wanted to come out West but still had to raise the funds. There, we sold our horses for seven hundred dollars.[28] That seemed a fortune to us but not enough to outfit a wagon and head out on the Trail.

I thought maybe I'd raise some extra cash by selling my Smith & Wes-son. This was the same twenty-two caliber pistol which I had attempted to shoot at prairie chickens and coyotes and game on our way. I wondered why in the dickens it was that I never could hit anything. I would shoot and shoot and never hit a darned thing. So there, in Omaha, I began to clean my pistol before trying to sell it off. And I found every gol blamed[29] ball that I had tried to fire jammed in that pistol barrel. It was just plugged chock full of lead![30] No wonder we went hungry!

We put up at the Farnum House, which was said to be the best hotel in town. There I met an old friend of mine, Kemp Caldwell. He roomed with me and three other boys there at the Farnum. Room and board was $21 per week.[31]

I told Mrs. Farnum I wanted to go west. I asked her to have her husband do his best to get employment for us so we could afford to go. Not long after, Mr. Farnum told us of the Powder River Army Expedition of Indian fighters. He said a Mr. Leighton was sutler for the outfit, and he promised he would do his best to get us a job with him.[32]

That's just how it happened. When Leighton asked me what I knew about mules, I told him I had had my heels kicked bloody and raw many a time, trying to break them. Besides, I was a Missourian.[33] Nobody knew mules like Missourians. He hired me straightaway.

We didn't go very far into Iowa to get the mules we needed, as the farther east we got, the scarcer the mules became. The government had bought all of them up, you see, for the War.

But we managed to get what Leighton wanted: thirteen four-mule teams, six dozen in all. They were all young mules. Only one span was over three years old. They cost us an average of five hundred dollars a span. Then we had them shod and all rigged up with harnesses and the like. That cost us $5.00 a span, at $2.50 an animal.[34]

On the first day of March, 1865, Kemp and I left Omaha with Leighton for the Powder River Army Expedition, for the West. Joe got cold feet and stayed behind. I never saw or heard about him again.

We followed the Mormon Trail, stopping at Fremont and Columbus, which were both just little villages with a store, blacksmith shop, and barns. Then Loop Fork and Wood River. That was a settlement of Hollanders, the farthest farm west in Nebraska . . . or anywhere, until you reached

Utah. We hit the crossing of the South Platte near old Fort Kearny nine days out of Omaha. There, we had to ford.[35]

Just as soon as it was light enough to see in the morning, we divided the fifteen teams into two teams. Then we hitched those mules onto two wagons, putting all fifteen men around them to drive them across. That's how we forded the river, time and time again. The Platte at this point was way over a mile wide, anywhere from six inches deep to way up under my arm, and had a bed of quicksand. We had to keep the teams moving, for the instant we'd stop, we'd feel the wagon go down. And if a mule stopped, he sank right up to his belly, and there he stuck. This happened several times. Then, one of us would have to sit on the mule and hold his head out of the water till others could pull him out and get him going. In the slush ice that was running in the river then, I can tell you that was no fun. And I had to do it two or three times.[36]

There were several islands in that river, and Mr. Leighton sat a case of whiskey on each one of them. He told us to drink it to keep warm as we worked. Of course, we were chilly and cold all the time, so we drank it down as if it were water. About nine o'clock at night, we got the last team across—it had taken us all day. I put on dry clothes and climbed up on my seat in the wagon, only to find I was in no condition to sit up anywhere! I crawled on top of the load, pulled the reins back of the seat, and laid on my stomach. I was drunk! That's the last thing I knew about until the next morning when I woke up in my bed.[37]

At Dobe Town, two miles west of Kearny, we rendezvoused with a wagon train loaded with supplies for the Powder River Expedition. Its wagon master was Bill Paxton.[38] He led us on the next leg of our journey to the West, what they called the Overland Trail.[39]

We had no trouble from there to Old Fort Laramie, except when the Indians would try to get the mules. We didn't lose a man. In all, there were thirty-six teams and thirty men in the train. My bed was a buffalo robe and two blankets. By doubling up with Kemp, we had two buffalo robes and four pairs of blankets. That made a good bed, anywhere we'd care to lay it.[40] Wages were $5.00, plus room and board. Of course, the "room" in that equation was the great outdoors.

On the 1st of April, a month after leaving Omaha, we arrived at Fort

Laramie. We had made a humming fast trip, which suited me just fine. I was able to spend my twenty-first birthday in relative comfort there at the fort.

While we were there, Indians brought two white women to the fort. Mrs. Larimer was one of whom you may have heard, for she wrote a book later about her life. These Indians, I was told, had murdered all the people of a certain wagon train some time ago, sparing only these two women. The women, they took prisoner. Now, at long last, they were returning them in exchange for a certain amount of money and a certain amount of horses. This was the result of an agreement negotiated with one of the fort's previous commanding generals.[41]

When the women were brought in, Fort Laramie was garrisoned by a part of the 11th Ohio Volunteers. The 2nd Colorado was also located there, plus the 2nd California Volunteers. When Mrs. Larimer and the other woman were finally safe within the fort's walls, they told what terrible treatment they had received at the hands of the Indians. They detailed the abuse and the horrible things that had happened. That's when the 2nd California and the 2nd Colorado men said the Indians should be hung instead of being paid. They attacked the guard house where the Indians were being housed for safety, and they threw a rope around one of the Indians. Little Thunder was his name. They tied him to the flag pole in the middle of the parade ground. Then, they got Mrs. Larimer to agree to scalp him. They gave her a knife, and she said she would, but her heart failed her when it came time to do the deed, and she couldn't go through with it. So they locked Little Thunder back into the guard house with the others.[42]

Then they telegraphed the general who had made this agreement with the Indians about returning the women and asked what he wanted them to do. I was standing in the telegraph office with a number of others, waiting for the general's reply. When the dispatch came, I read:

"Tomorrow morning, at nine o'clock, hang Little Thunder, Walks Under The Ground, and Two Face with fifth chains. After hanging twenty minutes, fire a volley of 20 pieces at them, and leave them hanging until further orders." That was the dispatch, word for word. I have never forgotten it.[43]

We left Laramie soon after, for Fort Sedgwick. That's where we were when the War Between the States ended. Peace was declared. But real peace didn't follow for a long time. We were at Julesberg on April 14 when Lincoln was assassinated.

We stayed in the area around Laramie until about the first of May. Then we were ordered to Platte Bridge. They said the Powder River Expedition would be organized from there and start across the country. We had an escort of the 11th Kansas under Colonel Moonlight.

Moonlight had a great reputation for making forced marches, and he drove us until we were all worn out. He even had us marching at night! In the middle of one night, after we'd all bedded down, the sentinel fired his gun. I had been sleeping soundly by a wagon and jerked up to peer towards the soldier's camp. I thought Indians were attacking. But what I saw was no Indian. It was a bear![44]

I could just see him on the skyline, and he was big. He had run out across the ridge, and when the sentinel had fired at him, it frightened the bear so much, he had run down through the camp and under the picket line. Of course, all the commotion stampeded the horses and threw the whole camp into an uproar. One fellow was sleeping outside on the ground—like me— and the bear ran over his bed! Stepped right in the middle of his stomach! He said he didn't think he was ever going to get his breath again![45]

From that same high ridge in the daylight, Indians seemed to delight in pretending that they were going to charge down upon us. We would fire at them with a 12# Howitzer brass piece,[46] and they would drop behind the hill. After the explosion, they would pop their heads up, and do it all over again. There wasn't a day that the Indians didn't skirmish us and make some show of attacking.[47]

But I can't say we were paralyzed with fear. Whenever events would settle down a little, we could usually find something to amuse ourselves. Five or six of us had never been to the mountains before, so we decided to climb above the falls on Garden Creek when we thought it was safe. We had a great sport rolling boulders down the mountainside, prying a big one loose, and sending it crashing down the mountain, tearing up trees in its path.[48] Who says a soldier's life is dull?

We quartered in Camp Dodge until early June. Our train was loaded with supplies for the different stage stations along the Overland Trail: as far west as Burnt Ranch on the Sweetwater River: one at Poison Spider, one on Horse Creek, and one at Independence Rock. When we were camped at the Rock, I looked over the names folks had scrawled on it, and there were hundreds. I couldn't believe my eyes when I discovered my uncles' names, George and William Asbury, painted there in pine tar! They had passed that way in 1852,[49] thirteen years before, en route to California.

Beyond Independence Rock, there was another station at Split Rock, one at Three Crossings, one at St. Mary's, and then the farthest station west that was guarded by the 11th Ohio Regiment, called Burnt Ranch. The Overland Trail from Platte Bridge to Burnt Ranch was well marked by the graves of the soldiers. Some had died of scurvy, but most had given their lives in protecting the emigrants. Originally they had been marked by piles of rocks and boards stuck in the ground, but by the time we arrived many had their rocks scattered, and their headboards were mostly decayed away.[50]

We started our Powder River Expedition on July 5, 1865, under the command of General Conner. Our division consisted of the 11th Ohio, the 2nd California, the 2nd Colorado Regiment, the 7th Iowa Battery, plus 90 Pawnee scouts, and 180 Winnebago Indians. Jim Bridger was chief of the scouts.[51]

Bridger was sixty-five years old that year. He stood about five feet ten inches tall, but a little stoop shouldered. He was a blood brother of the Crow Tribe, he said. His Crow name was *Kash-sha-peese*, which meant Fine Cloth. I asked him how he came by that name.

"I was one of the boys, when I was a young man among them," he told me. "They used to buy this broadcloth a yard wide or more, and they would take two widths of it to sew together. Then the women would bead them with a fancy strip with porcupine quills and beads right down the back. That was our dress-up blanket." The Crows thought a lot of Bridger, it was plain, and honored him as being a great chief and warrior.[52]

Our trail across the country left the Overland Trail and went north, following what they called then the Gold Trail, or the Bozeman Trail. We established a fort on Powder River, and I helped haul the first load of logs to build it. We put up some buildings and a stockade, and they called it Fort Conner.[53]

Frequently, small parties of Sioux would ride in our vicinity, especially when we were camped away from the fort. Our Pawnees would find them, though, and never allow them to get away. From the time we left the Platte River until we were ordered to cease hostilities, I'm sure no hostile Indian ever saw our camp and got away alive to tell about it.[54]

No fight of any consequence happened until we reached Tongue River, when our Pawnees reported a train of emigrant wagons ahead, surrounded by a body of Sioux. We couldn't go directly to the rescue of the train without letting the Indians know we were in the country, so we marched in secret down the Tongue, surrounding their village. At daylight, we commenced firing. Horses packed with buffalo robes and beaver skins and Indian paraphernalia of every kind went racing. The Pawnees—instead of fighting, as they had been ordered—commenced trying to catch these horses, so quite a few Sioux warriors escaped. Even so, we captured the village, most of their horses, and a number of their women and children. We burned all of their lodges and destroyed everything left in camp.[55]

Some of our men were wounded. The arrow points they used then were made of iron, you know. It was just ordinary iron, but when the point struck a spot, it would bend over and clinch down. They were awfully hard to extract from a wound. Our Indians taught us that when an arrow was embedded in flesh, we had to push it through instead of trying to pull it out. The points, or heads, were attached to the arrow with windings of sinew. Blood in the wound softened that sinew so much, it would pull back and leave the point, if the arrow was pulled. Always. So, instead, the Indians would break the feather off the end of the arrow and push it out at the nearest place. Most of them had great skill in doing this, missing vital organs, and the like. They said it was part of their war training.[56]

We had taken about twenty-five or thirty women and children prisoners. These, plus the horses, were taken back to our camp on the Tongue. The women were very sullen the next morning, and we couldn't get them to talk; not even to say a word. We found it impossible to get anything out of them about their people—even through our half-breed[57] French/Sioux interpreters. Finally, we told them they could go to the corral and select whatever horses belonged to them, and return to their people. Then they began to talk and laugh and tell everything about what the Sioux had been doing and planning in regards to the wagon train. They said they had had the train surrounded for two or three days, and if the Pawnees hadn't discovered them, everyone in the train would have been killed the next day. It was a big train, 30 or 40 wagons and probably 150 people.[58]

Just a few days later, our Pawnees located a Sioux village further up the Tongue. We thought it to be the main village of the tribe. We made ourselves ready for another fight. But on the night before our attack-day, two companies of the 6th Michigan came galloping into our camp. They had orders, they said, from Headquarters: "Close hostilities. Return to Fort Laramie."[59]

It took all of the commissioned officers to persuade General Conner not to disobey orders and attack the village. He was a red-haired Irishman, full of flash and temper, and they just had to beg and coax him not to go. They told him it would ruin his life. Conner felt—as I did—that if the order had only been delayed twenty-four hours, we could have ended the Sioux War. We were, after all, an army of veteran Indian fighters now; we were practically invincible. There were not enough Indians living to have defeated our expedition.[60] But the orders came when they did, and in the end, we obeyed.

We had no further trouble then, on our return trip, until we crossed the South Platte at Julesberg, on the Overland Trail. An emigrant train arrived, and they were put under our protection. We were told to take care of them until they were out of danger from the hostiles. We started on down the road with them till we got about four miles west of Alkali Station. Then we saw it, just ahead: two trains being attacked by Indians.[61]

The valley was broad. The trains stood about half a mile apart, ten wagons each. We sped ahead on our horses to help them. The Sioux were determined to drive us back, but we persisted. We finally managed to drive them away from the train that was camped just west, up the river. Most of the emigrants had escaped to the other train, but the Indians had set fire to this one anyway. First the grass around it, then the wagons themselves. We hurried down and succeeded in putting the fire out. Groceries and provisions were strewn all over the ground. The Sioux had scattered most of them over the prairie but had ripped the flour sacks open and emptied all of them out. There were white cones of flour everywhere. The flour sacks, they took for the cloth.[62]

The people from the other train came back up when it was safe. They told us the other wagons were loaded with corn in hundred-pound gunny sacks to supply the different government posts along the Trail. First, we unloaded their corn. Then we built breastworks around and under the remaining wagons. Inside the circle, we buried the dead. We built camp-fires over the seventeen graves, to obliterate all traces of them. Then, when we felt they would be safe enough in our absence, we rejoined our emigrant train and rode on.[63]

In less than three days, two companies of cavalry caught up to us and took over protection of the wagon trains. We were ordered back to Leaven-worth. We had no more trouble with the Indians after that.[64] I thought my adventures were over. But I was wrong.

About forty miles west of Marysville, Kansas, we were overtaken by a prairie fire. It was October, and the grass was dry. Flames raced as fast as the wind could push them on both sides of the road. The road itself was very broad, probably one hundred yards wide, so wagon trains could travel in two lines, side by side; made it easier to corral the animals between them and to protect themselves from the hostiles. Well, the width served us well. We lined up our wagons in the middle of the road and tied our mules securely to the wheels. Then, we lit the grass afire on each side and back-fired against the oncoming wall of fire.[65]

Soon the road was full of game: antelope, deer, wild turkeys, wolves, coy-otes, and every living thing of the prairie, all racing together down the road ahead of the fire. It was the most remarkable thing I ever saw. They came charging by us and didn't pay any attention to us or to one another at all. Their only thought was getting away from those flames. The prairie chick-ens and turkeys would fly as far as they could then light in the road and run.[66]

Those flames jumped thirty feet at a time in that tall prairie grass. The smoke was so dense and hot, we almost suffocated. And the sound! But our back-fire worked. The flames died down where they came together, and at last the smoke cleared up enough where we could go forward. Quite a way to end things up on my Powder River Army Expedition, I must say!

When I got to Leavenworth, my employer Mr. Leighton was waiting. My contract with him was up. When it came time to settle up my salary, I found he had credited me with not only my own time, but that of two other men who had deserted him on the Expedition, as well. I was grateful but I told him I had had enough of the Trail and enough of the West. I wanted to go home. He tried to persuade me not to go, said I wouldn't be satisfied living a civilized life. "You're wrong," I told him. "I've had enough of Indians. I never expect to cross the Missouri River again in my lifetime."[67]

Leighton just shook his head.

I made my way back to Canton on the Mississippi, and settled in with my family once again. I had a lot of tales to tell, all right, and a lot of catching up to do. But six weeks came and went . . . then two months. Everything seemed so quiet and dead in Canton. It got to where I couldn't resist the itch to get up and move on.[68] The Trail was calling.

So, I wired Leighton: *Need a good hand going West? See you in the spring of '66.* And I never returned to Missouri for another forty years.

SUMMARY

Finn Burnett went on to become a frontiersman and Indian fighter of note on the Far Western Frontier, participating in many major battles in what the U.S. Government termed the Indian Wars. His was an especially volatile era of transition for tribal peoples who were displaced by the ever-increasing onslaught of settlers and gold-seekers. Government policy was to protect the interests of American citizens.

Even before the Oregon Trail, tribal peoples were regularly displaced by the arrival of white settlers. From colonial times forward, civilized boundaries pushed westward from the Eastern seaboard, sending tribal people farther inland. In the early years of the Oregon Trail, this push translated into removal of indigenous peoples to smaller and smaller reaches of their traditional lands. Later, it resulted in separation from traditional tribal homelands onto strictly enforced (and oftentimes very distant) reservations. In some cases—especially in Finn Burnett's time through the late 1870s—it meant outright tribal extermination.

The lure of gold in what are today California, Oregon, Montana, Colorado, and the Dakotas; the desire to escape the issues of the Civil War (and later, its effects); the enactment of additional legislation granting more free land to homesteaders—all these inducements added legions to the throngs already headed west. And all deepened the deadly conflict between cultures.

Burnett saw and participated firsthand in this conflict. He spent most of his adult life fighting and killing Indians. Yet, in his later years he professed a deep respect for some. He particularly admired the Shoshone people and chose to live for some time on Wyoming's Wind River Reservation, teaching them how to farm. Not everyone believed that *the only good Indian is a dead Indian*, even in Burnett's tumultuous time.

Emigrants generally had contact with at least ten distinct groups of tribal people en route from Missouri to the Oregon Country.[69] Their first encounters were with those tribes they termed *civilized*, because they readily assumed the language and customs of the whites: the Fox, Sauk, Shawnee, and Potawatomi. The neighboring Oto, Missouri, and Winnebago tribes were also generally friendly, as were the Omaha, Quapaw, Osage, Ponca, and Kansa (called Caw and Kauza by Farnham).[70]

Upon reaching the Platte River Valley, emigrants regularly came in contact with the Pawnee, who were mainly agricultural and rarely fought with whites. Next were the Arapaho and Cheyenne who were—until the 1870s—known for their friendliness and desire to trade.[71] Beyond these, came the Plains tribes.

The Sioux (Nakota, Dakota, Lakota) were made up of fourteen main tribes. They were not welcoming to the tide of emigrants. Hostilities grew as the buffalo—central and essential to Sioux survival, both physical and cultural—were hunted by whites to near-extinction. Their homelands were overrun by emigrants and settlers. Their sacred places were ripped apart by gold seekers. The Sioux responded with no-holds-barred aggression.

Beyond the Plains, emigrants encountered what they often termed the Snake Indians. This included the Shoshone, the Bannock, the Ute (or Utahs), and the Paiute. As the wagon trains neared the Pacific Northwest and entered into Oregon Territory, diaries regularly mention the Nez Perce, the Cayuse, Umatilla, and Walla Walla tribes.

Then, along the Columbia River and into the Willamette Valley, the Teninos, Wascos, Klickitats, Chinooks, Calapooyas, Clackamas, Santiams, and Multnomahs. Many of these tribes had had white contact from the Pacific for many years. Still, they could not foretell the cataclysmic impact this massive influx of Oregon Trail settlers would have on their culture and, ultimately, their survival.

Discussion 1

"I just jumped out of the frying pan into the fire [when conscripted for service in the Union Army] . . . for that's when I made up my mind to head West."[72]

—FINN BURNETT, recalling 1865

"One day Green drove up . . . looking more serious than usual. . . . [He told my husband, Angus] 'I am for the South. If it comes to war. . . . in Oregon, we shall be on opposite sides. I am willing to shoot other Yankees, but I am going to fire over your head, Angus. I couldn't stain my hands with your blood. . . . . [My husband] extended his hand and said 'We have come to a parting of the ways, old friend.'"[73]

—NANCY JANE MCPHERSON, recalling 1865

"In the Cherokee country, where the contending [Union and Confederate] armies have moved to and fro [and] where their foraging parties have gone at will, sparing neither friend nor foe; where the disloyal Cherokees in the service of the rebel [Confederate] government were determined that no trace of the homesteads of their loyal [Union] brethren should remain for their return; and where the swindling cattle-thieves have made their ill-gotten gains for two years . . . the scene is one of utter desolation."[74]

—REPORT OF THE INDIAN BUREAU, 1865

The Civil War (also called the War Between the States) had some unexpected impacts on the emigrants who traveled the Oregon Trail. Some emigrants fled to Oregon to escape the fighting, yet those from the Northern states oftentimes found themselves at explosive odds with those from the Southern states. Sometimes individual wagon trains disbanded en route; sometimes they just split up at night into two separate camps. Some tribal people and some Blacks fought in the Civil War then found themselves displaced and excluded after the fighting stopped. What would your choices have been if you were a young man of soldiering age during the War? What would they have been if you were an emigrant traveling on a divided train? What reasons do you think compelled tribal people and Blacks to fight in the Civil War?

Discussion 2

"We didn't go very far into Iowa to get the mules we needed, but the farther east we got, the scarcer the mules became. The government had bought all of them up, you see, for the War."

. . . .

"The Overland Trail from Platte Bridge to Burnt Ranch was well marked by the graves of soldiers. Some had died of scurvy, but most had given their lives in protecting the emigrants."

. . . .

"Just a few days later, our Pawnees located a Sioux village further up the Tongue [River]. . . . We made ourselves ready for another fight. But on the night before our attack-day . . . [we got] orders. . . . 'Close hostilities. Return to Fort Laramie.' . . . [General] Conner felt . . . that if the order had been delayed 24 hours, we could have ended the Sioux war."[75]
—FINN BURNETT, recalling 1865

Many soldiers were pulled off the frontier during the Civil War to fight on the front lines. Suppose you are an emigrant, traveling within the 1861–1865 time frame. How do you think you would feel to discover that many soldiers, who had previously been posted along the Trail for your protection, were now absent? How do you think their absence would have been viewed by the tribal people? What was the Sioux War Burnett talked about? How did its timing fit with the timing of the Civil War? What is its connection with the Powder River Army Expedition that Burnett joined?

"These Indians . . . had murdered all the people of a certain wagon train some time ago, sparing only these two women [whom] they took captive. Now, at long last, they were returning them in exchange for a certain amount of money and a certain amount of horses."[76]
—FINN BURNETT, recalling 1865

"For four years, she lived among us [again, after being returned from captivity], but she was a grieving, unsatisfied woman, who shook one's belief in civilization. [We could never erase] the wild life from her heart."[77]
—SUSAN PARRISH, 1850

Many tribes regularly raided other tribal camps to take women as captives or slaves. This was accepted—even expected—behavior among some. Girls were usually made into slaves or workers for the capturing tribe but sometimes acted as substitutes for daughters that had died or were killed. Abducted young women were given or traded as mates. Some were eventually adopted into the tribe as full members. Boys and young men were almost never taken. How might this practice have been viewed by white emigrants? How did they react when white women were taken captive? Based this chapter's text, how did the white women react to being reunited with white people? How is this different from the woman described in the quotation by Susan Parrish? What might have contributed to this difference in reaction?

Discussion 4

"We started our Powder River Expedition on July 5, 1865. . . . Our division consisted of the 11th Ohio, the 2nd California, the 2nd Colorado Regiment, the 7th Iowa Battery, plus 90 Pawnee scouts and 180 Winnebago Indians."

.   .   .   .

"Frequently, small parties of Sioux would ride in our vicinity, especially when we were camped away from the fort. Our Pawnees would find them, though, and never allow them to get away. From the time we left the Platte River until we were ordered to cease hostilities, I'm sure no hostile Indian ever saw our camp, and got away alive to tell about it."[78]

—FINN BURNETT, recalling 1865

"I have heard that you intend to settle us on a reservation. I do not want to settle down in houses you would build for us. I love to roam over the wild prairie. There, I am happy and free. When [Indians] settle down, we grow pale and die. A long time ago, this land belonged to our fathers; but when I go up the river [now] I see camps of soldiers on its banks. These soldiers cut down my timber; they kill my buffalo; and when I see that, my heart feels like bursting."[79]

—WHITE BEAR, Kiowa, 1867

Why were the Pawnee and Winnebago fighting against the Sioux? Using this book's text for review, list additional tribes who historically befriended or helped white people during the Oregon Trail era. Now, using other historical sources and literature, list tribes or notable tribal leaders who have befriended white settlers since the establishment of Jamestown, Virginia, in 1607. (Begin with Powhatan and Pocahontas.) What was the effect of these friendships upon neighboring tribes? List known Indian wars with the whites. Were the causes of these wars similar, or were they different from those of the Oregon Trail era? What were the outcomes of these Indian Wars?

NOTES

1. F. G. Burnett, Life of F. G. Burnett: As dictated to his granddaughter, Verna in October, 1926. From the original account in the possession of his family, 1. Used by permission. Tad was a folk term, short for tadpole, indicating that the boy was quite young.

2. Ibid., 1–2.

3. Ibid.

4. Ibid., 3.

5. Ibid.

6. Ibid.

7. Ibid., 4.

8. Ibid. The Burnett family owned slaves. Burnett uses the term "negro," "colored," and the then-common "nigger" in his original account. "Negro" and "colored" will be used exclusively in this chapter. JBH

9. Ibid.

10. Ibid.

11. Ibid. Old Nate was a slave. Burnett attempted to record phonetically Old Nate's reaction: "Just listen at that, just listen at that!"

12. Ibid., 10.

Fincelius G. Burnett

13. Ibid., 9. Burnett's opinion. Treatment of individual slaves could vary substantially from owner to owner and from time period to time period. If Burnett's description of Uncle Ike and Aunt Stasia's positions within the family are accurate, the two slaves were far more fortunate than most.

14. Ibid., 10. In recalling this date, Burnett was mistaken. The Emancipation Proclamation was issued by President Lincoln in September 1862, and went into effect January 1, 1863. The proclamation, which freed Negroes held in slavery in the Confederate States, was subsequently confirmed by the thirteenth amendment to the Constitution. The thirteenth amendment freed slaves held anywhere in the geographic United States.

15. Ibid.

16. Ibid. Burnett cites Uncle Ike, himself, as using the term "nigger" in this quotation.

17. Ibid.

18. Ibid., 11.

19. Ibid.

20. At the beginning of the war, enlistment didn't automatically mean a soldier would be sent directly to the battle lines. Some were allowed to stay at home to safeguard their towns and farms until such time as they might be called up to fight at the front.

21. By this, he means they were of Americans of German extraction. He also refers to them as Dutchmen. They may have been what were termed Pennsylvania Dutch.

22. Burnett, The Life of Finn Burnett, 12.

23. Ibid., 13.

24. Ibid.

25. Ibid., 14.

26. Ibid., 15.

27. Ibid.

28. Ibid., 16.

29. "Gol blamed" was a typical expression of exasperation in this era, most commonly used by men. It was considered in polite society to be just one step away from swearing.

30. Ibid., The Life of Finn Burnett, 16.

31. Ibid.

32. Ibid., 16. A sutler in those days was a person who followed the Army with food,

liquor, etc., to sell to the soldiers.

33. Ibid., 17.

34. Ibid.

35. Ibid., 18.

36. Ibid.

37. Ibid., 19.

38. Ibid. William Paxton later became the founder of Paxton and Gallagher and was called *The Grand Old Man of Omaha*, one of the city's most noted men.

39. Another name for the Oregon Trail.

40. Burnett, The Life of Finn Burnett, 19.

41. Ibid., 20. The general who had negotiated the agreement is cited as General Mitchell. General Conner was in charge when the women were brought in.

42. Ibid.

43. Ibid., 21.

44. Ibid.

45. Ibid., 22.

46. Ibid. This would have been a howitzer cannon with a twelve-pound shell. Typically in the West, the Army used what it called Mountain Howitzers that, at 550 pounds, were lighter and more mobile than the traditional 1800 pound Field Howitzers. This meant they required fewer horses or mules to pull them. Sometime during this era, the mountain howitzers began to be mounted on what were called prairie carriages. Burnett doesn't mention whether the cannon he cited was wheel-mounted.

47. Ibid.

48. Ibid., 24.

49. Ibid., 25.

50. Ibid.

51. Ibid.

52. Ibid.

53. Ibid., 27. The name was changed several years later to Fort Reno when the War Department issued an order stating that no fort was to be named after a living soldier.

54. Ibid.

55. Ibid., 29.

56. Ibid., 30.

57. Ibid., 26. "Half-breed" was Burnett's term.

58. Ibid., 31. This is the last mention Bur-

nett makes of this incident. Whether the women and children were, indeed, permitted to take their horses and leave, is not known. Burnett does seem to indicate a great many of their horses remained with the Army: "Of the horses that we captured, several hundred head were used as remounts for the 11th Ohio Regiment."

59. Ibid., 32.

60. Ibid. Burnett's opinion was a common one. It wasn't until Custer was wiped out in 1876 that the Army began to acknowledge how severely it had underestimated the Sioux.

61. Ibid., 34–35.

62. Ibid., 36.

63. Ibid., 38.

64. Ibid., 39.

65. Ibid., 41.

66. Ibid.

67. Ibid., 42.

68. Ibid.

69. Jim Tompkins, "The Road to Oregon," USDI Bureau of Land Management, 45.

70. Ibid., 43.

71. Ibid.

72. Burnett, 13.

73. Lockley, 27–28.

74. Helen Hunt Jackson, *A Century of Dishonor* (Norman, OK: University of Oklahoma Press, 1995, originally published 1885), 289.

75. Burnett, 17, 25, 32.

76. Ibid., 20.

77. Glenda Riley, *Women and Indians on the Frontier, 1825–1915* (Albuquerque, NM: University of New Mexico Press, fifth printing, 1991), 21, 313.

78. Burnett, 26–28.

79. Russell Freedman, *Indian Chiefs* (New York: Scholastic, Inc., 1987), 37.

LUCY ALICE IDE
Trail's End—Thus We All Are Scattered

1878

ON MAY 2ND, I commenced my journey to the far, far west. The hardest thing of all was bidding farewell to our near and dear friends, many of whom I feared I was seeing for the last time on earth.[1] Some traveled with us for a few days, as far as our jump-off point. Others stayed behind at their gates, loading us with butter and cheese, baked goods, and little remembrances to take with us.

Everything was new and strange; we didn't get much sleep the first night we staked our tents. The next morning, it took us quite awhile to get our things together. It was a routine with which we would become *very* familiar in time, but in the beginning we were slow and awkward to the utmost degree. I wondered at the time whether we were making the right decision, whether we would ever be anything but a company of tenderfeet,[2] whether this and whether that; whether, whether, whether.

Blessed be they that expect nothing, for they shall surely receive it. That's my motto.

The day we crossed the Mississippi by ferry and passed through the city with our wagons, the people on the streets probably thought we were a circus, and we—the occupants of the wagons—its wild animals. We certainly didn't feel very tame, for it was cold and snowing.[3] The wind whipped us in every direction, making our painted wagon covers gap and dance.[4]

We camped on the city fairgrounds and made quite a spectacle. Some among our company, however, showed "the white feather" and went to one of the hotels for a warm supper and a soft bed. The rest of our camp remained in their respective tents to weather the storm. In the morning, we went to get some of the sweet cream butter which had been so kindly given to us, and we found it had been stolen by some dogs.[5]

"A bad beginning makes a good ending." That's what my husband said.

Maybe. But I couldn't help but think how delicious that butter would have tasted on the fresh dandelion greens I picked along our trail only a few days later! We were a week until proper baking and laundering could be done. Still, we were able to camp mostly on farm grounds and on the outskirts of little towns, where supplies were abundant. Local folk and peddlers came and visited us wherever we camped. We were, for the most part, quite comfortable and well contented.

Yet, at almost every farm house we passed, we found a shingle tacked up with this inscription on it: *This Farm For Sale*. After looking about, seeing nothing in every direction but a wide stretch of prairie as far as the eye could see—not a single hill, a tree or even a shrub, just dead level—we didn't wonder at their anxiety to sell.[6] Surely Oregon would be better than this!

As we traveled on, the weather became more unsteady. We still had hard frosts at night but often found ourselves axle-deep in mud during the day, owing to the incessant rain. Even so, we traveled upwards of twenty-five miles every day. Bogs, marshes, swollen streams . . . rain or no rain, we pushed forward. It was considerable work, but we had many hands to do it.[7] Everyone helped get us through: the men, the women, the boys and girls. Adversity proved to be the great leveler, for everyone—regardless of rank or station—pitched in.

I must admit, though, that the first time we got soaked clear through by the rain, I thought to myself, *Well, well, this is not so romantic after all*. And my thoughts strayed back to the comfortable home I left behind (in spite of my attempts to the contrary), then just as suddenly leapt forward. Was this a good move we were making? But echo answered not a word.[8]

Outside of Fort Dodge, the boys amused themselves by collecting coal which was located nearby. We thought to burn it in our stoves, you see. Burned biscuits were the result of that experiment! Faces were rather long that morning, as you can imagine. Then the rain once again leaked through the wagons, soaking everything. I was feeling pretty blue, too, until I found other wagons and other folks were in the same predicament. That cheered me right up. We stripped our wagons and dried things out as best we could.[9]

It had not been our plan to travel on the Sabbath, and for a while, we did not. We stopped here and there along the way to attend church services in the little towns, or a circuit rider would stop amongst us and deliver a sermon. Before long, though, the need for decent wood and grass dictated our spiritual disobedience. The motto *Still We Move On* became our reply to most every complaint.

I did try to hold the Sabbath regularly in my heart, if not in habit, and to be grateful for every blessing, large and small. Like the day I finally saw a hill again—I felt like running to it and kissing it[10]—and I praised the Almighty for this most welcomed relief. Or the days when we would pass through the towns and I could buy oats, codfish, pickles, and the like. Or the days I would find mustard greens free for the picking.[11] Sometimes the most homely of niceties were esteemed the most dear.

I will never forget the first mail delivery we received on the Trail. It was in Omaha, Nebraska. We had crossed the muddy Missouri River in box cars and went straight to the station where letters were waiting: one from Mother, one from Sister, several from friends. There were also a lot of newspapers from home. As we read them, it felt almost that we were back there on a visit. But all pleasant things must end, so all too soon we had to put our letters away and prepare for the next part of the journey. We bought supplies of woolen stocking yarn (at eighty cents per pound), oysters and lobsters,[12] flour, sugar, crackers, horse feed, and so on, then headed out five miles from town to camp for the night. Everyone had plenty to talk about, as all had received mail.[13] Family news was repeated, and repeated, and repeated again, while the newspapers made the rounds, with everyone trading. I hadn't realized how much I missed seeing the written word.

Several days later, just before North Bend on the Platte, we lost some of our company to the rails. One of the Hunter brothers had been bleeding at the lungs for some time, and it was thought best for him to go by rail car rather than wagon.[14] We agreed we would meet him in Cheyenne a month hence, when—hopefully—his health would be more recovered. How fortunate we were to have civilization readily at hand!

However, civilization had its drawbacks, too. Columbus was a large, dirty, foreign-looking town. Just in standing there a few minutes, waiting to buy supplies, I saw two men taken to the lockup;[15] I judged in glancing around that about 4/5 of the people I saw ought to go there as well.[16]

We were told by several of them that we shouldn't press on any further, on account of Indian trouble. But we didn't give that story credit. We were told that the hog cholera had run rampant in Columbus that season. That was a true story—our nostrils confirmed it. The loathsome stench from hundreds of carcasses lining the banks of the river assaulted our nostrils even in the city.[17] We hurried to finish our business before it began to rain again, then moved on.

By and large, we avoided the pitfalls of traveling from town to town. But one fine day, a certain man of our party was hunting rabbits on the outskirts of a little settlement, and he accidentally shot a farmer's steer in the leg. We thought he might have some trouble, all right, but were surprised when the Sheriff came into camp and arrested him. Off he went to jail. Well, as it turned out, the Sheriff was a brother to someone from back home. He became as cordial as could be with us. He even invited us to come see his jail and courthouse in town. This, we did, and posted the fine of $12.50 to bail our *hunter* out. That particular incident gave us considerable fun for a very long time![18]

One *needed* an amusement in the prairies of Nebraska. It was nothing but storm and thunder, thunder and storm. Often, we would have to chain our wagons together and wait out the fury without the benefit of supper, for we could not cook. Maybe we would have a bit of bread and dried beef to chew on, maybe nothing. But I can tell you many were the times we were so hungry, a piece of bacon between two pieces of bread actually tasted better than the best of cakes and pies at home.[19]

After one such storm, we discovered even the railroad tracks and bridges had been washed away. Where our wagons had stood just the day before, the water was ten feet deep! We counted twenty-five telegraph poles struck by lightning, as well as four horses—dead—that had been struck. I did not form a very good opinion of Nebraska, I can tell you.[20]

Yet, the storms brought one exciting thing: a stray pony belonging to Buffalo Bill Cody wandered into camp,[21] driven by the thunder and lightning. One man of our party was less than impressed. He said he had shot buffalo to feed the railroad crews, just as Buffalo Bill had. He poked fun at the *Bragging Blow Hard*, as he called him, for all the fanfare Bill later stirred up over that part of his illustrious past. This member of our train had run a Pony Express station, he said, when Bill had been a Pony Express rider. There must have been quite a lot of hard feeling lingering between the two men from those days,[22] as our gentleman refused even to go with us to return the horse.

Now, where once there used to be vast herds of buffalo, we saw vast herds of cattle in every direction. At one of the railheads, we were told there were 75,000 head of cattle driven there from Texas! And, in looking, we saw they were herded by Texans and Mexicans, each with a broad-brimmed hat, a couple of revolvers, and a Bowie knife that made them look quite formidable. Each also had a short-handled whip and a lasso twenty feet long, or more. These herders were a very rough class, that was plain. They shot at each other at the slightest provocation, especially after they had been paid and gotten liquored up. There was one shooting scrape while we were there, but thankfully, none of our men were involved.[23]

The plains were becoming quite settled. The National Homestead Act of 1862 made it possible to assume title to 160 acres of land after five years, when certain restrictions had been met. A dwelling of some kind had to be constructed, the land fenced, and a portion of it had to be plowed. They called that *proving up*. The homesteader had to actually live at the place a certain portion of the time, for the claim to meet requirements. He could prove up on a claim twice. After he had the first one for several years, then he could begin on a second one, and no taxes were collected during that time. It was quite an inducement for the uninitiated, I must say.[24]

Real estate agents ran advertisements in the Eastern papers, calling attention to this grand opportunity. Of course, they collected a sum of money from the prospective homesteader for putting him—or her—next to a favorable juncture of circumstances. They always failed to mention, however, that the unknowing homesteader had to have enough funds to sustain himself during the entire five years, as the land wouldn't pay anything and would hardly grow anything but grass during the required period. Yet, homestead shacks soon dotted the landscape.[25] There was scarcely any American Wilderness left anymore.

In Cheyenne, Wyoming Territory, we had a mail delivery. We all agreed it was a feast from friends at home. Here, again, we met Mr. Hunter, who had come ahead by rail for his health. Here we met his family who joined us with their wagons, and here we saw for the first time the snow-covered, ever-to-be-remembered Rocky Mountains.[26]

A week later, on July 2, we commenced our climb over them. As for giving a description of the beauty, grandeur, and wildness of these rugged mountain peaks, the deep canyons, and beautiful flowers, it is beyond my poor powers to describe. In fact, it was beyond description. Suffice it to say I felt repaid for all the hardships and boring landscapes we had come through so far.[27]

We camped on the top of a pass for dinner, where we found strawberries growing within an arm's length of lofty banks of snow. My husband said he thought these snow banks had doubtless been there for ages, as nearby canyons—many hundreds of feet deep—were filled full with snow. The snow was probably so hard, he said, that we could walk over them. The children, of course, didn't care to learn anything scientific. They immediately took to the snow banks for a rousing game of snowball.[28]

July 4 seemed very little like the Nation's birthday to us, although the cannon at Fort Laramie wakened us that morning, telling us that such was the case. Cannonade followed us to Fort Sunder, where we laid by to choose the best way to proceed. It was nightfall before we laid camp.[29] Plans for some sort of patriotic hoopla that night dissolved in the hard rain that overtook us. There would be no stirring recitations, no boisterous singing of "Yankee Doodle," no setting off of gunpowder, no dance. The storms sent us to bed straightaway, tired and hungry as usual.

The next morning, we drove down to the river and attempted to cross. Railroad ties were running like mad down the current. The river was full of them, washed in from the storm. It looked awfully dangerous, but we managed to get over.[30]

Our troubles were just beginning. The road on the other side was the worst road we had had in the whole trip thus far. It took five and six men to keep a wagon right side up, and things got considerably mixed before they got down the mountainside. We all walked, of course, to be safe. Safe! One of our party almost fell down an abandoned mine shaft as we walked, covered over as it was with overgrown bushes.

When we finally made our way to the river again, we had to pay 31 cents a team to cross at the toll bridge.[31] The water before us was swift and swollen from melting snows in the mountains. The men didn't want to tempt the danger. We paid.

But two days later, when we came to yet another toll bridge, they wanted to charge us 50 cents a team to cross it. The men took a vote and decided not to pay, even though the river was running like a torrent in that place. It didn't look good for us crossing on our own, particularly with the toll bridge owners in an ugly mood about us. But several members of our party went above the bridge a little ways and, with heavy poles, held the ties back while a team crossed, then let them go . . . then held the ties again until another team had crossed, and so on. Eventually, our entire train had forded the river safely—without paying 50 cents per team. We all joined in three hearty cheers at our own audacity and went on our way.[32]

After coming through Bridger's Pass, we came to yet another toll bridge. The usual rate was charged to cross it: 50 cents a team. But, after our men threatened to tear the bridge up and cross in the old ford the bridge had been built upon, they decided to let us pass at the rate of 10 cents per team. Over we went, victorious, and camped.[33]

On the other side, we found a tent pitched, with a family living there. They had ploughed up a little patch of ground and had vegetables growing: potatoes, peas, etc. I can assure you, we looked with wondering eyes upon that garden. It was the first of its kind we had seen for weeks and weeks.

These people told us there used to be a fort here and that it had been used also as a stage stop in the old days before railroads crossed the barren wilds. It had been called Sulphur Springs. Truly, it was rightly named. The water in the springs was pure sulphur. You could put your hands in, reach the bottom, and take out large pieces of the stuff. Sick and infirm people used to come from a great distance to take the waters—drink the water of the springs and to bathe—these people said. It had been a regular resort.

I was particularly interested in a little graveyard near the ruined fort. As I tried to make out the faded tombstones, I thought to myself, *Someone mourns their buried dead, likely never knowing where they rest in this lonely place among the Rockies.* Looking at what little remained of the fort and the tumbling tombstones, I thought I should like to be laid to rest nearer my friends, and much nearer civilization.[34]

The next day, we traveled all day . . . and all night. Fifty miles of it. It was the hardest trip we had yet experienced, and that was saying something! We came to Ritter Creek, a poison stream. We dared not stop or use the water ourselves, and we couldn't let the horses have it. We urged them on and on. It was a beautiful moonlit night, but no one could enjoy it. Our gloomy mountain road had high rocks standing guard through deep passes and over little valleys, but nothing could be seen but great beds of alkali. It gave us pause, I assure you.[35]

We stopped at twelve midnight to rest the weary horses and to eat. We gathered close around our little fire. Some were making tea; others were making oyster soup. Some were looking sad and lonely; some were making merry. It was a scene I knew I would remember, no matter how long and how far I traveled.[36]

Our horse Dolly had taken very lame. She could hardly hobble along, especially in the darkness. But she must. Poor thing, she *must*. This is what tried men's souls—and women's too—but thankfully, the next morning we reached fresh water and were able to lay by a day to rest.

Near us were camped a company of Princeton, New Jersey, college students. They were hunting minerals and fossils and petrified wood and just generally having a good time. They invited us down to see their collection, so I went. They seemed very nice, refined young men.[37] They had some intriguing samples of petrified woods and other specimens. They showed me the bones of animals that are now extinct. One gave me some specimens of petrified wood and a beautiful moss agate.

They related some of their adventures to us, and we, in turn, told them of some of our hardships. It seemed too strange to meet refined and cultivated people out here, hundreds of miles in this wilderness. Likely, we would never meet them again, but I shall always remember the day spent so pleasantly with them on Bitter Creek.

In the evening, the students came up to Henry Hunter's tent—it being the largest—and had a grand sing. They sang their old college songs, and we all joined in singing some of the Sankey and Moody's songs.[38] I thought it would probably never happen again that such a group of good singers would make the Rocky Mountains echo with music, hundreds of miles from any other human ear.[39]

We made noise of a slightly different variety when we discovered a cave large enough to hold 200 people! We carved our names upon its mammoth walls, beside the names of hundreds of others who had also "discovered" it.[40] The men and boys, especially, seemed to enjoy hooting and hallooing in the cave, testing whether the walls would bounce their exuberances back.

From there, we traveled over very rough roads—up and down and over mountains, through valleys, on and on—until at last, we came in sight of the railroad again. It looked like an old friend. We came through Devil's Teapot in high spirits, down to Green River.[41] It was the first town we had seen since coming from Laramie, 300 miles away, and our excitement was high. But the day closed in sadness.[42]

Only a short time before, two teams had joined our company from Utah: father, brother, husband, wife, and little boy. They were bound for Colorado, they said, to improve the wife's health. But as she came up the mountain, she began to fail, as she was scarcely able to breathe the thin air of those altitudes. We advised them to get her back home, if possible. Yet, they had pushed on to Green River, wanting to get supplies for the trip back. They had just unhitched their horses there when the lady began to die. She only breathed a few times and was gone.

They came to our wagon to tell us she was dead. She had had no lady friends traveling with her, so we told them to hitch up their teams and come over to us. We would do all we could for them.

It was heartrending. Her little child was only eight months old. It was afraid of us and would not let us hold it, so the father cared for it as nicely as a woman. Meanwhile, Lucinda and Mrs. Hunter and I washed and dressed the corpse. She had been a nice-looking lady in life, though very poor. She looked as though she had been sick a long time.

I went to her trunks and got out her clothes. She had everything arranged: suit after suit of under-clothing, and one suit beautifully made and folded by itself. It was almost, I thought as I fingered it, as if she meant it for this occasion. That thought so impressed me that I took it, and we put it on her.

The men went to town and bought a coffin. Then, when she was proper-

SEEING THE ELEPHANT

ly dressed and we had arranged her hair, they laid her gently in it. You can scarcely imagine how sad and odd we felt as we lay encamped by the river bank with this strange and lonesome lady lying dead, dressed for burial in a covered wagon only a few steps away.

Lucinda, Lena, Nellie, and I took turns sitting up by the wagon[43]—occasionally wetting her face so she would look natural—all through the night. We buried her the next morning in the little cemetery that lay at the base of the mountains, with the Green River rushing by in the distance.[44]

Ten days later, there was an eclipse of the sun,[45] matching our moods completely.

It was an ominous beginning to our passage through Devil's Gate. The scenery there was magnificent beyond description—throwing every other place we had passed into the shade. It was the wildest place a person could imagine, and then some. The Gate was one solid mass of rocks on one side towering hundreds of feet above us, and on the other side, a drop of hundreds of feet while the Weber River rushed madly over the great boulders in one seething mass of foam. You could scarcely hear yourself speak over the deafening rumble in the throat of this deep canyon.

The road was just wide enough for a wagon to get through, and barely that in some places. You can rest assured that we all walked while passing through the Gate. I, for one, kept just as near the middle of the road as I could. Even then, my head swam so much, I could scarcely walk.

It was only about half a mile through the Gate, I think, yet it seemed hours before we successfully made our passage. The scenes were grand, indeed, but terrifying.[46]

From there, we took the southern route, which put us into Ogden, Utah Territory. It was quite a pleasant place, entirely Mormon. There were beautiful fruit and shade trees in every yard and on every avenue. But oh, the dejected, degraded looking women![47] That was enough to condemn the Mormon Doctrine in my mind, leaving everything else out.[48]

They extended to us a cordial invitation to attend church at their Tabernacle on the Sabbath, but we declined.[49]

Instead, we pushed on to the little settlement of Corrine, what they call here a Gentile town. It was very dilapidated and poor-looking, typical for such towns throughout this Mormon country. The only thing to recommend it was the springs. Two springs, side by side, gushed out of the ground near Corrine. One was so hot, you couldn't bear to put your hand in it; the other was very, very cold. The water was very salty. We washed ourselves and our clothes in the spring and thought to travel on.[50]

But the local folks warned us about Indian trouble ahead. They said the Indians were burning dwellings, destroying property, and murdering people. Our men argued back and forth what we should do—go or stay. The train was divided. Some wanted to turn back and go to Ogden for safety. Others were in favor of going on. What was rumor? What was true? Finally they reached a decision: the train would move on.[51]

As it worked out, our most immediate trouble would come not from Indians but from a hotel owner in Marsh Basin. We had stopped for dinner, and some of our company went into town to have some tires set on their wagons. While they were there, the hotel landlord offered our girls $7.00 per week to stop and work for him! Seven dollars! Well, some of the older girls had quite a time making up their minds, but reasonable heads—those of their fathers—prevailed. In the end, none of them stayed behind.[52]

We traveled the stage roads as often as we could, which cut down on dust and assured us of receiving news at stage stops along the way. At some of the stops, we saw breastworks thrown up, protection ditches dug, and windows all boarded up. Indian trouble, the station keepers said. They'd robbed the stage many times and given the settlers no end of grief. A wagon train of soldiers—Indian fighters and scouts—was due there any day, that's what we were told. But still, we saw none.[53]

What we did see on King's Hill was an old freighter who seemed to be having some bad luck. Now, King's Hill was a pull about four miles long. This freighter had ten mules hitched to a trail wagon, and he couldn't make them go. He asked, as we passed, if our men couldn't help him drive them up to the top.

On the Trail, you tried to help your fellow travelers. So our men agreed. They tried and tried to get those mules pulling. But it was a fool's errand, indeed. They finally gave up the job, and we left the freighter swearing at those poor mules. We could still hear him swearing, long after he had faded from our sight.

At the top of the hill, we discovered a wagon that the old freighter had brought up previously. Some of the boys decided to explore the wagon's contents and found some cases of canned fruit in it. By the time we left the place, they had materially disfigured the Eighth Commandment.[54]

The next excitement I remember was pretty tame, by comparison. It was sitting in a real rocking chair outside Boise City. The ranch where we stopped was owned by Mr. J. W. Walling, who had crossed the Trail in 1847, he said, with a team of oxen and spares. He told us he had sold some of his oxen for beef to John C. Fremont's perishing soldiers and saved their lives. We were well-treated, indeed, and enjoyed the simple comforts of a real home. I can't tell you what a satisfaction it was to these trail-weary bones to settle into Mrs.Walling's prized rocking chair![55]

It was so pleasant there, we talked of staying. In Boise City, we could get considerable work: I, at a shop for $2.00 per day; and Chet, at $5.00 per day.[56] As we were out of money, this was a tempting situation. We decided not to go on. We pulled our wagons out of the train, and bid everyone goodbye. Crying, we left our Trail family.[57]

It wasn't long, however, until a representative of the train came after us. *You're not going to stop here*, he said. *Come along to the store and we'll help you get your supplies. You're going on with us.* When we rejoined our friends, they all rushed up and shook hands as though we had been gone weeks instead of about fifteen minutes. We bought our supplies with borrowed money, and moved on. It would have been pretty lonesome to have stopped, anyway, I told my husband.[58]

We crossed over the Snake River on the ferry (at $1.50 per team) and found ourselves at long last in the state of Oregon. The wind blew and the rain came down all night. I had to sit up with one of the men until nearly sunup, as he was sick with worms.[59] This was not the welcome into Oregon I had expected.

The autumn had arrived. It was only September, yet we could already see snow covering the mountain tops as we traveled. We all wore our wraps and were still cold. We built fires every night to keep warm. The men of the company worried we wouldn't make it over the Blue Mountains before they became impassable. They talked long into the night, after the campfire tales had been told, the stories recounted, and the songs had been sung. After the rest of us were huddled in our quilts and bedrolls, the men's tones grew serious, their faces grave. If there was this much snow here, they said, how much might there be up ahead?

They pushed us hard, to reach Walla Walla.

Aunt Sallie—who had never been strong—began to fail. We made her a bed in the wagon during the day and tried to make her comfortable. By night, we boiled clothes over the fire, wrung them out, and laid them on her lungs, which seemed to give her relief.[60] Still, the day came when she could not speak aloud. We didn't think she was long for this world.

Now and then we would see some lonely grave close by the roadside, and Aunt Sally's face would darken. She did not want to die in these wild mountains, with only the wind and wild creatures to bear witness. She hung on.

Even the best roads through the mountains were only trails. The one that confronted us could hardly be called even by *that* name. The markings along one side of the mountain showed us that we had the right route, but the trail itself was just one large boulder after another, with a slope so steep, all of us felt the wagons would surely turn over if we tried to pull them over. So the men got their heads together and came up with a plan.[61]

They found a long, straight tree and sawed it down. Then they lashed it under our wagon bed, with some branches sweeping the upper side of the road. All passengers, except the driver, walked . . . and Aunt Sally was carried. All of us with any weight swung to the upper part of the tree to keep the wagon from tipping over and going down the mountainside. That also seemed to help break the jarring of the wagon when it jolted from one big rock to another. Each wagon had to be taken over the trail in this same way. Despite all this care, the wheel on one wagon couldn't stand the strain, and some spokes cracked.[62]

When the ordeal was over and we reached the foot of the mountains on the other side, we stopped at a little cabin to repair the wheel and get Aunt Sallie a cup of tea. Though weak, she made it plain to us she was anxious to go on, so we pressed forward with all due speed. We bought apples and watermelons from the farmers en route and mashed these to a paste to feed her. Slowly, she began to improve. By the time we reached Walla Walla, she was able to be up and was feeling better. She even walked a bit, curious to see the white men there with Indian wives.[63]

One day more and her prayer that she might live to see her new home was answered. By nightfall on September 15, we entered Dayton, Washington Territory—the end of our Oregon Trail. Doctor Day, himself, gave us a hearty welcome then ordered beef and flour for us—a generous gesture as we were nearly out of all our provisions. We camped with our wagon train for the final time.[64]

This was the end of our trials and pleasures under the flapping canvas of an emigrant wagon. We intended to make Dayton our home, at least for some time. Others from our train decided to stop here for a while, others to go on to the Palouse country. Some still had far to travel, as they were headed to other parts of the Territory. It was a bittersweet encampment that last night together, full of reminiscences, laughter, and tears.

The sun came up in the morning as it had every morning since May the 2nd, and the wagons rolled out in different directions. Thus, we all were scattered.[65] Thus, life began again, anew.

SUMMARY

Lucy Ide's account of her family's travel across the Oregon Trail is especially important because it comes at the end of what scholars consider the Great Overland Migration. Ide's descriptions clearly show the changes that had taken place along the route. Towns—even cities—had been established and were thriving. Ide's original journal mentions thirty-five of them by name.

When members of her wagon train fell into difficulty, there were options for rescue just down the road, or across the campground: wheel smiths, doctors, hotel and mercantile owners. When feed or equipment was needed for the animals, a visit to the nearest resident farmer, supply store, or leather shop caused—at the most—a short delay.

Visitors were frequent to the train: local town residents, circuit riders, even a group of Princeton students, on a scientific holiday!

This certainly was not the emigrant experience of old. Rail lines along the route had been in use since 1869. Even the old stagecoach lines had been largely abandoned by this time for long-distance travel, and the Pony Express was a thing of the past. Mail call was regular, and newspapers kept the emigrants in touch with what was happening both back home and wherever they pulled in, in towns along the Trail.

By the time Ide's train crossed the plains, Custer's Last Stand (which more accurately could be called the Sioux's Last Stand, for the battle sealed their fate) was already three years in the past. In the Pacific Northwest, Nez

Perce Chief Joseph had already declared, *From where the sun now stands, I shall fight no more, forever.* The West, with the exception of a few, isolated pockets of futile resistance, was civilized.

Lucy Ide and her husband reached their destination in only four months without major incident. They eventually settled near Spokane, Washington, and founded a town of their own. They called it Mondovi after their old home town in Wisconsin.

The Oregon Trail continued to be used for emigrant travel throughout the rest of the nineteenth century, though fewer and fewer families traveled in organized wagon trains. More traveled in small groups or even as individuals. Often these journeys were in spurts or segments, with families moving from place to place. There are even records of isolated wagon passages being made over the Oregon Trail in the 1920s.

But, as our rural nation became more industrialized, family wagon travel gave way to travel by rail, then by automobile, and finally by airplane. Commerce and supply transport followed the same progression. When highways and freeways were paved across the nation, they often followed the same routes pounded into the earth by emigrant wagons.

Now, the ruts carved into the land by the Great Oregon Trail Migration have largely been grazed off, plowed under, or built upon. But the imprint the Trail has left upon us all remains indelible.

LET'S INTERPRET

Discussion 1

"We . . . cross the Ferry over the Mississippi River . . . [and] while [the train was] passing through Winona the people thought it was a circus and we occupants of the wagon the wild animals I guess for we do not feel very tame as it is very cold and snowing."[66]

— LUCY IDE, May 3, 1878

SEEING THE ELEPHANT

"One wagon just passing . . . with the motto, 'Root, little hog or die' . . . on both sides. . . . And on another cover is written, 'Bound for Origen.'"[67]
—E.W. CONYERS, May 25, 1852

"[Father bought] wagons . . . gorgeous in green and yellow paint, with stout canvas covers snugly adjusted over supple hickory bows."[68]
—CATHERINE SCOTT (Abigail's sister), recalling 1852

Purchased wagons were commonly factory-painted in bright colors. Farm wagons being outfitted for the Overland Journey sometimes also got a coat of paint. In addition to providing color, the paint helped seal the wood against the elements. It was also common practice for emigrants to paint slogans or designs of animals on the wagon canvases. What do you think is the meaning of *Root, little hog, or die*? What sorts of animal designs do you think might have been common for Oregon Trail travel? (Don't forget the title of this book and political symbols.) Suppose you are an emigrant. What designs or slogans would you decide to put on your wagon? Why? Now, think of the modern counterpart of placing slogans on wagons. In World War II, bomber planes commonly had what was called nose art. Where do you see slogans or designs on transportation vehicles today?

Discussion 2

"From here Cushman Hunter takes the [railroad] cars for Cheyenne[;] he was bleeding at the lungs and it was thought best for him to go by rail [rather than by wagon]."[69]
—LUCY IDE, May 30, 1878

"[This morning we] travelled over very rough roads up & down, over [mountains] through deep canyons on & on and at last we come in sight of the [railroad] again[. I]t looks like an old friend."[70]
—LUCY IDE, July 18, 1878

The transcontinental railroad had been completed in 1869. Since the mid-1870s, more and more people were using the rails as a viable passenger transportation system. What effect do you think this had on wagon train travel? Remember that shipping goods (that normally would have been hauled in a wagon) was still very expensive. What effect do you think the coming of railroads had on remaining buffalo herds in the Plains? On the tribal peoples? Why? What effect do you think a transcontinental railway had on end-of-the-trail towns and communities?

Discussion 3

"A few more passing suns will see us here no more, and our dust and bones will mingle with these same prairies. I see as in a vision the dying spark of our council fires, the ashes cold and white. I hear no longer the songs of the women as they prepare the meals. The antelope have gone, the buffalo wallows are empty. Only the wail of the coyote is heard. The white man's Medicine [power] is stronger than ours. His iron horse rushes over the buffalo trail. We are birds with a broken wing."[71]
—PLENTY COUPS, Crow, 1878

"The Government took the best warriors from the tribe, and made them lift their hands to God and swear that they would be true to the Government. They made out of these men, policemen who were to guard the Government and keep the [rest of] the Indians good. . . . [The Government] gave me implements with which to till the soil, and raise stock, and build a home, and it seemed to me I must obey every word they said. They told me that the wild game, now roaming the hills, would soon die off and that if I tilled the soil and raised stock and grain, I could get money for it; and money is what makes everything move along."[72]
—RUNS THE ENEMY, Crow, 1876

"A stray pony came along [which] proved to be Buffalo Bill [Cody]'s."[73]
—LUCY IDE, June 16, 1878

By this time, the traditional life of tribal peoples—even in the Far West—had been irrevocably changed, and in most cases, wiped out. All but a very few were now relegated to reservations. The *West of Old* was already being mythologized (and even parodied) in elaborate, traveling circus-type extravaganzas such as Buffalo Bill's Wild West Show. The packaging of the Overland Trail experience had begun. Suppose you are a tribal person and you had the opportunity to join Buffalo Bill's Wild West Show to re-enact wagon train attacks, massacres, etc. Would you do it? Why? Now, suppose you are a person whose parents (or even grandparents by this time) had traveled the Trail. You don't have any direct knowledge about the experience, only what you have been told. How likely would you be to believe that what you would see in Buffalo Bill's Wild West Show was true? How is this similar to or different from television today?

Discussion 4

"We cross the great muddy looking Missouri river in box transfer cars . . . and here we are at Omaha[. N]ow for our mail . . . the first news from home[.] I received letters . . . also lots of [news]papers . . . we bought oysters (a case) lobsters flour sugar crackers horsefeed & etc."[74]
      —LUCY IDE, May 28, 1878

"We have today seen vast herds of cattle such as I have read about but never expected to see[. A]s we pass through a town called Ogallala they tell us there is 75,000 head of cattle been driven in from Texas and I should not dispute it for the broad Prairie is one moving mass of cattle."[75]
      —LUCY IDE, June 19, 1878

"We stopped here and there along the way to attend church services in the little towns, or a circuit rider would stop amongst us and deliver a sermon. . . ."[76]
      —LUCY IDE, July 11, 1878

"Come to Marsh Basin . . . The [hotel] Landlord offered the girls 7 dollars a week to stop and work[. S]ome have quite a mind to stop, but after a time decide[d] to go on [with our train]."[77]
      —LUCY IDE, August 14, 1878

Lucy Alice Ide

"Went as far as McDowell's ranche & camp at noon . . . they killed a beef here & we bought some[. T]hey branded some cattle here the first we ever saw branded."[78]

—LUCY IDE, August 31, 1878

The Trail had certainly become civilized over the course of forty years! When supplies were needed, emigrants stopped in towns or at farmsteads along the way. Mail service was regular and reliable. Telegraph lines sped messages across the country in no time at all. In 1878, cattle were branded as a matter of course to identify legal ownership as there were so many of them. Railheads shipped people, goods, and livestock over long distances for the price of a ticket or a bill of lading. If you could choose the year you would prefer to have traveled the Oregon Trail—based on the chapter texts—which would you choose? Why? How do you think people one hundred fifty years from now will view us and our lives? What resources will they have available to them to research how we live? Do you think those resources will give them an accurate and complete understanding of who we are now, how we think, and what matters to us? Why, or why not? How complete is our understanding of the people of the Oregon Trail?

NOTES

1. Kenneth L. Holmes, ed., *Covered Wagon Women: Diaries and Letters from the Western Trails, 1840–1890*, Vol. 10 (Spokane, WA: The Arthur H. Clark Company, 1991), 61.

2. Folk term for someone new and/or untrained in the task at hand.

3. Holmes, 61, May 3.

4. It was common for wagon train canvases to be painted with slogans, names, figures of animals, etc.

5. Holmes, 62, May 3–4.

6. Ibid., 63, May 10.

7. Ibid., 63–64, May 15–16.

8. Ibid., 64, May 17.

9. Ibid., 64, May 18.

10. Ibid., 65, May 20.

11. Ibid., 65, May 24.

12. Most probably tinned or canned.

13. Holmes, 66, May 28.

14. By 1878, the railroad had become a popular and relatively common form of transportation in the West. In many places, it paralleled the Oregon Trail. It was still more expensive than wagon travel, however, so emigrants still often chose what they called the old-timey mode of transportation.

15. Jail.

16. Holmes, 67–68, June 1.

17. Ibid.

18. Ibid., 69, June 11–12.

19. Abigail Scott, letter to her grandfather dated July 18, 1852. Holmes and Duniway, 154.

20. Holmes, 70, June 14–15.

21. Ibid., 70–71, June 16–17.

22. Margaret Comstock Dalton, A Lady From The Golden West, unpublished. Private collection of her family, 5.

23. Holmes, 71–72, June 19.

24. Dalton, 20. The actual language of the Homestead Act granted the land "to any person who is head of a family or who has arrived at the age of twenty-one years, and is a citizen of the United States, or has filed intention to become a citizen." After January 1, 1863, one quarter section of land (160 acres) could be claimed, as long as it was in a legal subdivision of public land specifically opened for homesteading. The only stated fee was $10.00, to duly register the claim.

25. Ibid.

26. Holmes, 72, June 26.

27. Ibid., 73, July 3.

28. Ibid.

29. Ibid., 73–74, July 4.

30. Ibid., 74, July 5.

31. Ibid., 74, July 6.

32. Ibid., 75, July 8.

33. Ibid., 75–76, July 12.

34. Ibid.

35. Ibid., 76, July 13. "It gave us pause" means it gave them something to think about, something to consider or worry about. High concentrations of alkali poison the soil and water.

36. Ibid., 66, July 13.

37. In this age, it was very unusual for a woman to attend college.

38. The enormously popular and well-known evangelist team of Ira Sankey and Dwight Moody. They helped popularize evangelical hymns such as "Rock of Ages," "Onward, Christian Solders," "Whiter Than Snow," and "Jesus Loves Me."

39. Holmes, 76–77, July 14.

40. Ibid., 78, July 17.

41. Wyoming.

42. Holmes, 78–79, July 18.

43. It was customary for the corpse to be attended by friends and relatives round the clock until burial, to help keep evil or negative influences from gathering.

44. Holmes, 78–79, July 18–19.

45. Ibid., 81, July 29.

46. Ibid., 81, July 30.

47. Ibid., 81, August 3. Whether this description is objectively accurate or is a subjective interpretation by Ide, we cannot judge from the entry. It is important to note that in this era, opinions against Mormons were prevalent, particularly in regard to their practice of plural marriages, or polygamy. The Church of Jesus Christ of Latter Day Saints allowed polygamy until 1890.

48. Holmes, 82, August 3.

49. Ibid., 82, August 4.

50. Ibid., 82, August 6.

51. Ibid., 82, August 7.

52. Ibid., 83, August 14.

53. Ibid., 84–85, August 19–20.

54. Ibid., 85, August 21. The Eighth Commandment is *Thou shalt not steal.* (Hebrew Bible)

55. Ibid., 86, August 24.

56. Chet was a man. His wage would have typically been at least double what Mrs. Ide, a woman, could earn.

57. Holmes, 86, August 27.

58. Ibid.

59. Ibid., 87, September 2. Worms were a common complaint, usually the result of eating undercooked meat in which fly eggs had already been laid.

60. Ibid., 88, September 10.

61. Dalton, A Lady from the Golden West, 11.

62. Ibid.

63. Holmes, 88, September 13.

64. Ibid., 89, September 15.

65. Ibid.

66. Ibid., 61, May 3.

67. Sarah LeCompte, ed., *Westward Quotes from the National Historic Oregon Trail Interpretive Center at Flagstaff Hill* (Baker City: OR: Trail Tenders, Inc., 1997), 6.

68. Holmes and Duniway, 27.

69. Holmes, 67.

70. Ibid., 78.

71. Jos. K. Dixon, *The Vanishing Race*

Lucy Alice Ide

(1913; reprint, New York: Bonanza Books, 1975), 189.

72. Ibid., 68.
73. Holmes, 70.
74. Ibid., 66.
75. Ibid., 71.

76. Lucy Ide, July 11, 1878, letter to Mrs. N. K. Fisher, by permission of descendants of Lucy Ide.
77. Holmes, 83.
78. Ibid., 87.

SUMMARY

FIRST, there was the land. The route that became the Oregon Trail began as a series of simple wildlife trails across the landscape, following rivers and watering holes. Native people traveled on the heels of the animals, making the trails their own and establishing home territories around them. Next, came explorers, trappers, and traders—by shank's mare, on horseback, travois, and canoe. Missionaries followed. And the adventurers. The settlers. The Army.

Civilization, as defined by the Oregon Trail emigrants, arrived. In their own words, they opened up the West; liberated it from the tribal peoples who did nothing fruitful with the land. They claimed it as their own, swept it free of existing uses, and—certain they were elevating it to its highest purpose—rendered it to plowshare and homestead.

It is tempting to view the displaced and much-besieged tribal people as merely victims in this great process of multigenerational change. But it is unfair to relegate them to that completely helpless status. Many tried to adapt to the ever westward push of whites; some were successful for relatively long periods of time. Many signed treaties, agreeing to relocate. Some demanded—and got—payment in return for acquiescence. Others served as guides or translators for missionaries, emigrants, and soldiers.

The tribes were masters at adopting what worked, and adapting what didn't to fit—and sometimes redefine—their cultures. Some new goods introduced by the whites over the years—new technologies and products— were good and sought after. Even the horses upon which the tribes rode originally came from the loose stock of Spaniards in the 1500s.

But trying to adapt, without giving up tribal identity, land, and lifeways, was a losing battle.

George Washington was the first American President to suggest moving tribal people farther west, in order to avoid confrontation with "civilized society, which is expanding the known Frontier" (Limerick, 192). With each generation, that known frontier marched determinedly toward the Pacific Ocean and Rio Grande River, pushing the tribes before it. From the white perspective, there was plenty of unclaimed land for the tribes to populate. From the tribal perspective, this shove already caused problems, as more migrating Indians jockeyed for new homelands within already tribally populated areas.

This led to generations of bad blood among different tribal nations as more and more of them fought to keep their hunting territories and homelands from being overrun by other tribes. Long before the white man came, battles and wars among the tribes had been common. This geographic upheaval just succeeded in adding an extra layer of confusion and hostility to all involved.

President Andrew Jackson first implemented the official policy of Indian removal, setting a precedent that would grow to astonishing proportions during the Oregon Trail years. As Narcissa Whitman and her husband were setting up their mission in the Oregon Country, the Cherokee nation was being forced upon their Trail of Tears to Indian Territory. It was a trend that would only grow stronger.

With every acquisition of land mass to the United States, whether by purchase, by treaty, or the spoils of war, came increased impetus for (white) settlement. As citizens of a nation whose (Anglo, Christian) self-image stretched from sea to shining sea, is it any wonder the emigrants looked upon any who would question that image as obstinate, troublesome, and unworthy of consideration?

These views were not restricted solely to Native Americans. Irish, Africans, Hispanics, Orientals, mixed-bloods, Mormons, Jews. These and more came under the too-often bigoted judgments of the emigrants. Add to the list: women *of a certain sort* who worried the sensibilities of polite society, and men *of low class* whose morals missed their mark.

Were all emigrants this closed-minded and prejudiced? No. But many were. They were fallible human beings themselves, but by judging and classifying others harshly, they felt safer in keeping their own place among the civilized.

It is interesting to note the changes in such attitudes as the Oregon Trail matured. Some prejudices shifted; some softened or became silent altogether. Some became more firmly entrenched. All in all, the microsocieties of the wagon train accurately reflected what was going on in the nation as a whole.

Unfortunately, their very numbers ravaged the land over which they crossed. Vanished today are the earth-quaking herds of buffalo and waves of wild game. Vanished are the warming fires of the Story Keepers. Cities have grown up now where forts formerly stood; bridges cross the rivers, and railroads or freeways disguise the ruts.

But the land remembers. The legacy of the Trail has left its imprint upon us, just as surely as the emigrants left their imprint upon the land.

The story of the Oregon Trail is the story of the human spirit in uneasy partnership with the land. Scratch the surface and you will find—alongside the bigotry, short-sightedness, betrayal, and blind conceit—heroism, courage, self-sacrifice, and valor. You will find heartbreaking tragedy but also moments of compassion and joy.

Regardless of race, religious belief, culture, or gender, you will find the story of the Oregon Trail is an age-old story, echoing eternal truths.

And if you squint your eyes just right . . . you, too, will see the elephant.

Historical Photographs and Artifacts

The following photographs and artifacts, unless otherwise noted, are courtesy of the USDI, Bureau of Land Management National Historic Oregon Trail Interpretive Center, Baker City, Oregon.

ROUTE OF THE OREGON TRAIL

Oregon Territory

Wagon road guide book cover from San Francisco, 1858. Guide books became very popular among overland emigrants. Many were published. Unfortunately, some were compiled by misinformed or unscrupulous writers. These erroneous guide books often did more harm than good.

Above: Wagon with sail, *Frank Leslie's Illustrated Newspaper,* July 7, 1860. Perhaps finding inspiration in an idea recorded by Lewis and Clark forty years earlier, one man actually manufactured and advertised "Wind Wagons" as an alternative to the standard wagon and team.

Below: Map of John C. Fremont's expedition to the Rocky Mountains in 1942 and Oregon and California in 1843–44, published in 1845; compass and telescope, about 1850. Many guide books included detailed geographic maps, meteorological tables for telling time and predicting weather, and descriptions of what emigrants could expect from specific stretches of trail. Some were accurate. Some were not.

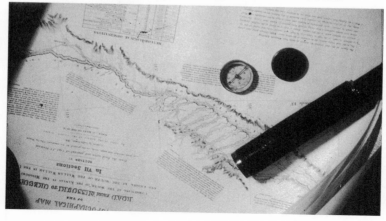

Sun goggles and case, about 1860. The blazing sun and seemingly endless dust of the trail wreaked havoc on travelers' eyes. These collapsible goggles (tied with hand-twined string) afforded some protection, and fit into their brass carrying case when not in use. Some goggles were available with green-tinted lenses, just like our modern sunglasses. Even so, "red eye" was common among emigrants. Some even went blind from the constant irritation of wind, sun, and alkali dust.

Native American beaded bag made by an American Plains Indian about 1860–90. Emigrants were both fascinated and afraid of Native Americans, and vice versa. Trading between cultures was common. Especially prized among pioneers was tribal beadwork such as this bag.

Traditional style Native American basket hat made by Rosa Thompson Minthorn, Umatilla Indian Reservation in northeast Oregon, 1973. Woven and decorated with plant fibers common to the Columbia Plateau, this hat doubled as a berry basket during the gathering season.

Meeker Marker. In 1906, Oregon Trail veteran Ezra Meeker placed Oregon Trail markers along its route, memorializing what he considered the prime years of overland migration: 1843 through 1857. Today these are most commonly known as Meeker Markers, and are helpful in pinpointing emigration routes where no ruts have survived.

Timber ruts or swale. In steep, heavily timbered mountains, wagons often had to be winched up the grades by muscle power, ropes, and chains. In some places, the passage between trees was so narrow that wheel hubs gouged them on both sides. Scars are still visible at this wagon swale at Blue Mountain Crossing.

Above: Ruts through rock. Some landscapes dictated that wagons travel single-file, one after the other for many decades. These ruts in Wyoming are worn through solid rock.

Below: Jenny Lind spool bed (about 1860–90) with "Basket of Flowers" quilt made by Mary Piesley Stephens, a pioneer to Oregon in 1848. Boards from the wagon boxes were sometimes used to build shelters at the end of the trail. Reminders of homes (and lives) left behind, such as this bedstead and quilt, were both practical and poignant.
Bed by permission of Sarah LeCompte; quilt by permission of
Schminck Memorial Museum, Lakeview, Oregon.

BIBLIOGRAPHY

Applegate, Jesse A. *A Day with the Cow Column, 1843*. Fairfield, WA: Ye Galleon Press, 1990.

Arthur, T. S.,ed. *The Lady's Home Magazine*, vols. 15–16, July–December. Philadelphia: T. S. Arthur and Company, 1860.

Articles of Agreement, Perkins Wagon Train, 1864. Unpublished document by permission of Nellie Perkins Edwards.

Bennett, Robert A. *We'll All Go Home In The Spring*. Walla Walla, WA: Pioneer Press Books, 1984.

Brown, Dee. *Bury My Heart at Wounded Knee*. New York: Holt, Rinehart and Winston, 1974.

Burnett, Fincelius G. Life of F. G. Burnett: As dictated to his granddaughter, Verna, in October, 1926. 1865. By permission of Ann Harman.

Carlson, Laurie Winn. *On Sidesaddles to Heaven: The Women of the Rocky Mountain Mission*. Caldwell, ID: The Caxton Press, 1998.

Cherokee Phoenix and Indians' Advocate, vol. 12, no. 14 (Wednesday, July 8, 1829), 2.

Child, L. Maria. *The American Frugal Housewife*. 1833. Reprint, Minneola, NY: Dover Press, 1999.

———. *The Little Girl's Own Book*. Boston: Carter, Hendee, and Co., 1834.

Coffman, Lloyd W. *Blazing a Wagon Trail to Oregon*. Springfield, OR: Echo Books, 1993.

Dalton, Margaret. Unpublished Papers. 1851-1900. By permission of Lois Comstock Franklin.

Deloria, Vine, Jr., ed. *Of Utmost Good Faith*. New York: Bantam Books, 1972.

DeVoto, Bernard. *Across the Wide Missouri*. Boston: Houghton Mifflin Co., 1947.

Dixon, Jos. K. *The Vanishing Race*. 1913. Reprint, New York: Bonanza Books, 1975.

Drotning, Philip T. *A Guide to Negro History in America*. Garden City, NY: Doubleday, 1968.

———. *Black Heroes in Our Nation's History*. New York: Cowles, 1969.

Drury, Clifford Merrill. *Elkanah and Mary Walker: Pioneers Among the Spokanes*. Caldwell, ID: Caxton Printers, Ltd., 1940.

————. *First White Women over the Rockies*. Glendale, CA: Arthur H. Clark Co., 1966.

————. *Marcus and Narcissa Whitman and the Opening of Old Oregon*. 2 vols. Seattle, WA: Pacific Northwest Parks and Forests Association, 1986.

————. *Marcus Whitman, MD*. Caldwell, ID: Caxton Press, 1937.

Emigrant's Guide to California, 1849. As cited in the interpretive exhibits of the National Historic Oregon Trail Interpretive Center. USDI, Bureau of Land Management. Baker City, OR.

Evans, James R. *Flagstaff Hill on the National Historic Oregon Trail*. Medford, OR: The Webb Group Research Group, 1992.

Evans, John W. *Powerful Rockey: The Blue Mountains and the Oregon Trail*. La Grande, OR: Eastern Oregon State College Press, 1990.

Farnham, Thomas J. *An 1839 Wagon Train Journal: Travels in the Great Western Prairies, The Anahuac and Rocky Mountains, and in the Oregon Territory*. 1843. Reprint, Northwest Interpretive Association, 1979.

Florin, Lambert. *Western Wagon Wheels*. Seattle, WA: Superior Publishing Company, 1970.

Franzwa, Gregory M. *The Oregon Trail Revisited*. Tucson, AZ: The Patrice Press, 1997.

Freedman, Russell. *Indian Chiefs*. New York: Scholastic, Inc., 1987.

Gazette (newspaper). St. Joseph, Missouri, 1847. As cited in the interpretive exhibits of the National Historic Oregon Trail Interpretive Center. USDI, Bureau of Land Management. Baker City, OR.

Gilliss, Julia. *So Far From Home*. Portland: Oregon Historical Society Press, 1993.

Haynes, Richard C., ed. *Oregon Trail Histories*. Portland, OR: USDI Bureau of Land Management, Oregon/Washington State Office, Cultural Series No. 9, 1993.

Helm, Mike, ed. *The Lockley Files: Conversations with Pioneer Women*. Eugene, OR: Rainy Day Press, 1981.

Hill, William E. *The Oregon Trail: Yesterday and Today*. Caldwell, ID: Caxton Printers, Ltd., 1989.

Holmes, Kenneth L., ed. *Covered Wagon Women: Diaries and Letters from the Western Trails, 1840–1890*, vol. 10. Spokane, WA: The Arthur H. Clark Company, 1991.

———— and David C. Duniway, eds. *Covered Wagon Women: Diaries and Letters from the Western Trails, 1840–1890*, vol. 5. Spokane, WA: The Arthur H. Clark Company, 1991.

Hunsaker, Joyce Badgley. *Oregon Trail Center: The Story Behind the Scenery*. Las Vegas, NV: KC Publications, 1995.

Ide, Mrs. Lucy A. In A Prairie Schooner, 1878. By permission of descendants of Lucy Ide.

Jackson, Edwin L. *The Georgia Studies Book*. Athens: University of Georgia, Carl Vinson Institute of Government, 1991.

Jackson, Helen Hunt. *A Century of Dishonor*. Norman: University of Oklahoma Press, 1995. Originally published 1885.

Jeffrey, Julie Roy. *Converting the West: A Biography of Narcissa Whitman*. Norman: University of Oklahoma Press, 1991.

Jessett, Thomas E. *The Indian Side of the Whitman Massacre.* Fairfield, WA: Ye Galleon Press, 1985.

Josephy, Alvin M. Jr. *The Nez Perce Indians and The Opening of The Northwest.* New Haven, CT: Yale University Press, 1965.

Katz, William Loren. *Black People Who Made the Old West.* Trenton, NJ: Africa World Press, Inc., 1992.

Kimball, Stanley B. and Violet T. Kimball. *Mormon Trail: Voyage of Discovery.* Las Vegas, NV: KC Publications, 1998.

Krech, Shepard, III. *The Ecological Indian, Myth and History.* New York: W. W. Norton and Company, 1999.

La Grande (Oregon) Evening Observer. Ezra Meeker dedication speech, 11 April 1906.

Larsen, Wes. *Field Folio of Indian and Pioneer Medicinal Plants.* Toquerville, UT: Third Mesa Publishing Co., 1997.

Lavender, David. *Land of Giants: The Drive to the Pacific Northwest, 1750–1950.* Lincoln: University of Nebraska Press. 1956.

———. *Westward Vision: The Story of the Oregon Trail.* Lincoln: University of Nebraska Press, 1963.

LeCompte, Sarah, ed. *Westward Quotes from the National Historic Oregon Trail Interpretive Center at Flagstaff Hill.* Baker City, OR: Trail Tenders, Inc., 1997.

Limerick, Patricia Nelson. *The Legacy of Conquest: The Unbroken Past of the American West.* New York: W. W. Norton and Company, 1987.

Lockley, Fred. *Conversations with Pioneer Women.* Eugene, OR: Rainy Day Press, 1981.

Mattes, Merrill J. *Indians, Infants, and Infantry.* Lincoln: University of Nebraska Press, 1960.

McLuhan, T. C. *Touch The Earth.* San Francisco, CA: Promontory Press, 1970.

Meacham, Walter. *Old Oregon Trail.* Manchester, NH: The Clarke Press, 1948.

Meeker, Ezra. *Ezra Meeker, A Brief Resume of His Life and Adventures.* Puyallup, WA: Ezra Meeker Historical Society, 1972.

———. *Ox-Team Days on the Oregon Trail.* Yonkers-On-Hudson, NY: Ezra Meeker and The World Book Company, 1923.

———. *Story of the Lost Trail to Oregon.* Seattle, WA: Ezra Meeker, 1915.

———. *The Busy Life of Eighty-five Years.* Seattle, WA: Ezra Meeker, 1916.

———. *The Ox Team or The Old Oregon Trail, 1852–1906.* Omaha, NE: Ezra Meeker. 2000. Reprint, Puyallup, WA: Windmill Publications for the Ezra Meeker Historical Society, Inc.

———. *Ventures and Adventures of Ezra Meeker.* Seattle, WA: Rainier Printing Co., 1908.

Miller, Susan Cummins, ed. *A Sweet, Separate Intimacy: Women Writers of the American Frontier 1800–1922.* Salt Lake City: The University of Utah Press, 2000.

Moynihan, Ruth Barnes. *Rebel for Rights: Abigail Scott Duniway.* New Haven, CT: Yale University Press, 1983.

O'Brien, Mary Barmeyer. *Toward the Setting Sun.* Helena, MT: Falcon Publishing, Inc., 1999.

O'Dell, Dee, ed. *Sagebrush Surprises*. Baker City, OR: Trail Tenders, Inc., 1997.

Oregon Donation Land Claim Act of 1850. Transcript housed at the Oregon Historical Society. Portland, OR.

Parkman, Francis (E. N. Feltskog, ed.) *The Oregon Trail*. 1872. Reprint, Lincoln, NE: Bison Books, 1994.

The Prairie Traveler: Handbook for Overland Expeditions, 1859. As cited in the interpretive exhibits of the National Historic Oregon Trail Interpretive Center. USDI, Bureau of Land Management. Baker City, OR.

Pringle, Catherine Sager. *Across the Plains in 1844*. Fairfield, WA: Ye Galleon Press, 1993.

Riley, Glenda. *Women and Indians on the Frontier, 1825–1915*. Albuquerque: University of New Mexico Press, 1991.

Shenkman, Richard. *Legends, Lies and Cherished Myths of American History*. New York: Harper and Row, 1988.

Smith, Helen Krebs. *The Presumptuous Dreamers*. Volume One. Lake Oswego, OR: Smith, Smith, and Smith Publishing Company, 1974.

Speer, Robert. *Presbyterian Foreign Missions*. Philadelphia, PA: Presbyterian Board of Publications and Sabbath School Work, 1901.

Stewart, Helen. Unpublished diary. 1853. By permission of her descendant, Walter Love.

Tobin, Jacquelin L. and Raymond Dobard. *Hidden In Plain View*. New York: Anchor Books (Random House), 1999.

Tompkins, Jim. *The Road to Oregon: Articles about the Oregon Trail*. In *Oregon Trail Histories*, Cultural Resource Series No. 9. Portland, OR: USDI Bureau of Land Management, Oregon/Washington State Office, 1993.

Unruh, John D., Jr. *The Plains Across: The Overland Emigrants and the Trans-Mississippi West, 1840–60*. Urbana: University of Illinois Press, 1979.

Ward, Jean M. and Elaine A. Maveety, eds. *Pacific Northwest Women 1815–1925*. Corvallis: Oregon State University Press, 1995.

Whitman, Narcissa Prentiss. *My Journal, 1836*. Fairfield, WA: Ye Galleon Press, 1994.

———. *The Letters of Narcissa Whitman, 1836–1847*. Fairfield, WA: Ye Galleon Press, 1986.

Wood, Joseph Warren. Journal, 1849. As cited in the interpretive exhibits of the National Historic Oregon Trail Interpretive Center. USDI, Bureau of Land Management. Baker City, OR.

INDEX

Shawnee Indians, 74, 211

Sioux Indians, 60, 62, 85, 104, 126, 173, 174, 194, 206–08, 211–15, 217, 231

slavery, slaves, 74, 93, 104, 108, 132, 146, 152, 155, 167, 168–72, 176, 199, 200, 214–16

Snake River, 2, 33, 60, 62, 91, 94, 116, 126, 139, 163, 164, 229

Snake (Shoshone) Indians, 30, 45, 60–63, 76, 78, 89–92, 211, 206, 138, 146, 152

Soda Springs ("Beer Springs"), 31, 62, 88, 89, 139, 163, 188

South Pass, 1, 88, 137, 138, 163

Spalding, Henry and Eliza, 1, 21–30, 33–37, 40, 42, 44, 45, 78, 122

Split Rock, 206

St. Joseph, Missouri ("St. Joe"), 9, 110, 133, 143, 147, 150, 152, 177–78, 182, 187–88, 254

St. Louis, Missouri, 21–24, 39, 43, 61, 78, 177, 198–200

Steamboat Springs ("Bellowing Rock"), 89, 139

Sublette Cut-off, 163

Sweetwater River, 83, 87, 187, 206

tobacco; smoking, 50, 56, 68, 70, 86, 96, 105, 184

Tongue River, 207–08, 213

Twain, Mark (Samuel Clemens), 198

typhoid, 114

Umatilla Indians, 128, 211, 248

Uncle Tom's Cabin (Harriet Beecher Stowe), 155

Ute (Utah, Utahn) Indians, 78, 211

vermillion, 63

Waiilatpu, 2, 36, 38, 46, 121, 128

Walker, Mary Richardson, 46

Walla Walla Indians, 37, 63, 67–68, 103, 128, 211

Wasco (Wascopum) Indians, 98, 211

Whitman Mission, 2, 43, 64, 66–67, 78, 94, 110, 115, 118, 120–23, 128, 240

Whitman, Alice Clarissa, 37, 122

Whitman, Marcus, 2, 21, 36, 37, 38, 40, 43, 65, 78, 117, 119, 121, 122, 128, 240

Willamette River; Willamette Valley, 62, 68, 70–71, 95, 99–100, 114, 118, 121, 128, 144–45, 147, 167, 188–89, 191, 211

Winnebago Indians, 206, 211, 214–15

wolves, 70, 51, 179, 183, 209

worm wood: *see* sage

Yakima Indians, 41

York (slave of William Clark), 104, 108